BESIDE THE POINT

Beside the Point

Close Encounters in the Global Classroom

Philip O. Chomak

Louisa Street Press

Published in the United States by Louisa Street Press,
Orinda, California.
www.louisastreetpress.com

Cover design by Andy Carpenter (acdbookcoverdesign.com)
Book design by Jim Shubin (www.bookalchemist.net)

Publisher's Cataloging-in-Publication data
Chomak, Philip O.
Beside the point: close encounters in the global classroom / Philip O. Chomak
pages cm
ISBN 978-0-9966198-0-6 (paperback)
ISBN 978-0-9966198-1-3 (eBook)

1. Chomak, Philip O. 2. English Language—Study and teaching—California—San Francisco Bay Area—Biography. 3. English Language—Study and teaching—California—San Francisco Bay Area—Anecdotes. 4. Adult education—California—San Francisco Bay Area—Anecdotes. 5. English language—Study and teaching—Foreign speakers—Anecdotes I. Title.
PE1128.A2 C56 2015
428/.007092—dc23
Library of Congress Control Number: 2015912725

For Joan and Ezra

Contents

Apparently, there is nothing that can't happen.
Autobiography of Mark Twain

"Son, anything can happen to anyone," my father told me, "but it usually doesn't."
"Except when it does," I thought . . .
Philip Roth, *The Plot Against America*

Prologue

The scene: an English-as-a-Second-Language classroom in Berkeley, California, 2006. Luis, a young Venezuelan student, starts to tell the class a story:

"My mother was in the chicken."

"Your mother was *where*?" I ask.

"In the chicken."

"Do you maybe mean she was in the kitchen, Luis?"

"Kitchen! Yes, yes, of course. Kitchen." He smacks his forehead. "Chicken is the big bird. I know, I know."

"That's right. I wouldn't expect you to have such a large chicken . . . or such a small mother."

"No," he laughs, "to tell you the true, my mother is a big one, a big mama. She's actually a little bit fat. But she's very very nice."

"I'm sure she is."

"And she have cooked many chickens in the kitchen," he proclaims, smiling broadly, showing off his new prowess in the language to his laughing classmates.

"I'm sure she has."

So many memories of so many students; most of them, like the one about Luis' chicken, make me smile. A few make me wince. They rise up and visit me often. It's part of the legacy of a career that snuck up on me.

In 1974, English as a Second Language was not something I was checking out, or even thinking about. I knew next to nothing about it and had no idea I'd be teaching it—for almost four decades.

My degree and interest were in literature, and I had hoped to find a place where they'd pay me to think and talk about great books. Nice thought. But, by that time, an M.A. in English Lit was no longer the passport to college teaching gigs that it once had seemed to be; nobody had spoken about expiration dates when they handed out those certificates six years earlier. I kept looking anyway.

On a Tuesday morning in the summer of that year, my casual search took me to Cañada College in Redwood City, on the peninsula south of San Francisco. At the conclusion of a fruitless job interview in an office of the English Department, Professor Somebody said, apparently as an afterthought, "You know, there *is* something you might look into. There's a language school on the campus of Holy Names College in the Oakland Hills. It's not the kind of job you're looking for—not specifically a Lit position. It's an ESL school, but perhaps they have something. You never know." I agreed that we *do* never know, and we shook hands. I took the contact information and thanked him, expecting nothing.

When I got back to my home in Berkeley, I called the academic director at the Oakland school and made an appointment for the next morning. That interview went well—which is not to say they had a job for me. The director told me they didn't need another teacher at that time but assured me he'd keep my application "on file" in case anything opened up. Sure, okay.

We repeated the standard less-than-grand finale: more thanking, more handshaking . . . the usual prelude to more waiting. I took solace in the thought that, although I needed the money, unemployment had its own reward—the sweet liberty of a schedule-free life. A "job" was not really what I was yearning for anyway.

So, again, I drove back to Berkeley and was about to tell my wife Joan that I'd come home empty-handed. But as I walked through the front door, before I said a word, she told me that the guy I'd just been speaking with in Oakland had called to say that one of their teachers had a family emergency (lucky me), would have to fly to Chicago immediately, and would be gone for at least a few weeks. Could I start tomorrow?

Of course I could.

Those few weeks of "subbing" turned into several months; eventually, in August of 1976, after a period of doing sundry odd jobs, I signed on at that school as a full-time teacher. Thus began my unexpected career. I never thought this "stopgap measure" would last so long, but I hadn't counted on how seductive it would be to hang out regularly with people who came from anywhere but here.

The typical ESL classroom both is and isn't America. Sure, they are visiting you, but you, in every sense but the geographical, are visiting them too, their cultures, their languages, and, most strikingly, the many-faced parade of their individual personalities. In some ways, it's better than physically traveling: on this trip, you can visit ten nations at once without suffering the expense of air travel or the indignities of body scans and luggage carousels.

Getting a job too often feels like the attaching of a leash (if not a noose), but finding myself in the midst of that multicultural crowd felt more like an *un*leashing. Happily, the freedom to be oneself need not be limited to periods of unemployment.

The kick that I felt at the beginning stayed with me, for the most part, until my last day, April 20, 2012. On that Friday morning, I handed in my keys and dry-erase markers and contemplated a future of *not* spending five days of most weeks inside classrooms, surrounded by students. Now, living that life, I find that my students are very much with me, my memories of them vivid—some, of course, more than others.

Teaching English as a Second Language is a good gig. It's satisfying to sharpen one's understanding of a linguistic point and then present it to a class with lucidity and life. But getting that point across is not what this book is about; it *is* about what happens in the endlessly unpredictable world *beside* the point—where surprises spring from the quirks of languages (theirs *and* ours), and, of course, from the quirky humans who speak them.

This memoir weaves together tales of my encounters with students from Argentina, Brazil, France, Germany, Italy, Indonesia, Iran, Iraq, Japan, Korea, Peru, Qatar, Romania, Saudi Arabia, Spain, Switzerland, Taiwan, Thailand, Tibet, Turkey, Venezuela, and Vietnam. It is also, naturally, about their encounters with each other.

Where I've forgotten students' names, I've substituted fictitious ones, and, while I was at it, I also changed some of the names I did remember, for the sake of privacy or, in some cases, safety. Thanks to the students, colleagues, and friends who have given me permission to use their real names.

For the most part, I have not attempted to stick to strict chronological order in the sequencing of these stories, but, in order to have a sense of the larger time frames, you should know this: I taught at that school (a branch of ELS Language Centers) on the Holy Names campus in Oakland from 1974 to 2003, at its sister school at Dominican University in San Rafael from 2003 to 2006, and in Berkeley, at a just-opened branch of the same company, from 2006 until that April day in 2012.

Students would attend this "intensive language program" for four to six hours each weekday. Typically, after stays of between one and twelve months, they would, with few exceptions, head back to their countries, either immediately or after subsequent studies at an American college or university. I felt, and still feel, an odd sense of privilege at the thought of becoming a part of all those far-flung memories of visiting this "foreign" land.

Teaching, for me, has embodied the paradox of relating to a group while trying to connect to each individual *in* that group. Many of those connections had enough wattage to stand out, to change the course of a lesson, or of a day—and to become stories.

Watching the Fish

One morning in the early eighties, I and about ten students sat around a rectangular oak table in a seminar room on the campus of Holy Names College, perched high on a bay-facing slope of one of the Oakland Hills. Behind my students' heads, through three large windows, was a cinemascope-like triptych of sky, bay, hills, bridges, and mountains. Bathed in late-morning golden light, that scene threatened to steal my attention away from my own lesson.

The goal for that day's lesson was to practice the simple present tense, so I asked my students to talk about the activities with which they typically started their days. "I do this. I do that . . ." The accounts held few surprises: showers, breakfasts, teeth brushing, etc. It was the quintessence of humdrum.

That is, until it was Dorje's turn. Dorje was a Tibetan Buddhist monk who was living with one of the homestay families which the school recruited for some of our students. You wouldn't guess that Dorje was a monk by looking at him. He was a stocky broad-shouldered twenty-something guy with a crew cut; he wore no robes or beads, just a blue and gold Cal Berkeley tee shirt, blue jeans, and white sneakers. He looked more like a football player than a holy man. His voice, however, was breathily gentle as he started his narrative:

"Every day, I get out of bed and watch the fish."

Ah, what a perfectly Tibetan Buddhist way to start the day, I thought, probably part of a meditation exercise. I imagined about a dozen exotic multicolored fish swimming silently and contentedly in the illuminated blue-green water of a large glass tank. I didn't own even one fish; that's how *un*spiritual *I* was.

"That's lovely, Dorje, that your host family has fish for you to watch. And about how many fish are in the tank?" Not that I really needed that statistic, but making conversation is part of the job.

He looked at me with total incomprehension. I knew that look. I obviously needed to simplify my English.

"When you watch the fish, Dorje, do you watch one fish or do you watch more than one fish?"

Now he looked at me as if *I* were the one learning the language. Evidently, *he* would have to simplify things in order for *me* to get it.

"Of course, I watch only one fish. I *have* only one fish. Everybody have only one fish. I only watch *my* fish."

Was there some arcane Buddhist wisdom here that was eluding my poor earthbound soul?

"Everybody has only one fish? No, no, Dorje, certainly some people have quite a few more than that. But most people have no fish at all, actually. Like me, for example. I have no fish. Some people collect them. And sometimes they can be pretty expensive."

Again, the blank stare of confusion, of near-desolation.

"Expensive? More than one fish? No fish? Huh?"

"Yes. Sure."

We silently stared into each other's eyes and *knew* that we were having two unconnected conversations. His classmates knew it too and seemed to be enjoying this little drama; perhaps they especially relished seeing their teacher as lost in this strange language as they usually were. Their attention level was cranked up: how would this detective story be resolved? Of course, not understanding long stretches of conversation in this country was the norm for them, but this was different: their teacher was a partner in this discussion *and* this confusion, so perhaps that would prevent it from being sucked into the void with all those countless others. Perhaps. I was starting to have my doubts that I could avoid disappointing them, but I was determined not to leave the classroom without at least *try*ing to clear up the mystery. I could see from his face that Dorje had the same resolve. I decided to resort to the traveler's trusty resource: body language.

"Okay, Dorje, let's start again, and this time, in addition to *telling* us what you do, *show* us too. Use body language." I stood up, walked back and forth, waving my arms around like a Sicilian to show him what I meant. He smiled and nodded vigorously to show he got it.

"Ah, good good, okay," he said as he rose from his chair. Then, delighting his classmates, he stretched out on the brown linoleum tiles of the floor-qua-bed. Rising again, he enunciated each word very carefully, peering deeply into my eyes to be sure I understood: "I . . . get . . . out . . . of . . . bed."

With my hopes rising, I nodded vigorously, almost chanting, "Uh-huh, uh-huh, uh-huh" to assure him that I was with him. So far so good. The whole class seemed to be hanging on each painstakingly shaped syllable.

"Then . . . I . . . go . . . to . . . sink . . . in . . . rest . . . room."

Uh oh. He was losing me again. It seemed very unlikely that his host family kept its lone fish in the bathroom sink.

"The sink?" I asked, hoping that he really meant something else. A fish tank, for example.

"Yes. Sink. In restroom. You know sink?"

"Yes, Dorje. Sure, I know sink. Sometimes in restrooms, sometimes in kitchens. That's what you're talking about, right?"

"Yes, that's right. That is sink. Exactly! Very good, teacher." He was laughing now, clearly having great fun with our suddenly reversed roles.

"Thank you, Dorje." I was committed to hanging in there and seeing where this would go. "Please continue."

"Good good. So. I go to sink and start water." Dorje mimed turning on a faucet, then placing his hands, palms up, under its running water, and applying it to his face, rubbing his cheeks with vigorous circular motions. "And . . . then . . . I . . . watch . . . the . . . fish." He kept massaging his cheeks until they began to turn red from the friction. "See me, Teacher? See me watch the fish? Watch . . . the . . . fish?"

Bingo! I finally got it. "You wash your face! You're saying you wash your face!" Laughter bubbled out of me despite the banishment of my serene delusion about Buddhist fish meditation.

"Yes, I already tell you. I watch the fish. Now you understand?"

"Yes, thank you, Dorje. I do understand! You're an excellent teacher." I could tell from their laughter that Dorje's classmates now got it too. We had all entered that little labyrinth together and emerged laughing on the other side. Dorje's pronunciation and grammar difficulties had brought me and my students to that richest of communal places: the unanimity of laughter. With every group, once we'd had our first good guffaw together, I felt I could teach them anything: we tend to trust the people we've laughed with.

We then spent a few minutes discussing the correct pronunciation of "wash" and "face" before moving on to the curious and sometimes confusing practice of generally using possessive adjectives ("my," "your," "his," etc.), *not* the definite article ("the"), for parts of the body.

After all that, it was obvious that there wouldn't be enough time to delve into the main grammar point of that morning's lesson—once again, the unforeseen had nudged us *beside* the point. No problem. We'd simply do it on the next day; the simple present tense would simply have to wait for the near future. The present was clearly the time to focus on those troublesome possessive adjectives. Which reminds me of the story of Jose, one of my Peruvian students, who, one weekend, decided to visit Yosemite National Park . . .

Jose in Yosemite

"What did you do on your weekend?" That question is probably the number one Monday-conversation-class warhorse, and for good reason. The memories of those two days of relative freedom are as fresh as they ever will be. There's also the fact that talking about one's weekend is an excellent way of continuing to experience it, prolonging the pleasure or, in some cases, seeking solace for the pain. One student's answer to that question on a summer Monday morning in the mid-eighties has remained clear, maybe because I've told this anecdote a thousand times.

Jose was one of the few Peruvians I have ever taught. Every woman in that Oakland class seemed to have gone a bit gaga over him. He looked carved out of stone: about six-and-a-half feet tall, coal black hair, impossibly broad shoulders, dark brown eyes, and an infallibly engaging grin. What man could compete with this guy, an Incan god with a winsome smile?

"So, Jose, tell us about *your* weekend."

"I went Joe-semight National Park."

"Ah, that's great. But the name of the park is pronounced 'Yo seh mih tee.' Try it, Jose."

"Joe seh mih tee."

"Yo."

"Joe."

"Listen, Jose. Yo. Yo. Yo. Not Joe, but Yo . . . Yo . . . Yo . . . Try saying Eeeeeeyo."

"Eeeeeeyo."

"Good. Now say it again, and then repeat it without saying the eeeee part, but remember the position of your tongue near your palate, which is what we call the top of your mouth, the roof of your mouth." I tapped my own palate, which tickled a little, and modeled this approach. "Eeeeeyo. Yo."

"Eeeeeyo. Yo."

"*Perfecto!* Now tell me again. Where did you go this weekend?"

"Joe seh mih tee National Park."

"Eeeeeyo. Yo."

"Sorry, teacher. Eeeeeyo. Yo. Yo seh might National Park."

"Mih tee. Yo seh mih tee."

"Ay, shit. Sorry, sorry. I got it now. Eeeeyosehhhmihhhteee National Park."

Looking around, I could see that some of Jose's classmates were starting to squirm. It was time to extricate us from this little pothole.

"Better. That's much better, Jose. We'll work more on this pronunciation later. I *know* you'll get it." Jose looked thankful that this ordeal seemed to be ending, for now.

"Anyway, let's hear more about your Yosemite trip. It's one of my favorite places in the world."

"Yes, is very beautiful the nature."

"Indeed. It's true. And who went with you to this magnificent place?"

"My brother and your wife."

Feigning outrage, I bellowed, "My wife! Oh now I know where she was all weekend! I'm going to murder *both* of you!"

Jose and all the others, without even thinking about it, broke into a fit of laughing. When one "gets" a joke in a foreign language, there's a special surprised satisfaction. Humor, in its mysterious sneakiness, exists in a deeper place than purely pragmatic communication. Even though the students in that conversation class were relative beginners, they had all seen enough American movies to know the meaning of "murder."

My "tirade" led into another mini-lesson on those pesky possessive adjectives and how, if you didn't get them right, they could get you killed.

From Brazil with Love

On the final Friday morning of a four-week session at our school on the Holy Names campus, I and my "Masters' class" students rolled down the hill in two cars, taking the tree-flanked Warren Freeway to Ver Brugge, a tranquil now-defunct little restaurant near the Oakland-Berkeley border. My memory of that small eatery is one of European elegance: white table cloths, burnished dark oak wainscoting, gleaming silverware, classical music. I'm not totally sure about the wainscoting. Or the tablecloths. But you get the idea. We'd spend the morning there instead of in our usual classroom: we were celebrating the lovely fact that everybody had passed the course.

After we had polished off our eggs, bacon, waffles, pancakes, etc., and were placidly sipping our second or third coffee refills, I distributed their "Final Reports," which listed the grades in all their classes. It also had their scores on what we called "The Michigan Test," a standardized exam concocted at the University of Michigan. Any student who scored an 85 or better received a fancy "Certificate of Proficiency," replete with gold-leaf embellishments. Nobody in the class hit that mark, but one came close. Thais (pronounced Ta-

eez), an attractive Brazilian woman in her early thirties, got an 84.

"Wow, Thais, that's great. You missed getting the Proficiency by only one point. You should be very proud of yourself." She blushed with the glory of it all.

"Thank you, Teacher. Can you believe it? Just one point!"

"Whew, I guess that's a little frustrating, huh?"

"A *little* frustrating? Way more than a *little!*"

"Yeah. I can see that."

"I knew you would understand."

"Of course I understand. I'd feel the same way if it happened to me."

"Great, Phil. That's why I'm sure you will give me that one more point. Just that one. I really want that beautiful certificate. Actually, I *need* it. You *will* do that for me, right?" She flashed a thousand-megawatt smile at me, using smile muscles that only Brazilians seem to have, a smile filled with gratitude for the life-changing favor she was sure I was about to bestow on her. I could see that she didn't have a shred of doubt that kind Phil, cool Phil, man-of-the-people Phil, would come through for her as he had always come through for *all* his students. Her question, as far as she was concerned, was purely rhetorical.

"I'm sorry, Thais, but I can't do that."

I knew a fuse had been lit when her hazel eyes doubled in size and bored into mine. The smile was gone. She looked incredulous, in shock.

"I thought you were my friend."

"Well, yes, I *am* your friend. *And* your teacher. And as your teacher, giving you that point would feel wrong to me. You know, unethical." As her face reddened with the rising temperature of her rage, I could see that she was not at all in the mood for my little exposition on pedagogical morality. I wasn't much in the mood for it myself.

"I don't believe this," she said a bit more loudly. Diners at the other tables were starting to look over at ours.

"Please try to understand, Thais. This is nothing personal. If I gave you that point, it would be unfair to Takashi, who got 83. I would have to give him *two* points."

"So *give* to him two points. You're supposed to be *his* friend too. I can't believe you even have to be thinking about this. You are not the person I thought you were. It's like I really didn't know you!"

It was becoming increasingly clear that, to Thais, this was a situation that was nothing *but* personal.

"Thais, please try to understand . . . "

"No, *you* try to understand!" She was screaming now. Everything else in that little restaurant stopped. "In *Brasil*, is very hard get a job, a *good* job. Every piece of paper is counting. A lot! This certificate make the difference between a good job and nothing, a good life and a shit life. I have a son in Rio. My little Roberto is everything for me, my whole world, my whole universe. I want him to have a life with joy, with always enough food, and security, but if I'm having a shit job, he can have nothing, and without the right pieces of paper, I can't get shit! So give me that one . . . little . . . point, Phil. Don't destroy my life. One fucking point! That's all what I'm asking. One fucking point!"

All my other students, and seemingly everyone in the restaurant, awaited my reply. I wished I could join them, step out of my key role in this movie, become a bystander, a member of the audience. Not a viable option. Thais was asking me to cheat—publicly. It seemed to me that there was only one choice I could live with.

"I can't do it, Thais. I'm sorry, but I can't." A few of the students nodded. In support of my position, I hoped. Thais was not one of them.

She got out of her chair and to everyone's astonishment, leaned toward the table and grabbed a knife, which, to me, probably appeared longer, shinier, pointier, sharper than it actually was, and pointed it at my chest, in the vicinity of my heart.

"You are murdering me *and* my son. You are murdering all our chance in this hard life. You are not my friend. You have no heart! I could *kill* you!"

I believed she could, and quite possibly was about to. Was my life really going to end right then and there, in that quaint little East Bay bistro, with inappropriately carefree Baroque music, maybe Vivaldi, accompanying us? Thais was the picture of a woman who was fully intent on ending it all for me with a few well-aimed stabs. But then she looked around at her classmates and at the other patrons and seemed to realize that murdering me in front of twenty or thirty witnesses would probably be worse for her future than not getting that bloody certificate. She dropped the knife on the table and stormed out, slamming the door behind her. I don't remember if, in that moment, I was shaking or paralyzed. Is it possible to be both?

I didn't see Thais again until the following Tuesday morning, on campus, just outside the building where, in about ten minutes, we'd have our first class of the new session. She walked slowly toward me, her arms dangling limply, her hands apparently devoid of weapons, her head a bit down, looking at my shoes, not my eyes, looking as condemned, as penitent, as if she *had* plunged that knife into my chest; this was not the madwoman who had been ranting in Ver Brugge. When she reached me, she raised her sad eyes to mine.

"Phil, I'm so sorry about what I did on Friday. I was crazy. Absolute crazy. I'm very embarrassed. Hoomiliated. You were right. I was *very* wrong. I was, how you say, bananas? Can you forgive me? Please forgive your crazy student."

How could I not? In the absence of grade and certificate obsession—and of lethal cutlery—suddenly the solution seemed ridiculously simple.

"Sure, Thais. I really appreciate your saying this. And I'll tell you what. I'm going to write a letter on the school's stationery. It's very nice stationery, with a red and shiny gold letterhead, very fancy. I will write about what an excellent student you are. That's not a lie. That will be a lot more valuable than that impersonal certificate."

"Oh, you shouldn't do nothing for me, Phil, but thank you very very very much. You really don't have to do this. I shouldn't get any helping from you after I was so bad. *So* bad."

"No, no, I'm happy to do this. I feel completely honest doing this. You really *are* an excellent student. Let's do this for Roberto."

She then thanked me, and thanked me again, and then again, and gave me a robust hug, which probably cranked up the intensity of the letter I wrote that evening. When I gave her the letter the next day, I got another world-class hug, Brazilian style. Four weeks later, Thais was flying back to Rio de Janeiro. That was that. Or so I thought.

About six weeks later, the school received a package from Rio with my name on it. I tore open the brown paper to discover a blue tee shirt with a white palm tree on its front. Above the left side of the tree was written *From Brasil*, and just below the right side of that white palm, under its roots, were the words *With Love . . . Thais*. A branch of the tree tilted up through the *B* and *r* of *Brasil*, and its tip pointed toward the left sleeve, on which one white word was stamped: Phil.

I brought the tee shirt home, showed it to Joan, and explained that it was from the Brazilian student whose knife-wielding at the breakfast table I had, of course, already told her about on the day it happened. I assured her that Thais and I did not have a steamy extracurricular affair going, and couldn't resist joking that, obviously, there's just something about me that drives women crazy. With that, rolling her eyes and smiling, she could easily agree.

The Trouble with Tee Shirts

The Thais story brings another student's tee shirt to mind. Tomoko, a short, super-slim Japanese girl, about seventeen, was a student at the Oakland school in the late seventies. She was not in any of my classes, so all I knew about her was that she was in our beginning level and that she was reputed to be extremely shy, which, at that time, was not a major distinction among our many Japanese students, especially the girls.

That's why, one day, during a break, as she walked toward me in one of the Holy Names' corridors, I did a double-take when I got close enough to read the two English words on her white tee shirt. In the upper left corner, in small purple letters, were two words, one above the other:

tiny
boobs

It was inconceivable that she knew the meaning of "boobs," and maybe hadn't come across "tiny" yet either. During that period in Japan, it was considered very chic to have English words on tee shirts, backpacks, sweatshirts, or seemingly any available expanse of cloth. The semantic content was unimportant; it was the fashion statement that counted. I often saw items bought in Japan that had utterly incomprehensible combinations such as, "Happy forgetting place honey to be examination society crazy." These unlikely verbal combinations reminded me of "word salad," the term clinical psychology textbooks use for similar statements made by schizophrenic patients. So, not expecting Tomoko's tee shirt to *mean* anything, her classmates didn't see anything funny or odd about those words either. Since I wasn't her teacher, I thought it would be best if someone else on the faculty (preferably female) taught her the meaning of her shirt's two-word phrase, an act which would probably take mortification to a new level. I spoke to one of Tomoko's teachers, and, after a bit of cackling together, she agreed to give Tomoko the news. That tee shirt was never seen again in Oakland or, I would guess, anywhere else on the planet.

To fill in an important part of the picture, I think it's worth noting that Tomoko really did have small breasts, a fact so obvious that it didn't need a caption. She was like a living breathing version of the picture dictionaries that are so popular with language students, books with labeled illustrations of common scenes such as a family having dinner, the table labeled "table," the fork "fork," the knife "knife," the father "father," and so on. For a brief time, poor Tomoko, with her tiny boobs labeled "tiny boobs," had become an unwitting participant in this graphic approach to language acquisition.

Another memorable tee shirt was worn by one of my Iranian students. Fatima was about Tomoko's age, but her larger frame and non-tiny boobs made her look older. She was a serious old-fashioned girl who had a few female friends but seemed uninterested in dating or partying with anyone at the school. I also knew that, although she didn't follow a strict dress code, she was fairly serious about her Islamic faith. That's what made me so sure that she didn't get the meaning of the English sentence on the tee shirt that she wore to my intermediate-level reading class one hot summer afternoon.

Taking up most of the front of her shirt was a large brown smiling face of a cartoon dog, its red tongue lasciviously lolling out of the right side of its mouth. Under that dog head was the statement "I'll go to bed with *any* dog." Whereas Tomoko had so little English that "tiny boobs" had absolutely no semantic significance for her, Fatima had just enough vocabulary to get the *wrong* meaning of *her* shirt's English—to take it literally. That was probably true of the other students in her class too. Of course, most native English speakers know the meaning of the idiom "go to bed with someone." They also know that, in this context, a "dog" is not a dog. Outside the safe walls of our classroom, Fatima was definitely sending the wrong message to the American men of Oakland. As her teacher, I felt that I had to let her know what she was advertising.

She was in a reading class in which each student had a lot of one-on-one time with me. On the day that Fatima wore her dog shirt to class, I was determined to set her straight when it was her turn to come up to my desk. After going over the reading exercises, as she started to get up, I stopped her.

"Oh, Fatima, I want to ask you a question before you go back to your seat."

"Yes, teacher?"

"It's about your shirt."

"Yes, teacher. It's nice shirt, yes? I like it so much," she said with a timid little smile.

"Uh, yes, but I was wondering . . ."

"Yes, teacher?"

"I was wondering if you know the meaning of the English sentence on it." Of course, I wasn't wondering at all; there was no way that she did.

"Of course, teacher. Very easy English. Very easy understanding."

"Well, Fatima, please tell me what you think it means."

"You mean like reading exercise?"

"Yes, that's right. It *is* a kind of reading exercise. What do you think the sentence on your tee shirt means?"

"Okay. It is simple. It mean dog very cute. I love dogs a lot. A lot. And it is so nice have cute dog be in your bed with you when go sleep. It make you feeling happy. You see, I understand this easy English, right?"

"No, sorry, Fatima. That's what it *seems* to mean. But actually it has a different meaning to American people. 'To go to bed with someone' means to have sex. And a 'dog' is an ugly person, sometimes a stupid or a boring person, what we sometimes call a 'loser.'"

Fatima looked confused and a little scared. The very mention of the word "sex" was like touching a powerfully charged electrode to her ear. Clearly, I was confusing rather than enlightening her. She looked incredulous that her formerly trustworthy teacher was now stripping words of what seemed to be their simple unambiguous meaning.

"What? Bed is not bed and dog is not dog?"

"Well, remember, we studied idioms? Words with special meanings in different cultures? Meanings which are different from the definitions in a dictionary? So knowing the dictionary definition usually won't help you to understand an idiom. Remember?"

"Yes, I kind of remember. So what good is dictionary?"

"Well, not much good in this case, I'm afraid."

Fatima was starting to catch on, and her look of bewilderment was changing to one of major embarrassment.

"Uh oh, teacher, please tell me exactly. Please tell me the exactly meaning of my shirt."

"I'm sorry, Fatima. I know this must be embarrassing. I think your classmates probably have the same idea that you do, but American men will certainly have a different idea. They will think that you are saying that you will be happy to have sex with everyone, with *any* man, even if he is an ugly bad person." Fatima was looking more and more horrified. "Now I think you understand why I think it's a bad idea for you to wear this tee shirt, right?"

"Yes, now I understand. Oh God, this is terrible! Thank you, Phil, for explain to me. English is crazy. Completely crazy! Maybe I will *never* learn it."

"Of course, you will, Fatima. Look at the important lesson you learned today. You're doing very well."

"Thank you, Phil."

"You're welcome, Fatima. Don't worry. And, by the way, the next time you buy a shirt with English on it, be careful. Make sure you understand the meaning."

"I will, teacher. I *will* be careful."

Fatima scurried back to her seat, and, despite the heat, grabbed the dark brown cardigan that she had been carrying from class to class since 8:30 in the morning, put it on, and buttoned it up to her neck. That shirt joined Tomoko's in tee shirt purgatory, where these garments waited, possibly forever, for wearers who understood them and would have no compunctions about transmitting their peculiar messages to the world.

Long after Tomoko and Fatima had returned to their countries, I would tell their stories to future crops of students, not only as tales that I knew would make them laugh (always one of my extracurricular goals), but also as cautionary tales. I joked that I was going to start a new business in which students could hire me to accompany them to clothing stores to give a professional "safety clearance" to any desired garment with English words on it, satisfaction guaranteed. Phil Chomak: Tee Shirt Consultant.

Sometimes, when I cracked that joke, some of my students looked like they were seriously thinking of taking me up on my proposition, but, trust me, I never made a penny on it.

While I'm on the subject, at least one more tee shirt deserves mention. It belonged to Anton, the only Romanian student I have ever had. He was in a conversation class of mine, level 105. (Each of the twelve "levels" at the school had a number. I've used this number system several times in this book since it's a convenient shorthand: 101-103 [Beginning], 104-106 [Intermediate], 107-109 [Advanced], and 110-112 [Masters].)

Anton prided himself on being an outstanding athlete and looked the part: tall, broad-shouldered, close-cropped blond hair that looked like peach fuzz on his enormous head, and rock-hard-looking muscles in all the usual places, and a few other places as well. He wasn't particularly swift in picking up the language and generally kept his emotions under wrap. Most of the time he seemed rather glum, unwilling to engage, loath to smile, loath to speak. This nineteen-year-old fellow showed up in class one day in mid-eighties Oakland wearing a white tee shirt with a picture of a red and blue soccer ball in the upper left corner of its front; right under the ball was this unlikely designation: "Soccer Dad."

Anton? Soccer Dad? The incongruity was funny in a surreal way, but I succeeded in keeping my laughter to myself. My intention was not to embarrass my student, but apparently it was time for another tee shirt clarification. Also, I was curious about Anton's take on his shirt's English—that is, if he *had* a take.

"Anton, I like your tee shirt."

"Thank you, Teacher. Soccer great sport. I love soccer."

"Yes, I know. But I wanted to tell you that it's kind of funny to see those English words on your shirt."

"Words? English words? Oh, I didn't look at words. I just like picture."

"Oh, I see. That *is* a very nice soccer ball. I like it too. But I was also wondering if you know the meaning of the words. Do you?"

He took hold of the shirt and pulled it away from his huge chest so he could read the words for the first time. From that perspective they were, of course, upside down and backwards. But it was still easy enough, Anton felt, to comprehend these two simple words, and, quite suddenly, his rather pale face turned a radiant crimson, a picture of fury and humiliation. He crashed his sledge-hammer right fist down on his desktop.

"No, no, no, no! I can't believe! I can't believe I buy shirt with stupid words on it. I am stupid boy! This is very very wrong! Soccer dad? No, no, soccer not dad, soccer living! All over world soccer living, not dad! Only in America soccer is dad! America don't love soccer, so it dad here! Stupid! Stupid! Stupid! America stupid! Anton stupid! Soccer alive in whole world! It never die!"

I tried to calm him down by explaining the difference between dad and dead. I told him what a soccer dad is and why it was kind of funny for a single Romanian teenager to be wearing a shirt that had obviously been targeted towards American fathers. He didn't see what was so funny about that and didn't surrender his rage easily. It was a fire that would not quickly be snuffed out by something as tame as a logical explanation.

By the next day, Anton's face had regained its usual pallor, and he wore a solid black textless tee shirt. Calm, for the moment, was restored. Of course, we never saw the Soccer-Dad shirt again. Yet another tee shirt had been sucked into oblivion.

The Zeal of Zaheen

Zaheen, a short skinny Saudi woman in her early twenties, was in my small 103 grammar class in Berkeley. In keeping with Islamic practice, her head was always covered; otherwise, she dressed in rather typical, if conservative, western clothes: jeans, sneakers, etc. Her nose looked as Jewish as mine. As an observant Muslim woman, she never went on dates or to parties. In fact, as she was careful to inform me and the other males in the room during our first class, she was not permitted to touch any male other than those in her family—her father or her brothers. Or her husband, if she had one, which she didn't. She added that she could only shake my hand if she or I were wearing gloves. I joked that I would go right out that afternoon to buy her a pair. She laughed sweetly. She had expeditiously and effectively drawn the line.

Zaheen's routine could not have been simpler. She went to school, went home and studied, read the Koran, and prayed. She had a student's life with no discernible distractions, ideal for her perfectionistic, perhaps obsessive, pursuit of the highest possible grades.

In that class, we aimed to cover about a third of the

material in the school's textbook for that level by the end of a four-week session. Zaheen, however, during her solitary evenings at home, had already gone through the entire book by the end of the second week. She had not only gone through it; she had seemingly mastered it. With every question I threw out to the class, Zaheen's hand would shoot up; whenever I called on her, she had the right answer. The other students may have been having more fun at night, but I could see that they were quite awed by the daytime triumphs of their more industrious classmate, and perhaps more than a little envious. Zaheen, basically shy, seemed both proud and embarrassed by her conspicuous academic distinction.

Since it was the middle of the session, it was time for me to give the students their midterm exam. I had put together a fairly lengthy test with six pages of questions about the course's grammar, vocabulary, idioms, and so on. With one exception, the students looked quite daunted by the heft of it; that exception, of course, was Zaheen, who gazed upon her test like a gourmet about to dig into a feast laid out on the table before her.

I gave the students an hour to complete that test, and, near the end of the hour, Zaheen was still poring over it. She assured me that, in fact, she had already finished everything and was just going over it to make sure that each answer was perfect. How many times had she already checked and re-checked it? I wondered if she'd still be there checking it, "making sure,

Teacher," if I had given her two hours. Or three. When it was time to take a break and move on to our next classes, Zaheen reluctantly surrendered her paper to me.

"Don't worry, Zaheen, I'm sure it's excellent. As always."

"Inshallah."

"Inshallah" is an Arabic word (and now an English one too) that means "If God wills it," or as we would usually say in English, "God willing." Saying it leaves the door open for the unexpected, always a good idea, and prepares one in advance to accept graciously whatever fate is waiting in the wings; one needn't be religious to appreciate the wisdom in that perspective. Although, as a representative of the total-immersion approach to ESL teaching, I'm supposed to strictly enforce the dictum of "English Only!" in the classroom, I've always backed off on that so I can selfishly continue to extract goodies from the international grab bag. It's also fun to toss some words from my students' languages at them when they're least expecting it and watch their reactions. But more about that later.

"Yes, sure, inshallah. Of course, I'm not at all worried about how you did today, Zaheen. I'm sure you did an excellent job."

"Thank you, Teacher."

Somehow, she didn't look as confident as I'd expected her to. She departed with a concerned look on her face that made it clear that she would not breathe easily until the next day, when I would give everyone their corrected and graded tests, and then discuss whichever questions might still be unclear to them. It was going to be a long night for her, I was sure.

That evening, after dinner, I sat at my desk, sipping a cognac and correcting those exams. There were no significant surprises; each student had performed pretty much as expected. Then I came to Zaheen's. Here too, her performance was completely predictable: Page One, perfect. Page Two, perfect. And on and on like that until one of the questions on Page Five. It was a multiple choice question, always the favorite form among my students, since, even if they have no idea what the correct answer is, they have a 25% chance of being right just by guessing, just by circling A, B, C, or D. The problem with Zaheen's answer to that question on Page Five was that she had circled *two* letters, B *and* D. B was the right answer, but I couldn't just give it to her. What kind of precedent would that set? Why not circle A, B, C, *and* D?

Her grade was 99%. I was sure that the news of the lost 1% would enter her like a knife; in her eyes, this would be an excruciating failure. I had another idea, one which seemed like a good compromise between justice and mercy. In class, on the next morning, before handing back her test, I said to her, "Zaheen, just as I expected, your test is excellent. In fact, it's almost perfect. But there *is* one problem. Here, on Page Five." She suddenly had a guilty look I'd never seen on that face before; she knew exactly where I was heading. I pointed to the question in question. "You circled both B *and* D. Only one of them can be the right answer. In fact, one of them *is* the right answer. Of course, that means that the other one is wrong. You have to choose only one. I'll give you a chance to get 100%, since I know how important it is for you. Think very carefully and choose B *or* D. If you choose correctly, you can have the point *and* 100%. If you choose the wrong one, you will stay at 99. Sorry."

"Oh," Zaheen said with a quivery voice, sounding grateful and worried at the same time. "Right now? Here? Today?"

"Sure. Take your time, Zaheen."

The other students sat there with their lesser grades and watched the drama of the agonizing perfectionist. Zaheen *did* take her time, weighing each choice, dreading a fatal misstep. I started wondering if I really *was* doing her a favor or simply extending her self-torture.

Finally, she looked up at me and said, still shakily, "Okay, teacher, I try now. I choose one."

"Okay, good, Zaheen. Which one is your final answer? B or D?"

She hesitated for a few more highly charged seconds and said with resignation and apprehension, "B, Teacher. I choose B."

"B? Did you say B? Or did you say D?"

I was starting to sound like Regis Philbin.

She looked a little more nervous, but repeated, "B, Phil. I choose B."

"B . . . is . . . right! You did it, Zaheen. 100%!"

A grand smile broke out on her face. She was radiant, ecstatic, suddenly beautiful.

I got carried away with that flood of joy and relief and raised my hand in the standard pre-high-five gesture. Zaheen, caught up in the same wave, raised hers in perfect choreographic synchronicity. Those two palms, hers and mine, flew toward each other, and, just as they were about to produce that climactic slap, we simultaneously came to our senses and pulled them back, as if from a blazing fire.

"Whoa, Zaheen, I'm sorry. I forgot."

Zaheen was shocked at what she had almost done but said, laughing, "I forget too, Teacher. But is okay. We both forget."

I laughed too, a little nervously. "Good. Good, Zaheen."

As all the students joined our laughter, Zaheen and I looked at each other and smiled, both of us knowing that we had shared something profound in that feeling, forgetting, approaching, remembering, withdrawing, and laughing. I would have liked to teach Zaheen a new vocabulary word, some grand amalgamation of all those gerunds, but I didn't have one.

It takes just a moment like that to establish a lasting bond. That session ended, and several months went by without having Zaheen in any of my classes. We'd always greet each other warmly as we passed in the hallway or ran into each other in the cafeteria, but I didn't have the chance to interact with her as her teacher again until she showed up in my Masters' class during the following summer.

She was, predictably, still studious, but was showing some signs of easing up on her relentless pace. She had made several friends since she'd last been in my class, and an actual social life had started to infringe on her formerly hermitic study program. She looked happier in general though maybe just a bit burned out. On the first day of class, we exchanged big smiles (but, of course, no hugs) and told each other how glad we were to be together in a class again.

Her work in class continued to be very good, and on one morning, she outdid herself. I had posed an especially difficult question to that group of fifteen students. It was the kind of question that was virtually rhetorical since I really didn't expect anyone to know the answer and was just using it to segue into the next part of the lesson. In fact, no hands went up, and I was about to answer my own question when Zaheen, seated to my left in the circle of students, cautiously raised hers.

"Yes, Zaheen?" I said, thinking she had a question of her own.

"I think maybe I know the answer."

"Great. Let's hear it."

She then proceeded to give a complex explanation of the issue at hand, perfect in every detail. I was nodding and smiling, so all the other students knew that Zaheen's answer was an excellent one. And Zaheen knew it too, of course. That answer was so amazing that we all applauded.

"Wow, Zaheen. I am very impressed. That was a perfect explanation."

"Thank you, Teacher," she said, blushing and smiling.

I walked over to her and said, with a winking reference to the in-joke that was part of our shared history, "And don't worry, this time I will remember *not* to give you a high five. I learned my lesson months and months ago."

Zaheen laughed and said, "It's okay now, Teacher. I'm becoming different. I'm changing. It's okay now to do high five with me. Really."

"Really?"

"Really, Teacher. Please give me high five."

A squeamish part of me felt like saying "In front of all these *people?*" but I went with "Okay, you've certainly earned it."

I approached her desk with exhilaration and just a bit of trepidation. We raised our palms high, and, then, with great gusto, completed the triumphant slap that we'd aborted seven months earlier.

Zaheen's cheeks were flushed with excitement. I knew that she had crossed over a line. I wondered what other lines she had crossed—and had yet to cross. Some of her Saudi compatriots were already criticizing her, I knew, for other deviations from their norm, from their code. Life was not going to be easy for her if she continued on this path, but, by this point, it would be at least as hard to go back to her old life, her old ways. She had perhaps painted herself into a corner, but it seemed to have giant windows with grand views. And an unlocked door.

It seems that so many acts can be seen as liberation from one angle, transgression from another. Sometimes, as I suspect was the case with Zaheen, we feel a heady mix of both. Her only reliable resource was, as the cliché goes, to trust her own heart, its beat quickening as she felt the textures of this new world. Without gloves.

What's in a Name?

It was the first class of a session in Oakland, and my students and I were in the usual business of getting acquainted: names, brief bios, questions and answers. I started things off.

"Welcome, welcome, my name is Phil . . ."

As usual, I had arranged the seat-desks (or as they're sometimes called in the classroom-furniture business, "tablet arm chairs") in a roughly circular configuration. On the circumference to my right, a couple of my Saudi students were unsuccessfully trying to suppress a sudden fit of tittering.

"Is something funny, guys?"

"No, no, teacher" Khalid insisted, but his grin shouted yes, something is *very* funny.

"So, if nothing is funny, why are you laughing?"

Shrugs.

I tried his friend. "Mahmoud?"

"Well, it *is* a *little* funny. The sound of your name in Arabic have meaning, kind of funny meaning."

"Oh. Okay. Cool. You *must* tell me, so I can laugh too. Also, I'll learn another Arabic word."

"Well, teacher . . ." Clearly, Mahmoud was reluctant

to say anything that might offend his teacher or fall below the minimum level of respect. Especially on the first day of class. His face had turned bright red.

"Really, Mahmoud, it's okay. This kind of thing happens a lot between languages. It can be very funny sometimes." Which was true. "Don't worry. I'm sure I won't be insulted or embarrassed." Well, maybe not sure, but close.

"Okay, teacher. I tell you." A few more chuckles (somewhat nervous, somewhat apprehensive) bubbled up and out as I watched him silently composing his short but, to him, hilarious sentence. "'Feel' in Arabic mean 'elephant.'" That *was* funny, and my guffawing freed up those Saudi guys to join me, freed them from fears of incrimination. In fact, the whole class joined in.

"That *is* funny. I even have an elephant's trunk." I displayed my profile to showcase my sizeable nose. "But I have to tell you that my name is actually not Feel. My name is Phil, which is a nickname for Philip. Phil, not Feel. So, you see, I only look like an elephant, but, actually, I'm human."

Mahmoud laughed at my joke but looked as if something in my explanation had befuddled him.

"Do you have a question, Mahmoud?"

"Yes, Teacher. I can't understand when you say 'Feel, not Feel.' The two words sound same. Exactly same." Of course, to his ears, they did.

"Well, actually, the sounds are different. Listen: Phil. Feel. The first is a short vowel sound—Phil. The second is long—Feeeeeeeeeel. Listen to the difference: Phil. Feeeeeeeeeel."

I wrote the two words on the board, and we examined and practiced the difference between the two vowel sounds until everybody could pronounce Phil correctly. I regally proclaimed that anyone who backslid into calling me Feel would be required to call me Prince Philip, an edict which, of course, I never enforced.

There are some homophonic coincidences which are potentially more embarrassing. For example, one time in Oakland, in the late seventies, I used the names of a couple of friends of mine, Jerry and Marla, in one of the sentences in a verb-tense review. When we came to that sentence, several of my Japanese students began to giggle. Never wanting to be out of the loop, I asked what had struck them so funny.

"Oh, we tell you later, teacher," said Hiroshi, a twenty-one-year-old guy, slyly grinning under his anachronistic flat-top.

"Why later? Is it embarrassing?"

"Yes. Hee Hee. Embarrassing."

"Okay. Since it's embarrassing, I can hardly wait."

During the break, Hiroshi told me that, in Japanese, there's a word whose pronunciation is very similar to "Marla"; it was something like "*marra*" or "*malla.*" In the Japanese language, he explained, there is no character which is pronounced as a pure "r" or pure "l" sound. There *is* a character which is a sort of hybrid of the two. That's why Japanese people have so much trouble pronouncing English words containing l's and r's. Before he could continue with his mini-disquisition, I interrupted him:

"That's very interesting, Hiroshi, but you still haven't told me the meaning of *this* funny word."

"Oh, right, yes, that's right. I didn't."

"So?"

"Well, it's mean, how you say? Ball? You know, what man have? He have two. Balls?" During his explanation, Hiroshi was pointing, with his finger at a discreet distance from its object, at his groin. "Here."

"Ah, I see, I see," I laughed, "testicle!"

"Testicle mean ball?"

"Yes, that's right."

"Okay, Phil-San. So that is meaning of Marla. Marla mean testicle. Now you understand."

"Thank you, Hiroshi. Thank you for the excellent Japanese lesson."

He laughed, "You welcome, teacher."

For years, I somehow had never told Marla how her name gave a funny wrinkle to one of my lessons, and why she might consider adopting a less provocative moniker if she visits Japan. When I recently read this story to her to make sure she was comfortable with its inclusion in this book, she laughed even harder than I had.

Many students, especially Taiwanese and Korean, arrive in ESL classes in the States feeling that their foreign names are impediments to bridging the gap between themselves and the Americans they expect to meet. Consequently, they change their Asian names to what they think of as typical American names. There have been spates of Amys, Andys, Brads, Alices, Joyces, Janes, Keiths, Kens, Peters, Roberts, Stevens, and Thomases flying here from Asia. Sometimes the students choose their own American names and sometimes a well-meaning friend or teacher, here or abroad, assists them with the selection.

The bonding with their new name happens very quickly and strongly. Back in the early nineties, we had a very gifted harpist in our school, a young Taiwanese woman who was simultaneously enrolled in our English school and the Holy Names Music Department. Her Taiwanese teacher in Taipei had given her the "American" name, Daphanie. This was a clear-cut case of spelling following pronunciation. I explained to my student that the English name was actually Daphne, that the correct pronunciation of that name had two, not three, syllables, and that the spelling was actually D-a-p-h-n-e.

"Oh, thank you, teacher. I didn't know that."

"You're welcome, Daphne."

We practiced pronouncing the English name a few times until she said it perfectly.

"That's great! So now you can change the spelling

of your name to go with the correct two-beat pronunciation," I said, hoping to appeal to her sense of music.

"Thank you for teaching me that, Phil. Now I know how to spell and say English name Daphne. Two beats. But my name is Daphanie. Three beats."

Clearly, I was too late.

"You know, you are probably the only Daphanie in the whole world. You're certainly the first one *I've* met."

"That's okay . . . because that's who I am. I am Daphanie."

"Yes. Of course. That *is* who you are. You *are* Daphanie."

In fact, after having been Daphanie for over a year, she was inseparable from that name. She *was* Daphanie. Who else could she possibly be? Her sweet round-cheeked smile could only be Daphanie's smile.

"I am so pleased to know the only Daphanie in the world. Daphanie, would you be so kind as to play your harp for us, as only you can?"

I knew she would. She had never said no to that request. Unlike most students, Daphanie was never shy about making music for her classmates and teacher; it was always a joy for her to play for us, to enchant us.

"Yes, I be glad to."

The other students were happy to join us in one of our several strolls over to the practice room on campus where Daphanie's harp lived. Its wooden frame, with many intricate carvings under a gleaming coat of gold paint, looked huge next to its player. After tuning up, Daphanie played something by Bach: sweet, yearning, crystalline, and free, straight from the soul, Bach's soul, Daphanie's soul. These were tones plucked from heaven, music to make one forget about all the Daphnes of the world; not one Daphne, I was convinced, could coax such glorious sounds from strings, wood, and air.

While editing this story, I did something that I wouldn't have been able to do when I'd met Daphanie: I googled her name. I'd simply wanted to see if I could find my old student; I couldn't, but what I did find surprised me: a handful of other Daphanies. The name, I learned, is, in fact, a very rare variant of Daphne, which is derived from the Greek word for "laurel." So perhaps she *wasn't* the only one back then. But perhaps she *was*.

Around the same time, I was tutoring a Korean student individually. His Korean given name was Young Man. This eighteen-year-old was about thirty years younger than I was, so his name seemed sharply apt, more like a descriptive label than an actual name. After two or three months, we got to know each other rather well and felt quite at ease, so I told him about an ongoing little private joke that regularly played out in the silent confines of my head: often, when he answered a question correctly, wrote a particularly good sentence, or nailed a difficult pronunciation, I'd say something like, "Well done, Young Man!" and then imagine him responding respectfully, "Thank you, Old Fart."

"Oh, is that right way to answer? May I call you 'Old Fart'?"

I laughed. His question was funnier than my secret joke. I explained that "Old Fart" was actually not respectful, then, what a fart is (even though, of course, the idiom "old fart" has nothing directly to do with literal flatulence), and that a simple thanks was a perfectly sufficient response.

The next time I commended Young Man, he showed me that he had listened well to me: he simply nodded and said "Thanks, Phil."

We looked at each other and laughed at the same time. It was obvious that my little joke was now sounding in two heads instead of one. It was as though he had actually said it aloud. But even louder.

"Go ahead, it's okay, you can say it, Young Man. Sometimes friends can feel friendlier by using typically unfriendly expressions in a friendly joking way. Do you know what I mean?" I didn't have high hopes that he *would* after my convoluted explanation.

"I think maybe I do," he ventured. "Like when friends call each other idiots or say 'drop dead,' but everybody can laugh because is clear that the words are just being used for kidding around, to have fun together. These bad words not really bad because they are not spoke in serious bad way. Is that correct understanding, Phil?"

"Absolutely! You understand me perfectly. You are truly an excellent student, Young Man."

"Thank you, Old Fart."

It's usually on the first day of classes that any issues related to my students' names arise. In San Rafael one afternoon, I was calling out the names on the list of an intermediate reading/writing class and came to the name Hak-Sun Lee. When I called it out, a twenty-something Korean man responded:

"I'm here. But please don't call me Hak-Sun. Please call me Harris. That is my American name. Harris."

"Oh, okay. Harris." As usual, I wondered if he had chosen that name or whether someone had laid it on him, here or back in Seoul. It seemed a somewhat odd choice. But, of course, odd name choices among my students were anything but rare.

"Yes. Harris. That's me. Harris."

"I'm curious, Harris, did you choose that name yourself?"

"No, no, I not choose. My home-stay father he give it me."

"Ah, I see. And how long have you had this name?"

"He give it me yesterday. Just one day. Just one day I have it."

"Oh, good, so you're not really too used to it by

now. Because, I was thinking that it might cause a little confusion since Harris is usually a last name, I mean a family name, so when you tell people that your name is Harris, they might ask you what your 'first' name is, your given name." The potential for confusion here is even exacerbated since, in Far Eastern countries like Korea, Japan, Taiwan, and China, family names come first and given names second. Hak-Sun looked a bit unsettled, even perhaps somewhat put upon, but I pressed on. "What do you think about this suggestion? How about Harrison instead of Harris? I think it's better for at least two reasons: first, in English-speaking countries, Harrison is used as both a last *and* a first name; in fact, there's a very famous American actor you've probably heard of, Harrison Ford." He nodded without changing his seriously glum expression. "Also, HarriSON sounds a lot more like Hak-SUN than Harris does, doesn't it?" He gave me another grim begrudging nod. "So, since you've only been Harris for one day, it would be easy to make this simple switch to Harrison. Don't you think so?"

His answer was all business: "My name is Harris. Please, teacher, call me Harris." As I said, the bonding process is swift and strong. That was that.

"Okay, no problem. Harris it is."

After the next day's lunch hour, we all returned to that classroom. Following the daily ritual, I again went through my student list, reciting the names, one by one. When I got to Hak-Sun's name, I was careful to respect his explicitly stated preference:

"Harris?"

"Yes, present, teacher, but . . . " He looked somewhat sheepish.

But? Had I somehow still managed to screw up?

"I was thinking about what you say yesterday, and I thought probably you are right about Harris and Harrison. Then I talk with my host father because I don't want to hurt his feeling, and when I talk with him he say yes of course. Yes of course your teacher right. Harrison is better. So thank you, teacher, for my name. I am Harrison."

It was strangely satisfying, and I told Harrison why.

"You know, you're the first student I've ever given a name to. I almost feel like I'm your dad because the only other guy I've ever given a name to before was my real son. Now I've added a Korean son to my life." He laughed, and I discovered that he actually had a rather winning smile.

"That funny."

Then, for the rest of that course, and later, when he wasn't my student anymore, whenever I'd pass him in the hall or see him on campus, I'd wave and say, "Hi, son." Invariably, a big smile would break out on his face as he'd wave back and boom out, "Hi, Dad!"

Ah, the pleasure of paternity without the responsibility or expense; not a bad arrangement.

Group activities and games can be fun and instructive, but some have the inherent drawback of being vulnerable to the vagaries of spotty attendance. Take debates, for example. Each team has a set number of members who prepare their arguments and rebuttals together. If even one student is absent, the debate probably has to be shelved until everyone returns.

During a session in Oakland, I co-taught a group activity class with my colleague, Robin. One afternoon, two student teams were scheduled to square off for the final, decisive round of a debate on one of the standard topics: probably abortion, or nuclear energy, or women's rights, or smoking, or euthanasia, or whatever. That's not important here. A few minutes after the beginning of the class, the teams, in two little round huddles on opposite sides of the room, were already going over their strategies.

But there was a problem. One of the students, a Japanese guy named Makoto, wasn't there yet. Five minutes passed, and he still hadn't arrived. Ah well, it wouldn't be the first time Makoto was late, Robin and I assured each other. Another five minutes passed, and still no Makoto. After a quarter hour had gone by, we reconciled ourselves to the obvious: we'd have to scrap the debate plan for that day and do something else. No big deal. Improv is good for the soul.

Just as we were about to announce to the students that the debate would be postponed to the next day, we heard the sound of running footsteps in the hallway, a crescendo of slapping sneakers right before a very winded Makoto made his appearance, gasping for breath, in the doorway.

"Ta-Dahhh!" sang Robin with relief.

"No, not Tadao. Makoto," explained our surprised student, still huffing and puffing, apparently wondering how his teacher could get his name wrong after they'd known each other and worked together for three weeks. "Robin, I am Makoto. Not Tadao."

"Of course you are Makoto, Makoto. 'Ta-Dahhh' is just something we say when we're very happy that something we've been waiting for has finally happened," explained Robin. "Like your arrival here today. It's like blowing a trumpet. Ta-Dahhh! It's not a name. It's a sound. Ta-Dahhh!"

"Oh, uh-huh, so you *did* remember my name."

"Of course," Robin assured him.

But, of course, there was no "of course" about it. We ESL teachers have to learn so many names, thousands over the course of our careers, that it's virtually impossible to remember them all. Robin herself tells the story of dining in a Berkeley restaurant one evening and being surprised by one of her former students, an Iranian man, someone who had been her student several years earlier.

"Hi, Robin, it's so wonderful to see you again."

"Yes, it's great to see you again too!" Robin gushed.

"Do you remember my name?" he asked, naturally hoping, even expecting, that she would.

Robin had no recollection of his name whatsoever and was somewhat embarrassed to be in the spot of showing him that he, or at least his name, was, in fact, *not* unforgettable. She reasoned, rightly, that a large portion of the Iranian male population was named "Mohammed" or "Abdullah," and decided that she'd take a chance and gamble on choosing the latter. It seemed like a long shot but preferable to conceding defeat at the outset and admitting that she had simply and utterly forgotten.

"You are Abdullah," she said, drumming up a confident tone.

"Yes!" he exclaimed, "you *do* remember my name!"

"Of course," Robin, relieved, assured him. "How could I forget?"

Each four-week session in Oakland began the same way: we teachers would interview the new students, assess their skills, and do our best to place them in the right level. On one of those days, a student wearing a faded red baseball cap and loose-fitting sweatshirt and jeans walked into the large lounge area in the Holy Names dormitory where we were going through those paces. With hair and body so well cloaked, I couldn't immediately determine this new person's gender. Not that that information was essential or even germane to the business at hand, but curiosity is curiosity. The Thai name at the top of the registration form didn't help. But, as soon as I saw it, I knew I'd be talking about it for years: Tittiporn.

Keeping a straight face, I greeted our new student.

"Hello Tittiporn. Welcome to our school."

Shyly, guardedly, almost inaudibly, a female voice answered me. "Thank you."

Now that I could see her thin wrists and hear her voice, I decided that I was probably in the presence of a woman. I asked the usual interview questions and sent her off to take our placement exam.

She wound up in one of our "high beginning" levels, 103. Some students show an understandable timidity during the first few days and then seem to bloom as they get more comfortable with their new acquaintances and surroundings. Not Tittiporn. The little that she spoke never seemed to increase in volume, so I generally found myself straining to make out what she was saying. My hunch was that her "shyness," for lack of a better word, was a regular part of her life in Thailand too, that she may not have fit in better there than she did here. She continued to seem so emotionally fragile that none of us felt comfortable or skillful enough to try to find an inroad to gently inform her that her name, with its very common Thai "porn" suffix, carried radically different semantic cargo in English.

We generally don't encourage students to abandon their original names and pick "American" ones in order to better "fit in," but sometimes it seems advisable, and sometimes consequences themselves push the student to do it autonomously. For example, a Korean man, Bum Suk Lee, was taken aback when, several times, upon introducing himself as Bum Suk to an American, he saw the other person unsuccessfully try to suppress an amused grin. Eventually, someone explained the meaning of his name in English, and he asked everybody to simply call him Lee. No harm done. Not much anyway.

With Tittiporn, none of us ever felt confident that we had earned enough of her trust to unload potentially mortifying information on her. So, life went on, day to day, and it became rather clear that Tittiporn would probably remain Tittiporn for her duration at our school, despite that name's connotations to Americans. At least, I was fairly convinced, her name didn't have the same association for most of her classmates.

One gets used to most names after repeatedly using them, but "Tittiporn" never lost its punch. With that name, there was simply no way to acquire the usual numbness that accompanies habit. I remember a day when I was co-teaching with a colleague, Martin, in the Holy Names language lab, a triple-sized room where our students could practice their English using a variety of electronic programs and devices. On that day, Tittiporn was seated quite far from the teachers' control module. Martin needed to speak to her about something, so he called out to her, quite loudly, across the room:

"Oh, Titti, can you please come up here for a moment? I need to talk to you."

Somehow, the nickname that Martin had created on the spot sounded even less acceptable than the original. *Titti?* Standing next to him, I muttered, "Martin, I don't believe you just called her that." A slightly guilty smile on his face, he threw his hands up. Translation of his body language: "Do you have any better suggestions?" Of course, I didn't. "Tit" was no improvement, and "Porn" would have been even worse since *its* meaning was probably much more widely known among our students. So Tittiporn remained Tittiporn. Until one day.

She arrived at school wearing a new baseball cap, red like her old one. However, across the front of this one, in big white capital letters, was the name "BILL." Shyly (of course), she requested that we now call her by that name. Clearly, someone had found a way to let her know about the waves that her original name stirred up in English.

Of course, her choice of this particular American name revived the initial air of mystery that surrounded her sexual identity; we may have been thinking of her as a woman, but that was not, it now seemed, how she saw herself; assuming, of course, that she understood that "Bill" is almost always a man's name. Of course, with English as well as with sex, there is apparently an infinite potential for jumping to wrong conclusions.

So Tittiporn was now Bill. Secretly, and, I guess a bit guiltily, many of us still silently heard echoes of the spicy original in our heads as we uttered its bland replacement. Tittiporn/Bill continued at our school for another few weeks, until the end of that session, before transferring to our San Francisco branch.

We didn't hear much about their new transfer

student from our colleagues across the Bay, until, one day, we got a third-hand account (maybe true, maybe apocryphal) that Tittiporn/Bill had been busted for shoplifting somewhere in San Francisco. Hearing that, I realized how much I cared about that lonely soul, and found myself hoping that the story was just an empty tale from an overactive gossip mill. True or not, the mere possibility of that scenario made all the snickering we'd done seem especially off, callous, narrow, and our reticence more cowardly than sensitive. For all we knew about her, if we *had* mustered the courage to tell her about the ribald meaning of her name in English, she might have even laughed with us and easily agreed that it *is* funny. But, when I contemplated the woes that might have befallen her in the city, all traces of jocularity evaporated. What was left, what lingered, was a sad sense that, if we had only taken a break from reveling in our little irresistible joke, there was more we might have done for that gentle refugee from Bangkok . . . and from Oakland.

I remember another Thai student whose name turned out to be more than the simple label names usually are. As she took her seat, I glanced at her first name at the top of the registration sheet that lay on the wooden desk between us: Som-Chai.

"Good morning, Som-Chai. How are you today?"

"I'm good, sir. Thank you."

"Good. So, Som-Chai, I'll be asking you a few

questions, just to find out a little about you, and also to see how well you understand me when I speak English to you and, of course, to listen to you when you speak English to me." I went through the routine first-day queries and comments, my standard mantra, and was about to finish up:

"So, Som-Chai, it's been very nice to meet you. I hope you'll enjoy your time here."

"Thank you, teacher, but can I ask you a favor?"

"Sure, of course, Som-Chai. Whatever I can do to help . . . "

"Please don't call me Som-Chai."

"Oh, I'm sorry. Did I pronounce your name wrong?"

"No, no, teacher, you pronounce it right. Perfect. But you sing it *not* right."

"Ah, so the tone, the intonation, is wrong. Does that affect the meaning?"

"Yes, it change meaning. In Thai language, the singing sometime change meaning."

"Please tell me how it changes it with *your* name."

"Well, my name real sound is 'Som-Chai????'" She intoned her name with an upwardly lilting second syllable, giving it an interrogative quality. "It mean 'Like a real winner.'"

"Aha. That's a good meaning. And," I asked with more than a touch of trepidation, "what did *I* call you?"

"You call me Som-Chai." And this time, the pitch of that second syllable dropped with a thud, like a solemn declaration. "It mean 'Like a real man.'"

I apologized for my faux pas, and, not surprisingly, she was gracious and understanding:

"Is not your fault, teacher. You could not know this."

I asked her to repeat the proper "melody" a few times, and I imitated her as well as I could. We kept up this little drill until we were both satisfied that I had it right. As Som-Chai got up to leave, I tried it one more time, aiming that second syllable, hyper-interrogatively, at the ceiling:

"See you tomorrow, Som-Chai????"

Her broad delighted smile revealed her suddenly conspicuous dimples.

"Perfect!"

Several times during the remains of that day, in bed that night, and on my way to school the next morning, I practiced singing her name: "Som-Chai???? Som-Chai???? Som-Chai???? . . . " I was confident that I had nailed it.

As it turned out, she'd placed into my Masters' class. I went down the list of students' names, and when I came to hers, I looked her straight in the eye and sang out, almost operatically:

"Som-Chai????"

Her brow wrinkled with obvious concern.

"Present. But can I ask you other favor? Please don't call me Som-Chai????"

That threw me. What she was now asking me *not* to call her sounded, to my ears, exactly like what she had asked me *to* call her on the previous day. I really thought I'd gotten it down.

"Am I still not saying it correctly?" I asked, mystified.

"No, no, teacher. It's perfect. But nobody *else* say it right. I'm very tired explaining, demonstrating, showing everyone right singing of my name, so I take English nickname."

"Yes?"

"Please call me Judy."

"Okay, Judy. But are you sure it's not Judy????" I intoned, almost squealing, raising that second syllable about three octaves.

Shaking with laughter, she joked, "Pretty sure."

Some names just grab you. Who can explain it? In the early nineties, in one of my Oakland classes, there was an Argentinean Jewish teenager named Horacio Teitelbaum. Teitelbaum was and is a fairly common Jewish surname in Brooklyn, where I grew up, but I had never heard it linked with an Horacio or any other Latino name. In Brooklyn, Latino names seemed to be exclusively reserved for Puerto Ricans. Something about the conjoining of those two names delighted me, and still does. I would tell friends about this name and would separate a loud "Horacio" from a quiet "Teitelbaum" with a little hiatus. I'd be sure to exaggeratedly roll Horacio's "r" with as much Hispanic grandiosity as I could muster before pausing—then with more than a dash of a Yiddish accent, mundanely invoke Teitelbaum like the kosher pickle of a name it is.

"O-RRRRRRRRRRRACIO . . . Teitelbaum."

I told Horacio how much I liked his name. Of course, not being from Brooklyn, he didn't see anything unusual or funny about it. "Hey, Horacio," I joked, "if I ever write a novel, I'd love to create a character with your name. Do I have your permission to use it, to make it part of a book?"

"Sure, why not?"

"Thank you, Señor Teitelbaum."

"You're welcome, Mister Phil."

Well, I haven't written that novel, and this is not a novel, but it *is* a book. I don't have any amazing stories to tell about Horacio, and I don't remember much about him; there's just that euphonious name.

Just taking attendance, calling out the names on a typical class list, was like reciting found poetry, an international smorgasbord of sound and evocation. I have long suspected that my rigorous attendance-taking at the start of each class had less to do with institutional requirements than with delight in the music of that list.

A Little Afternoon Music

In the story about Zaheen, I alluded to my little hobby of hitting up my students for bits and pieces of their languages in order to surprise their compatriots in other classes by spouting a word or expression in, hopefully, the right context. When I was able to pull it off, it usually elicited amazed laughter, not to mention a bit of cultural pride at hearing their native tongue coming from the mouth of their English teacher.

"Hey, teacher, how you know that? Who teach you that?"

"My students, of course."

"Your pronunciation perfect. Just like native speaker." I always suspected that some of them said this whether it was true or not, but I always lapped it up. Of course, if my few little nuggets provoked a flood of actual sentences in return, I would throw my hands up, wave the white flag, and my foreign "conversation" would be over before it began.

The surprised and amused responses to showing off my piecemeal knowledge were nothing compared to the shock and occasional embarrassment that my former colleague, Phyllis, could spark among our

Iranian students. Phyllis, a diminutive white-haired woman who dressed a bit more formally (relative to the rest of us), had, with her husband, Jack, lived in Iran for many years and was fluent in Farsi, a fact of her bio that she generally didn't advertise to her students. Sometimes, while overhearing a few of our Iranian students chatting away among themselves in their language, she'd pick up some impolite comments; of course, those barbs carried an extra charge if they happened to be about *her*. As that American "little old lady" chided them in the river of Farsi that was at her command, they could not have felt more mortified had they been caught with their pants down.

I couldn't hope to compete with Phyllis in this arena, but I was happy to settle for the surprised laughs I got for my far more modest displays of a word here, a phrase there. Of course, I didn't always get it right.

Case in point: San Rafael, 2004. In a morning grammar class, I asked Amy, a twenty-something Taiwanese student, to teach me how to say "Good morning" in Chinese. "*Zao ahn*," she said. I repeated it until she assured me I had the pronunciation down. One of Amy's friends, Shirley, was in my afternoon reading class, so, planning to surprise her with a Chinese "Good afternoon," I asked Amy how to say that too. "*Oo ahn*," she modeled. Once again, I imitated her until I got it down.

That reading class met right after lunch. The ten or so students, including Shirley, filed in and took their seats. Going down the class list, I arrived at Shirley's name. Geared up for my little surprise, I smiled at Shirley and said, "*Oo ahn.*"

"Excuse me, teacher? I don't understand. Please repeat." Looking concerned, she cocked her head at a forty-five-degree angle.

"Sure. *Oo ahn.*"

"I sorry, Phil. I still no understand you. Please, one time more."

"Hmm. Maybe I'm not pronouncing it right. But, here goes. *Oo an.*"

"What language is that words? Is English?"

"No, no. It's not English. I thought it was *your* language. I thought it was Chinese! I just learned how to say it. This morning. Or I *thought* I learned it. Your friend Amy taught it to me this morning."

"Chinese? Really? But I don't know this saying. What it means?"

"Well, Amy told me it means 'Good afternoon.'"

"Oh. 'Good afternoon.' Say again."

"*Oo ahn.*"

"Oh. I see, I see. Now I know problem. 'Good afternoon' is '*Oo ahn?*' in Chinese, not '*Oo ahn.*'" The pronunciations sounded exactly the same, but the melodies were starkly different. The former was a lovely two-beat phrase in which the second note rose jauntily above the first, but the latter version, *my* version, was unmusical, dry, literally monotonous. I couldn't help but think about my Thai student Som-

Chai and how my wrong intonation of her name had an entirely wrong, potentially offensive, meaning. Chinese, like Thai, is a tonal language. What new insult, I wondered, had I unwittingly hurled at poor Shirley?

"Oh, Shirley, I see. My tones are wrong. I'm not *singing* it right."

"That right. My language have tones, like song. Very important."

"I hope my 'song' doesn't have a bad meaning. What *does* it mean?"

"No meaning. Nothing. I never hear it before today."

"Oh, okay." I guess no meaning was preferable to a bad one. Still, why bother to speak if you communicated nothing? It didn't even succeed on the surprise-your-students-by-speaking-their-language level. If I wanted to try this one again, I needed to find a way to remember that two-note melody.

"Please, Shirley, say it again for me. Or maybe I should say 'sing it again.'"

"Okay," she laughed, starting to enjoy the ridiculous importance this had taken on for me. "*Oo ahn*?" There it was again, that lovely little tune, rising interrogatively, like Som-Chai's name. Hearing it again, I realized that there was something very familiar about it. I sang it again for Shirley to be sure I had it right.

"*Oo ahn*? Right?"

"Yes, right. You sound like Taiwanese person."

"Good, good."

Silently, I repeated the little phrase a few times in my head until—*voila*—it came to me. Mozart! *Eine Kleine Nachtmusik*. In the first movement, the famous allegro, the second and third notes have exactly the same melody as Shirley's "*oo ahn*?" That two-note phrase is then repeated a few times before it rises in pitch. I was inordinately delighted by this connection; language teachers as well as language learners routinely use mnemonic aids, but rarely are they as classically satisfying as this one.

"I've got it, Shirley. I figured out how I can always remember the right melody for '*oo ahn*?' Do you know Mozart's *Eine Kleine Nachtmusik*? In English, that German title means 'A Little Night Music.'" Her face was blank. I looked to her classmates.

"Anyone?" With the exception of one Swiss student, it didn't ring a bell for any of the others either. So I sang it, starting with "*ahn?*" as the downbeat: "*Ahn? oo ahn? oo ahn? oo ahn? oo ahn?*" and so on, singing through an absurdly large portion of that movement, the joy of discovery definitely carrying me over the top. All the students, including Shirley, started laughing with recognition; apparently, that melody was famous just about everywhere. And to make things even easier, both "good morning" (*Zao ahn?*) and "good evening" (*Wan ahn?*) were "sung" to that same Mozart tune, so, naturally, sing them I did, *con gusto*. Why avoid the ridiculous when you can revel in it with people from all over the world?

In future classes, when I'd intone one of these

Chinese greetings, I'd usually tell the story of how I memorized that mini-tune, and add, "You know, most people think that Mozart was Austrian, but, as you can plainly see and hear, he was obviously Chinese. I'm probably the only person who's told you the truth about this. You won't see it in any biography of Mozart. Ever."

Generally, everyone laughed at this silly riff, but I always scanned the room to make sure that no one was taking me literally and jotting down this new-found "fact" in order to share it with the folks back home. Only once did I feel the necessity to actually smile and wink at a student who looked at me quizzically after my delivery. Well, maybe twice.

La La La

Many Japanese students are bedeviled by the pronunciation of "r" and "l." It's a real problem that should not be dismissed as an unfair stereotype. As Hiroshi made clear in his explanation of why the name "Marla" sounds funny to him, part of the problem stems from the fact that neither sound exists in Japanese. This confusion affects not only speech, but writing as well; we tend to spell words the way we visualize and pronounce them. For example, in a memorable film review by a young Japanese guy, he wrote about his first visit to an American movie theater: "The movie was so funny that everybody crapped." That line earned a place on the bulletin board in the teachers' staff room in Oakland for the next ten years.

I had a student in Oakland in the early nineties, Taka, who had a fairly stubborn case of this syndrome. When introducing himself to the class on the first day, there were several examples of his r-l problem; for example, while mentioning a few of his hobbies, he said, "I rike baseball."

Gently, I said, "Taka, I see you sometimes have a problem with the 'r' and 'l' sounds, hmm?"

"Oh yes, Teacher, but not sometimes. Maybe always."

"Okay, I want to help you with this."

"Thank you for your kindness, Teacher."

"You're welcome. But, before we start, I want to tell you that I understand how hard it is to break these old speaking habits. I know that even if you say something right today, you may slip back into your old way tomorrow or the next day, and I'm sure that your classmates know it too. So don't feel bad if that happens. Okay?"

"Okay, yes, Teacher. I try not feel bad."

"Good. Let's start. You said 'I rike baseball,' but it should be 'I *like* baseball.'"

"Oh. Okay, I try. I rike baseball."

"No, Taka, you're still saying 'rike.' You're making an 'r' sound, but you need to make an 'l' sound. To make the 'l' sound, touch the top of your mouth, your palate, with the tip of your tongue, and say 'La la la.'"

"Ra ra ra."

"You're not touching the top of your mouth with the tip of your tongue. Look into my mouth. Watch what my tongue is doing." I then opened my mouth as widely as I could, as if I were at the dentist. Taka peered in as I sang, semi-operatically, "La la la la la la la."

"Oh, I see now, Teacher. I see what your tongue doing. Now I try again. La. La. La."

"Great! Now do the same thing with your tongue to say 'like.' La la la la. Like!"

"La la la la like!"

"Perfect! Now say 'I like baseball.'"

"I la la la like baseball."

"Great! Now say it without the la la la part. Just say 'I like baseball.'"

"I . . . like . . . baseball."

"Perfect again. I like baseball too."

A smile spread across Taka's face as he enjoyed his success. The transformation of his "l," however, was, as expected, not a permanent one. On the very next day, he asked me to explain something in that day's "resson." I repeated the previous day's instructions: "Remember, Taka, in order to make the 'l' sound, touch the top of your mouth with the tip of your tongue and say 'La la la.'" We went through the routine again until Taka was able to say "lesson" perfectly.

As the four-week session progressed, the intervals between Taka's "l" mispronunciations got longer and longer. During the first week, with each occurrence, I would repeat those tongue-to-palate directions: "To make the 'l' sound, touch the top of your mouth with the tip of your tongue and say 'La la la.'"

By the second week, it was no longer necessary to go through the full explanation. It was sufficient to simply say "La la la." Taka would then carefully position his tongue and quite quickly nail the offending "l" word:

"Runch."

"La la la."

"Lunch."

"Perfect"

"Rater."

"La la la."

"Later."

"Very good."

"Engrish."

"La la la."

"English."

"Yes!"

By the fourth and final week of the session, Taka had successfully incorporated a very natural, clear, and automatic "l" into his speech. I don't think I had to la-la-la him even once that week. On graduation day, before he left my classroom, I congratulated him, we shook hands, he thanked me, and we both felt a solid sense of accomplishment.

As I was gathering my papers before I too left, Rasheed, from Qatar, came up to my desk and said, "Can I tell you something, Teacher?"

"Sure, Rasheed. Of course. What is it?"

He had a funny little grin. "Well, I wanted to tell you that 'la' is Arabic word for 'no.' So whenever you interrupt Taka to help him with 'l' sound, it sound very funny to me. When you shake your finger at him and say 'La la la,' it feel like you saying 'No no no.' In Arabic. And it make sense because you are telling Taka he make a mistake, right? 'No no no, Taka.' But funny thing is you are American teacher. Speaking Arabic. To Japanese student! And you don't know it. And he don't know it. But he understand you perfect!"

We enjoyed a good laugh together, and I could see that he was feeling the special satisfaction of knowing that he'd been able to communicate something funny and slightly complicated in English.

"That *is* very funny, Rasheed. Thank you for sharing that with me."

"You're welcome, Teacher."

Before he left, I thanked him again for his additions to both my vocabulary and story collections. Both Taka and I had learned something new that month.

For many years after that, when an Arabic speaker would make a mistake in English, I would often seize the chance to surprise that student by whipping out Rasheed's one-syllable gift. It never failed to get a laugh, and even some double- or triple-takes, as I waggled my finger in the air in mock reprimand and chided like a schoolmarm, "La la la."

Nothing to Sneeze At

One of my earliest attempts to play my vocabulary-surprise game met with some stumbling blocks which had nothing to do with the tonal problems I'd run into with Chinese and Thai. I had wanted to surprise some of my Japanese students by being ready with the Japanese equivalent for "God bless you," just in case one of them happened to sneeze. The first step, of course, was to learn the correct word or phrase. When a Japanese guy in one of my beginners' classes sneezed, I seized the opportunity:

"What do Japanese people say when someone does that? When someone sneezes?"

"Oh, English word is 'sneeze'?"

"Yes, that's right. Sneeze." I wrote it on the board. "What do Japanese people say when someone sneezes?"

"Oh, okay. I help you, Phil-san. Japanese word is *kushahmi.*"

"Ah, okay, great. *Kushahmi*. That's a nice-sounding word. *Kushahmi*. Thank you."

"You welcome, Phil-san."

I jotted down my own crude transliteration and waited for a Japanese student to sneeze in one of my other classes. That wait lasted at least a couple of months before I got my chance. One morning, Toru, a Japanese guy in his early twenties, split the air with a whopper of a sneeze in the middle of a grammar lesson, which reminded me that I had a response hidden somewhere in my chaotic notes. It took me a few seconds to locate it in the jumbled contents of my briefcase:

"*Kushahmi!*" I bellowed.

"Huh?"

"*Kushahmi.*"

"Ah, *kushahmi*. I see. You practicing Japanese."

"Yes."

"So you know this Japanese vocabulary."

"Yes, I learned it from one of my other students two or three months ago. I learned that *kushahmi* is what Japanese people say to someone who has just sneezed."

"But, no, teacher, we don't say *kushahmi*. We say *ki ōtsukete*."

"It's not *kushahmi*?"

"Yes." (In Japanese, when someone agrees with a negative question, the answer is in the affirmative. For example: Person A: "Greece *isn't* in Asia?" Person B: "Yes." That seems more logical than *our* practice of saying "No," since, in effect, that "Yes" is short for "Yes, what you said is true." It can sometimes be a little confusing.)

"Wow, my other student was so sure. You're not kidding me? It's really not *kushahmi*?"

"Yes."

"No?"

"Yes."

"Okay, so what does *kushahmi* mean?"

"It just mean 'sneeze.' It just Japanese word for 'sneeze.' But we don't say 'sneeze' to people after they sneeze. You don't say that either in America. It sound funny. Don't you think so?"

"Yes, I do."

"So, remember, if Japanese person sneeze, say *ki ōtsukete.*"

"Okay, I will, Toru. Thanks for correcting me."

"You're welcome, Phil-san."

I wrote down that word too. Toru seemed to be allergic to something that was blooming in Oakland that spring, so he provided many opportunities to practice my new Japanese vocabulary. When that session ended, however, I had another longish wait for my next Japanese sneeze.

When that sneeze finally arrived, several weeks later, I was armed with my new improved knowledge. I turned to the sneezer, my student Mayumi, and said to her, confidently, "*Ki ōtsukete.*" When she started laughing, I thought it was simply the usual result of being surprised at my knowing this inside information. But not this time.

"No, no, Phil-san. We no say *ki ōtsukete* after sneezing. We say *o daiji ni. Ki ōtsukete* mean something like 'Be careful. Maybe is something dangerous here.' Or sometimes if someone going on trip, we say it too, like, you know, 'Take care' before travel?"

"Oh? And *o daiji ni*? People say *that* after someone sneezes?"

"Sure. Like when you say 'God bless you.' It mean 'I hope you get well soon.' Like 'Take care of yourself so you get healthy again.'"

"That sounds perfect, but it seems that every time I ask, I get a different answer."

"Trust me, Phil-san. Other ones wrong. I have right answer for you. I sure. Believe me. Okay?"

"Okay." She definitely sounded the most confident so far, and her explanation was spot-on specific, so, yet again, I whipped out my pad and jotted down this latest candidate for Japanese post-sneeze politeness. During the next interval of waiting between sneezes, I was not quite so confident.

My chance came just a few days later, in my Masters' class. Masayuki, a big barrel-chested fellow who looked like a wrestler or a football player, let loose with a full-throated blast that we all felt as much as heard.

"*O daiji ni!*" I bellowed, half expecting an objection or correction.

"Thank you, Phil-san." All right! It worked! I felt like, after a long trip, I had finally arrived.

"Uh huh. So that really *is* what you say in Japan when people sneeze."

"Well, not usually." Uh oh. There we went again. I hesitated before asking him for a clarification, not really wanting another addition to my growing list. Enough was enough. But ask I did.

"Not usually? Mayumi told me it's *o daiji ni.*"

Masayuki shrugged. Feeling more amazed than frustrated, I pressed on: "Okay, Masa, if it's not *o daiji ni*, what *do* people say after a *kushahmi*?"

"We usually say nothing. It not necessary. Not important. We silent."

"Nothing? Never *o daiji ni*?"

"Oh, sometimes, maybe, if you know someone very well. But usually nothing. Silent."

"So, Masa, it's not considered impolite to say nothing after a person sneezes?"

"No, never, Phil-san. Don't worry. It's okay."

"But what if Mayumi sneezes? Maybe she comes from a different part of Japan, a region where saying *o daiji ni* is expected."

"If Mayumi sneeze, it's okay. You can say *o daiji ni* to her. She teach you that, so you don't want her to think you are bad student. Right?"

"Right. Of course. Thank you, Masa. That's what I'll do."

But, clearly, as a rule of thumb in these situations, silence had become my safest option. Nevertheless, safety in the classroom not being a high priority, when a Japanese student would sneeze, I'd usually offer my *o daiji ni*, unlike the other Japanese students in the class, who generally said nothing on those occasions; it was almost always an amusing surprise and seemed to be appreciated as a gesture made by a foreigner who didn't know enough to avoid being unnecessarily polite.

I thought of all that recently in the locker room of my health club in El Sobrante. I was alone in there except for a guy, probably in his early twenties, who had more than fifty percent of his muscle-bound body covered with tattoos. I had seen him around the club before, but we had never exchanged a word. Suddenly I sneezed, and the sound was magnified by standard locker-room reverb.

"Bless you," said the surprisingly soft-spoken tattoo guy.

"Thank you," I replied.

"No problem."

Yeah, it was no problem for him; he hadn't tried to figure out how to say it in Japanese.

Ay, There's the Rubber

"English as a Second Language" is not always an accurate descriptor of what students are trying to learn here in the States. Some of them have already studied one or more foreign languages. And many of them have already studied English in their countries, but sometimes that English is British, which is not quite the same as what we speak in this country. Yes, of course, Americans and Brits can usually understand each other, but there are enough differences in accent, grammar, vocabulary, and idioms that I'd sometimes joke with my students that the real reason for the American Revolution was to free ourselves from having to speak like them.

For those who've studied the Queen's English as a second language, American English can sometimes be confusing. Perhaps, for them, "AETL" ("American English as a *Third* Language") would be a more apt course title than ESL.

Very soon after I started teaching at the Oakland school, I bumped into one of those many British-American discrepancies. On one of the first days of that session, I had written a sentence on the front blackboard which included the word "color." As I was proceeding with the lesson, Koji, one of my Japanese students, a serious man in his early thirties, slowly, with an air of caution, raised his hand.

"Yes, Koji, do you have a question?

Looking both sheepish and peeved, he said he didn't have a question but wanted to point something out to me.

"Sure. Go ahead."

He then said what he'd felt compelled to say: "I don't mean not respect, Teacher, but you spell a word wrong. 'Color' is not spelt like that way. I'm sure about this." His left hand gripped an open little dictionary (this was a couple of decades before electronic dictionaries and dictionary apps for cell phones became ubiquitous). He went on: "My teacher in Tokyo teach me word is spelt 'c-o-l-o-*u*-r.' And just in order be sure I check in my very good dictionary. It say same thing." At which point, he lifted the pocket-sized book above his head like a crusader's torch.

"Well, Koji, was your Tokyo teacher Japanese or from some English-speaking country?"

"My teacher in Japan is from UK."

"Uh-huh, I'm not surprised. And I'm sure your dictionary is also British."

"Here. Take look. And please look at correct spelling of 'colour' on this page," and he indicated the left-hand page of the open book. There it was: "colour," c-o-l-o-u-r.

I then checked the title page of his *Collins Gem Pocket English Dictionary* and, of course, read that it was indeed published in England. I gave some other examples of differences between the two Englishes to Koji and the rest of the class. He was a bit red-faced about his presumptuousness and apologized (with a zee, not an ess, and certainly not with a zed) about his having jumped to that negative, potentially insulting, conclusion. At the same time, I sensed his relief at discovering that his teacher actually did know something about the language he was getting paid to teach (at least in this case) and was not some moron who couldn't even spell "colour."

The Koji incident was only the first of many in which I had to point out the discrepancies in English one routinely ran into after crossing the Atlantic. There were also times when my students were not the only ones learning something about that. For example, while one of my intermediate grammar classes was taking a quiz one morning in the early eighties, I noticed Rie (pronounced *Ree*-ay), a pretty twenty-five-year-old Japanese woman, speaking to her closest desk neighbor (not "neighbour"), Francisco, a twenty-something Venezuelan guy. Of course, conversation during tests is routinely discouraged, so I gently informed her of that. She looked chastened and somewhat fearful, which was not my intention.

"So sorry, Phil-San. I not cheating. Really, Phil-San. It's the true."

"It's okay, Rie. It's just best not to talk to the other students during a test."

"Okay. I sorry."

"It's no problem. Don't worry about it. If you have a question, or if you need something, just ask me. Okay?"

"Okay, Phil-San. I do that."

"Do you need something right now? What did you ask Francisco? Maybe *I* can help you."

"Yes. Maybe. Probably."

"Yes?"

"What I ask Francisco is 'Can I borrow a rubber?' I need a rubber. Maybe you have one, Phil-San?"

I tried to hold back my laughter but didn't even come close to succeeding. It was almost unthinkable that she was asking Francisco if he had a spare condom. But I couldn't totally rule it out. On several occasions, Japanese women had surprised me during a break to explain an absence or a listless performance in class by confiding that they had been dealing with "woman sickness" or that it was "menstruation time of month," or other variations on the same theme. It was not a subject that women typically mentioned to their male English teachers, or even to their female ones, and the first time I heard it I wondered if I had somehow misunderstood. But no. It was a level of openness about matters that were usually ultra-private that I hadn't seen with women of other cultures, including my own. So, now, with Rie, I couldn't be 100% sure that she wasn't casually mentioning a need for a condom . . . only 99.9.

"Something is funny, Phil-San?"

By that time, of course, all the other students had stopped thinking about the quiz and were waiting to find out what their teacher had found so humorous. I got right to the point: "Well, Rie, in this country, 'rubber' is a slang word for 'condom.'"

She and about a quarter of the students knew the meaning of "condom," and, after they explained it to the others, everybody was laughing, Rie somewhat embarrassedly.

"Oh, Phil-San, I didn't ask Francisco to lend me condom. Please believe me."

"Of course, I believe you. Why would anyone ask to borrow one of those during a quiz on the past perfect tense?"

She laughed more unabashedly now that she'd been reassured that her *sensei* (teacher) didn't suspect her of being so overwhelmed by desire that she couldn't even wait for the end of the quiz to make sure she'd have all the necessary equipment at hand when she needed it.

Rie then explained what I had by then guessed and what those of her classmates who'd studied British English already knew: she'd asked Francisco if she could borrow his eraser. What could be more fitting in the context? "Eraser" was a new word for her;

although it existed on both sides of the pond, she was accustomed to using that British slang equivalent, which was a new one for *me*.

"Thank you, Rie. I guess you studied British English in Japan, right?"

"Yes, that right, Phil-San. American meaning of 'rubber' very different."

"Oh yes."

Then, Yves, a French student in his late twenties, asked a sensible question: "So, Phil, how you can know which meaning of rubber someone is using?"

"Well, I guess an English person would probably be talking about an eraser, and an American would be referring to a condom. Also, as with all slang and with vocabulary in general, the context usually makes the meaning clear. Right?"

"Uh, maybe is not so clear to me. Please explain more, Phil."

"Well, if you needed to erase a mistake on a quiz, like Rie, you would not ask for a condom; you'd ask for an eraser. Of course, a condom, especially a rubber one, might do the job, but not nearly as well as a good eraser. Not to mention that it would be a bad idea to use that condom for its intended purpose *after* using it to rub out your error." That got a good laugh, always one of my primary goals.

I went on: "Also, imagine a situation in which two lovers are embracing, and, in the heat of passion, one asks the other, 'Do you have a rubber?' I don't think there'd be any confusion about whether that question was about a condom or an eraser. An eraser of *any* type would be a terrible choice for birth control *or* disease prevention."

"I got it," said Yves, laughing with all the others. "That's context."

"Yes, that's context indeed. Okay, everybody, you'd better get back to your quizzes or we might run out of time."

Rie's hand shot up. "But, Phil-San, I still need a rubber." With a mischievous grin, she asked, "Do you have one?"

I dug around in my briefcase and found a brand new never-sharpened pencil, its rubber tip pink and clean, and handed it to Rie with an ostentatious flourish.

Turkish Delight

In the late seventies, while filling in for a sick colleague, I met Fehmi Baykan, a Turkish student in his twenties. It was a balmy spring day in the Oakland Hills, so I decided to take the small Masters' class outside and have our lesson on the plush green mattress-like grass of the Holy Names campus. There were about seven or eight of us, and we sat in a circle, facing each other. Since I was meeting these students for the first time, I asked them to introduce themselves. Fehmi said that he was a philosophy student at his Turkish university; that alone was quite enough to distinguish him from the pack. His appearance too was somewhat different from that of my typical students: diminutive, skinny, and mustachioed, he looked like he was analyzing the world, as if it were a complicated but intriguing text.

The class ended, and all the students except Fehmi and a Swiss woman, Kristina, left. That was the final class of the day, so the three of us were free to continue basking in the hot sun, which pulled strong green fragrances out of the newly mown grass, smells which covered us like a tent, made us drunk with late-afternoon languor, and freed our tongues to yak away about books, life, music, philosophers, food, films, what have you, as if we'd known one another forever.

To make a short story shorter, Fehmi and I became friends and got together a few times, away from the campus. It was enlightening to look at my world though his eyes. For example, I might be driving us to somewhere in Berkeley and Fehmi might shake his head in amazement and exclaim: "Wow, it's fascinating how Americans actually stop for red lights, how the intended symbolism of those lights actually affects the behavior of—it seems like every driver. In Istanbul, they have virtually no meaning, those red lights, even for police. It's like nobody even sees them. The safety idea behind them is excellent, and it is so good seeing how drivers here obey them, but in Istanbul, their endless going on and off and on and off with nobody seeing is waste of electricity." I made a mental note to avoid renting a car in Turkey.

I invited Fehmi and Kristina to dinner at my home on Sacramento Street in Berkeley. Right after they arrived on a Thursday night, Kristina handed Joan a box of Swiss chocolates, and, a couple of beats later, Fehmi handed her a box of Turkish Delight, that white chewy candy, embedded with fruit and nuts, that's as good as anything for yanking out dental fillings. It was the prelude to what turned out to be an evening filled with excellent food and wine, stimulating conversation, and lots of laughter. We said good night a few hours later, feeling like old friends.

Six days a week, our mail would arrive through a slot in the front door and land on the living room floor. The clank of that slot's iron lid, as our postman completed his delivery, was like the ringing of a Pavlovian bell; my pulse would quicken, I'd stop whatever I was doing, and rush over to that pile of paper on the floor in the hope of finding something more satisfying than the usual array of ads and bills. Crouching down to check out Saturday morning's stack, I found an envelope from Kristina: inside was a greeting card in which she had written a sweet note thanking us for the lovely dinner, our hospitality, etc. Nothing from Fehmi. Yet.

Monday's mail, however, did contain an envelope with Fehmi's name and address on the back flap. I picked it off the floor, opened it, and removed the Hallmark card. The cover had a close-up of a bouquet of roses, their deep burgundy petals against a midnight blue background. This was, of course, Fehmi's thank-you card, his Turkish Delight to Kristina's Swiss chocolates, as it were. Always the diligent student, Fehmi was emulating his Swiss social mentor in every detail of proper American guest-etiquette.

When I opened the card and saw its factory-printed greeting, I started laughing like a lunatic. In that very small house, Joan heard me from our bedroom and came out to see what was causing the commotion.

"What's so funny?"

She was already grinning before she got her answer.

Without saying a word, I handed her the card which, I was certain, our new philosopher-friend had selected with great attention to its semantics, doing his best to make sure that its words precisely communicated the nuances and fullness of his feeling. When she opened it, her smile doubled, and she too laughed as she read, in addition to Fehmi's inked thanks and signature, the three words in Hallmark's most stately calligraphy:

With
Deepest
Sympathy

The Education of Yaqub

In the mid-nineties, Yaqub, from Saudi Arabia, was about sixteen or seventeen. A tad shorter than average and almost but not quite chubby, he had a jovial, teddy-bear quality: milk chocolate skin, frizzy hair, very large brown eyes. This amiable young guy was well-liked by his classmates and teachers; after all, how many people have an antipathy for teddy bears? At the time of the following incident, Yaqub had been at our Oakland school for a few months and had already been in several of my classes. He was my favorite kind of student, one who loved to learn as much as he loved to horse around. We enjoyed and seemed to understand each other from the start.

During one summer session, Yaqub was in one of my afternoon conversation classes. I remember that room clearly: it was on the ground floor and had windows looking out on a grassy courtyard that had about a half dozen picnic tables placed under leafy trees. Inside the room, I had the individual seat-desks arranged in a horseshoe configuration to encourage face-to-face relating. The emphasis of this advanced class was on practicing spoken English, and the plan for that day's lesson was for each student to speak about "an interesting aspect of your country."

The students spoke about things I had heard many times: temples in Kyoto, idyllic Jeju Island in South Korea, the Night Markets of Taipei, the museums and restaurants of Paris, the cultural pluralism of Switzerland. When it was Yaqub's turn to speak, I expected to hear one of the usual Saudi cultural references: the oil industry, the alphabet, the cuisine, the marriage customs . . .

"Okay, Yaqub. You're on. What aspect of your country would you like to share with us today?"

"Well, Phil, I would like to talk about our thinking about Jewish people, how we Saudis feel about that."

"Ah, good, Yaqub, that's an interesting topic." Of course, being Jewish myself, I had a special interest in what my young friend had to say about the Saudi-Jewish connection, or rather, disconnection. I certainly knew what Saudis generally felt and said about Jews, but here was an opportunity to hear the perspective of the more open-minded younger generation.

"We hate the Jews," Yaqub began. "We have nothing to do with them." His use of the first person plural took me by surprise.

He continued. "For example, Steven Spielberg movies? We would never watch those. Never. Not in my country. No books, no music, no nothing from Jewish people. We are very strict about that. There are no exceptions."

Again, the shock of "we," not "they." It didn't take

long for a surprising realization to dawn on me: Yaqub had no idea that *I* was Jewish, even though it was literally as plain as the nose on my face. What was planted in the center of my face was, to Yaqub's eyes, not a "Jewish nose," but a normal one, one that so many Arabs had too. Semitic standard issue. He went on. He was just getting warmed up.

"When I am in the same room with a Jewish man, I want to take off my shoe and hit him in the face with it!"

The faces of the other students reflected my own shock, disbelief, and confusion. None of us had a precedent for dealing with a teddy bear who had suddenly turned into a grizzly. I snuck a peek through one of the windows, at one of the picnic tables under an oak, and imagined myself relaxing there, reading something, sipping something, listening to birdsong, basically enjoying the solitude of the unconnected. But that was a dream that lasted one, maybe two, seconds: inside that room, the pressure was building, and there would be no escape on that day, though I didn't yet know exactly where we were heading, or how I would handle it. Part of me didn't want to embarrass this young guy, but another part wanted to "teach him a lesson," literally and figuratively, or maybe it was the same part. Lessons are where you find them. Resigned to my entrapment, a "lesson plan" began to take shape, at least the first step of one.

"Let me ask you this, Yaqub. Can you always *know* when you're in the presence of a Jewish man?" I detected a slight unwelcome quiver in my voice, so I tried, with only moderate success, to sound calm, collected, unshaken. I was the man, after all: *he* was the boy.

With no hesitation at all, he snapped back, "Yes, of course I can tell. Every time."

My next steps couldn't have been clearer to me, or more irresistible. It was not a question of *if* I would detonate the bomb, but when. I wondered if any of the other students had sensed the direction this "discussion" had taken. I was sure that Yaqub had not.

I upped the ante. "You're saying that there can be no exceptions, that you have no doubt that you will always have 100% accuracy in this, that if a Jewish man is in the same room with you, you will always know it."

"Of course, Phil. Always. That's what I said."

The time had come to light the fuse.

"Yaqub, *I'm* Jewish."

Yaqub looked completely confounded; he opened his mouth as if to speak, but nothing came out. There was no place in his frizzy head to stow this anomaly, much less process it. He just stared at me for several seconds. It was the look of a man who'd just been shocked, but, also, betrayed, deeply hurt. Jewish? Of all the things I could do, or be, this was the absolute worst.

His rejoinder, when it finally came, was seething with resentment: "That's *your* problem."

I felt, in fact, like I'd been hit in the face with a shoe.

Enraged and probably humiliated, he was now glaring at me. I decided to use logic to try to pin him down, clear him up, settle him down, which, as usual in emotionally supercharged moments, only made things worse.

"Yaqub, we've known each other for several months. We always joke together, we laugh together, we respect each other. You know what I'm talking about. It's always been good between us. It's unmistakable. You know I've always liked you, and I'm sure you've liked me too. I *know* that. I'm *sure* of it. You know that's true. You can't deny that."

Again, Yaqub took longer than usual to fashion a simple sentence. After two or three seconds, he said, icily:

"I never liked you."

Now *I* was the one silently staring at *him* as he turned his head away and looked through the windows. I felt like crying.

"I don't believe you, Yaqub."

He turned from the windows, faced me again, and shrugged, as if my believing him or not was the least important thing in the world. And then we ran out of time. Our fifty minutes had run out, like a therapy session that is seconds away from a breakthrough. Or not.

"Well, it looks like we've run out of time. I'll see you all tomorrow. Enjoy this beautiful afternoon," I chirped, failing, I'm sure, to sound on top of things, "professional," whatever that is.

Everyone then left the room. Except for Enrique, one of my Venezuelan students.

"Are you okay, teacher?"

"Sure, sure, Enrique, I'm fine," I lied. "I'll see you tomorrow." Enrique, looking unconvinced, gave me a grim little smile, nodded, and left. I sat at my desk alone for about ten minutes, staring at I-don't-know-what before packing up and proceeding dispiritedly toward the parking lot to get into my Camry and drive back to Berkeley.

It's funny. Part of the wonderfully strange alchemy of my job is rooted in forgetting: forgetting the culture and nationality of my students, forgetting my own culture too, and relishing the relationship between individuals, Phil the individual person and Dorje the individual person, Phil and Enrique, Phil and Thais, Phil and Fehmi . . .

Phil and Yaqub. But, of course, the world rarely allows us to casually push aside our inherited affiliations, which, more often than not, cut us off from each other by placing suspicion above trust, history above immediacy, cultural identity above individual integrity. Yaqub had brought me back to this reality, this remembering. Once again, the teacher had become the student.

On the next afternoon, when that class re-convened, I did see all my students again. Except Yaqub. The lesson that day was okay, ordinary, had no big surprises. The fifty minutes passed, and again I said goodbye to the students, and they left to enjoy another sunny Bay Area day. As I was packing up, I heard someone at the doorway. It was Yaqub. I was very surprised. And curious. I had no idea what to expect.

"May I come in, Phil?" Yaqub was strangely formal, but, considering the explosions of the previous day, not surprisingly so.

"Yes, sure, Yaqub. Come in. Come in."

"I want to talk with you. May I?"

"Of course, Yaqub. You can always talk with me. What's up?"

"Well, Phil, I want to tell you that my Saudi friends talked to me in cafeteria after they heard what happened yesterday, and they said, 'Yaqub, you were wrong when you spoke to Phil. You lied. We know you always liked Phil. You always told us that. It's not right that you said you didn't like him. You should be honest, Yaqub. But you lied. You should say sorry to Phil.' They are right. So, Phil, I *am* sorry. What you said is true. I *do* like you. I always liked you."

"Thank you, Yaqub. It means a lot to me to hear you say that. You know, as I told you, I like you too. You have been one of my favorite students. So thank you for saying this."

"You're welcome, Phil. It is important to me that you understand why I said what I said to you. Please understand that my whole life I have been taught that I must hate the Jews. My father, my grandfather, my uncles, all say same thing. 'Jews are bad. You should hate them. Have nothing to do with them. All Jews are bad. All of them. Every one of them.' Phil, I don't know what to do with what happened here yesterday. It's so confusing. You are Jewish, but you are not bad man. Your life make my father and my grandfather and all my uncles wrong. Like liars. Can you see this is so confusing? Can you see this makes me feel sad? And crazy? Maybe even kind of afraid?"

"Yes, I do see. I do." A talking camel would have been no less surprising to him than a good Jew. Technically, I was not supposed to exist.

"When I go back to Saudi Arabia, I will have to keep this new understanding secret. I can't tell no one. But I want you to know that I now see that it is possible to be a Jewish man and still be a good man. You are Jewish and you are good. That make me feel crazy and afraid. Like I don't know nothing. But, at same time, it make me feel right, like when you correct my grammar. I don't know *what* I feel right now. Is there an English word for what I am talking about?"

"Maybe not, Yaqub, but I understand you. I know that, on this trip, you have learned something far more important than English."

"I think that's true, Phil. But what do I do with it? What do I do with what I learned?"

"That *is* the question, isn't it, Yaqub?"

Moi, THE JURY

On a spring morning in the early eighties, about a dozen of my advanced students and I got into three cars, one of them mine, and made the descent from Oakland's hills toward its flat downtown. Field trips in teachers' and students' cars were common in those days, before the company got concerned about its liability in permitting such casual transport. Our destination on that day was the Superior Court of Alameda County, just off the shore of Lake Merritt. That huge white pillared building always reminds me of a two-tiered concrete wedding cake. Our plan, mixing real-world English with a bit of cultural exploration, was to visit one of its many courtrooms and spend an hour observing a trial, hopefully a juicy one.

After finding three parking spots, a formidable accomplishment, we walked to the courthouse, entered it, and stood in front of that day's roster of cases posted on a huge bulletin board in the main lobby. This *was* Oakland, so, fortunately for us, and sadly for Oakland, there were several homicide cases to choose from. We selected one and proceeded to its room, a solemn chamber with highly polished oak benches, desks, chairs, and matching wall paneling. This was clearly a room where fateful life-altering decisions were routinely made. We sat quietly as the jurors, attorneys, and others filed in. Anticipation? You could almost taste it.

When the bailiff asked us all to rise for the entrance of the judge, it felt like a curtain going up at a weighty Shakespearean drama. We stood up and waited for the judge, silver-haired and black-robed, to sit down on his "bench" behind an enormous oak desk, flanked by an American flag on his right and the flag of California on his left. We all sat back down, and then the judge gave a synopsis of the case.

A woman had been murdered in her bedroom in Montclair, an upscale village in the Oakland Hills. Ostensibly, a burglary had taken place: entry had been gained through a broken window, drawers had been pulled from their dressers and emptied onto the floors in most of the rooms, all the closet doors had been flung open, jewelry and high-end audio equipment had been taken. The woman had had the bad luck of being home when the thief arrived. She was found dead on the floor of the bedroom, its heavy curtains ripped from their windows and wound tightly around her throat; the strangle knot had been expertly tied.

Several relatives and friends suspected that the whole burglary scene was a stage set which was conceived and constructed by the victim's husband; it was he who sat in the defendant's chair that day. That their marriage had had plenty of problems was no secret. And it definitely didn't help his case that just about everybody knew he had a girlfriend on the side.

We ran into a bit of luck, from a theatrical perspective: the business of the day was the cross-examining of the husband. He was a handsome guy in his forties with meticulously coifed black hair. In his expensive-looking, perfectly fitting gray suit that looked like it was made of steel, he exuded wealth and confidence. He stuck to the story of coming home from work and being shocked to find, first, his house turned inside out and upside down, and then his wife lying dead and blue-faced on their bedroom floor. He repeatedly affirmed his love for her and lamented that he'd never feel whole again. Of course, the prosecutor was buying none of it.

The hour flew by, and the judge proclaimed that the trial would resume on the following day. When we left the courtroom, it was as if we were walking out of a theater before the end of the play. We would be back in our regular classroom on the next day, so, if we were curious enough, we'd simply have to follow the case's progress in the news.

Driving back to Holy Names, I wondered what my students thought about the trial. In my Camry were a Venezuelan man, a Japanese woman, an Iranian woman, and a French woman. As we rolled up to a red light, I posed a question to the little group:

"So. What do you think about the case? Do you think the husband is guilty or not guilty?"

Without a gap, needing not even a second or two to ponder, the French woman, Françoise, proclaimed her verdict:

"Guilty. Habsolutely. No question. Completely guilty."

"Françoise, how can you be so sure?"

Her widened eyes, under raised eyebrows, looked back at *my* eyes in the rear-view mirror and silently shouted, somehow with a French accent, that it was incredible that I had even asked a question about something that couldn't be more self-evident. She explained the unimpeachable basis for her certainty, as if to a child:

"Because, Pheel, 'e 'as ze face of a murderer."

About six weeks later, there was a small article about this case on one of the last pages of the *San Francisco Chronicle*'s Bay Area section: the jury had reached the same verdict. They could have saved themselves a lot of time by just asking Françoise, for whom investigation was just a matter of looking: "'e 'as ze face of a murderer." Guilt by physiognomy: one's face was the prime witness against one.

I wondered what was written on mine.

Two by Two

I've had twins in my classes twice, identical ones: one pair from Korea, 14-year-old boys Duk-Ju and Hyun-Ju, and the other from Spain, 28-year-old Ana and Carmen. Neither pair made it easy for their teacher or anyone else to tell them apart. They wore identical outfits every day. At the beginning of class, I'd have to nail down who was who, so I'd know who said what, and how much each one knew or didn't know about the language I was teaching them.

Duk-Ju and Hyun-Ju were distinguished not only by the fact of being twins, but also by being the youngest students I'd ever had. They were in San Rafael with their nineteen-year-old sister, whose English, fortunately, was at about the same intermediate level as theirs, so she was in their class and could keep a custodial eye on them. For the first couple of days, I had to play who's who, and they'd accommodate me: "I'm Duk-Ju." "I'm Hyun-Ju." It's a point of professional pride for ESL teachers to quickly learn the unusual names of students in their classes, to let our students know that we are not typical Americans for whom, they believe, foreign names are hard, or impossible, to learn or pronounce. I've done what many teachers have done, made notes on the class list, scribbled entries like "mustache," "glasses," "crew cut," "tall," "acne," etc. With these Korean boys, the challenge was cranked up; finding a mnemonic device to distinguish one from the other was not going to be easy.

I studied both of them head to toe, toe to head. It took me a couple of days, but, suddenly, bang, there it was, subtle but clear: at the top of Duk-Ju's head, two small curved hairs stuck up, one leaning left and the other right, like a little rabbit-ear antenna. Hyun-Ju's hair lay perfectly flat. There. I had my memory trick: Duk-Ju, Duk, Duck, Daffy Duck, Donald Duck, Saturday-morning cartoons on TV, the antenna sitting on top of the set, bringing animated fun to this Korean boy with crystal clarity. I was ready to wow them, to mystify them, *and* their sister. Not to mention the other students. (The enjoyment of teaching often entails being a magician, standup comic, actor, and general ham. The hope, of course, is that your students are enjoying it as much as you are.) For the next two weeks, I'd find that antenna each day and say to the boy beneath it, "Good morning, Duk-Ju," then turn to his brother and say, "Good morning Hyun-Ju." I relished the mystified looks on everyone's faces, especially the boys themselves. Obviously, no one else had detected Duk-Ju's antenna.

On Monday of the third week, however, the jig was up. The brothers arrived, together as usual, wearing their proud weekend purchases: identical San Francisco Giants baseball caps. When I saw those orange-and-black lids tightly clamped to their heads, I knew that they had defeated me, even if they didn't know it themselves. I thought about saying "Good morning, Duk-Ju" to one of the newly capped Giants' fans and hoping I'd be lucky, but I knew it was only a matter of time before my luck would run out and my fallibility would be on display to all. I realized that it was time to spill the beans. Looking directly into those four fourteen-year-old eyes, I started giggling about my forthcoming confession. Now the students' wonderment had a different cause: their teacher was laughing at something that no one else could see or hear. Perhaps he was losing his mind. Perhaps he had already lost it.

"Duk-Ju. Hyun-Ju. The time has come for me to tell you my secret, to tell you how I know who is who."

"Good. Good. We try to figure out how do you do that, but we cannot," said Duk-Ju or Hyun-Ju. "Do it one more time before you tell secret. Who am I?"

"I don't know. You are either Duk-Ju or Hyun-Ju, but I don't know which one anymore. I can't do it if you guys wear those baseball caps."

"Why not?" asked Duk-Ju or Hyun-Ju, looking even more stymied, and turning to his brother to see if he had any guesses, but his twin was identically lost.

I then explained about the antenna and the cartoon ducks.

Now *they* were the ones laughing, along with everybody else. Simultaneously, Duk-Ju-or-Hyun-Ju and

Hyun-Ju-or-Duk-Ju lifted their hands to the brims of their caps and doffed them at precisely the same moment, a coordinated choreography fourteen years in the making. At first, they were still indistinguishable due to the hair-flattening that caps are infamous for. But, in only a few seconds, those little rabbit ears started to resurrect themselves on top of the head of the quieter brother, the one who had not been asking the questions that day.

"Aha, good morning, Duk-Ju," I greeted him. "And good morning to you too, Hyun-Ju," I said to the more vocal one, whose hair continued to lie flat. Those Giants caps look really cool, so I don't want to ask you not to wear them. I guess I'll just go back to asking you who's who every day."

"Well, actually, teacher, we're not exactly the same. I will tell you secret. You can know who is Duk-Ju and who is Hyun-Ju, even when we wearing our new hats," said Hyun-Ju.

"You would really tell me this very big secret, Hyun-Ju? I feel very honored."

"Honored, teacher? What is 'honored'?"

"I'll tell you later, but first tell me the secret. I don't want to wait another second."

Laughing again, Hyun-Ju rose from his seat and walked across the room to where Duk-Ju was sitting. He pointed to a small brown birthmark on Duk-Ju's cheek, just beside the left corner of his mouth. "See, teacher? You see Duk-Ju has spot right there, but I do not. My face clean!" He found his own joke hilarious and started laughing again, wildly. It was contagious: Duk-Ju joined him, as did their sister and all the other students. I did too, of course, grateful that these little guys were still too young to grow substantial beards.

As I said, those Korean guys were not the only twins to visit my classes. About a decade earlier, Ana and Carmen flew in from Madrid and landed in one of my advanced classes in Oakland. Both of them were engaging, witty, sexy, stylish, and meticulously studious. I know that some twins are irked by other people's apparent blindness to each sibling's individuality, but Ana and Carmen seemed to get an almost perverse pleasure out of emphasizing their sameness and confounding everyone: they would arrive each day in the same outfit, their brunette hair done up in the same chic pixie-ish fashion, both of them looking at the world through identical brown horn-rimmed glasses. This was not going to be an easy case to crack; I wasn't expecting any help from *las hermanas*, and the competitor in me didn't want any.

A full week had passed without my making any progress. I'd start each class with an implicit admission of failure:

"And you are . . . ?" I'd say to Ana or Carmen.

"I'm Carmen!" Carmen, for example, might say, with a tone and a face that implied that it should be obvious to anyone with a brain and two eyes. Who else could she be?

"Yes, yes, thank you. Good morning, Carmen," I'd say before turning to Ana and greeting her too.

"Good morning, Ana."

"Good morning, teacher."

They were like a couple of flamenco dancers, their fiery eyes exuding victory through those horned rims. I half expected them to jump to their feet, stomp their shoes on the floor, and shout "Olé!" The gauntlet had been thrown down, and it was my pleasure to take it up. An English teacher doth not live by English teaching alone.

I remained clueless for several more days. Then one morning, in the second week of the course, I was helping the students write their essays. This sometimes necessitated getting physically closer to a student in order to check out a word or sentence. While I was helping Ana construct a sentence at her desk, my eyes were oscillating between her paper and her angular face. Carmen, who didn't always sit beside her sister in class, *was* sitting next to her that morning. Which enabled me to make a startling discovery: whereas everything about *las hermanas* appeared identical, their horned-rimmed glasses were *not* exactly the same. The slots in the tiny screws at the corners of Ana's frames were in horizontal repose, while those in Carmen's screws were perfectly vertical, were, to my eyes, exclamation marks, no less exclamatory for their smallness.

I couldn't suppress an "Ah!" Ana was understandably curious.

"What? What is it, teacher?"

"Oh, I just thought of a good way to make this sentence better," I lied. I went on helping her with her essay, but I was already imagining the coming triumph of the next day. How delicious taking attendance would be.

Unlike my antenna trick with Duk-Ju and Hyun-Ju, I wasn't able to see these new ID markers from across the room. Each day, on one pretext or another, I needed to get close enough to Ana or Carmen to see the orientation of those screws. Then, either right there, near her, or a minute later, while taking roll from my desk, I'd say, "Good morning, Carmen" to Carmen or "Good morning, Ana" to her sister. The first day I did this they looked surprised but didn't question me about how I'd pulled it off. I'm sure they just chalked it up to a lucky guess. After another three or four days of correct identifications, they realized that I really *had* devised some kind of system. I could see that it had started to drive them slightly nuts.

"Hey, okay, teacher, tell us. How you know?" Carmen asked between my taking attendance and the start of that day's lesson.

I was enjoying their bewilderment entirely too much. Donning my slyest wise-guy grin, I answered, "Oh, it's simple, Carmen. Even though you and Ana are identical physically, you are unique spiritually. When I look deeply into your eyes, I can see your souls, your very souls, your immortal and distinct identities."

Both sisters looked a bit spooked for a moment, possibly wondering if I actually was one of those California shamans left over from the sixties. Or perhaps just one of the innumerable lunatics who found refuge in the open-minded open-door city of Berkeley. Then skepticism, appropriately, took hold. Of course, they knew that Phil the joker was kidding; this was pure chicanery, not priestly insight. Ana's right eyebrow seemed to jump halfway up her forehead as she peered right at *my* soul:

"Hey, come on teacher, what's the trick?"

I only laughed and turned my palms up in the classic shrug of the falsely accused.

My savoring of this victory lasted for about another week. Then, one morning, firmly confident, I sauntered over to one of the sisters, who was seated to my left, espied her vertically slotted frame screws, and said, "Good morning, Carmen."

A playful smile bloomed on her face as she replied, "Phil, I'm surprised at you. I'm not Carmen. I'm Ana. Look into my soul."

"Good try, Carmen, but you can't fool me. I *know* who you are," I said in the shaman's omniscient tone.

From the opposite side of the room, to my right, the other one, the one with the horizontal screws, said, "No you don't, teacher, you *don't* know. *She's* Ana. *I'm* Carmen."

"Good try, Ana, but I know something about you that even you don't. So it's no use trying to fool me. In this case, two heads, or maybe I should say *twin* heads, are *not* better than one."

Their full lips, painted neatly with, of course, the same burgundy-hued lipstick, spread into knowing, mischievous smiles; they rose from their seats, and with graceful, apparently rehearsed, precision, met in the center of the room, right in front of my desk. They removed their glasses, exchanged them, and donned the now correct ones.

"Whew," said Ana, "That's better. Carmen's glasses give me headache! Her prescription is not at all identical to mine. It's for lenses much more strong. So you see, the screws are not the only things that are different about our glasses, Phil. They *are* called screws, right?"

Feeling screwed, but impressed with their detective work, I said, "Yes, yes, that *is* the right word. So tell me, how did you figure it out?"

"Well," said Ana, "after three weeks of watching you watching us, we wonder why, every day, *every* day, you come really close to us and look into our eyes. We talk about it, study each other's eyes, study our own eyes in the mirrors, and we didn't see any difference between them. Then Carmen had this great idea, a real discovery. She thought this: maybe you weren't looking at our eyes at all. Maybe you were looking at our *glasses*. So we look very carefully at our glasses to see if something, *any*thing is different about them, and I notice that the screws are not the same. Carmen's screws stand up. My screws lie down. Right?"

"That's exactly right!"

They flashed twin grins at me, and stood tall, both of them with arms triumphantly akimbo. "What you think about that, teacher?" Carmen prodded.

"I think you have won the contest. *Brava! Brava!* You have slain this bull. I am vanquished! Congratulations, *toreras*!"

Again, it was time for them, for me, for everyone to have a good laugh. They truly *were* excellent students and had, through careful investigation, figured out my simple but subtle trick. *Las hermanas* had indeed won.

As they swaggered back to their seats, strains of Bizet's *Toreador Song* were playing in some distant corner of my mind. They didn't need to say a word—*the* word—but I could hear it loud and clear: Olé!

Onions

The hardest thing to do in a foreign language (and, sometimes, even in one's own) is understand someone on the telephone: no facial expressions or hand gestures can finesse the meaning, and the voice that fills the single engaged ear is sometimes corrupted by crackling static, a buzzy electronic tone, or insufficient volume. That's why even people who have been studying a foreign language for a long time will quake at the thought of receiving important information via this sometimes torturous device. Generally confident experimenters with English, this "foreign" tongue, frequently lose their nerve when they contemplate the challenge of surviving an entire phone conversation. Often they'll ask a native speaker to stand in for them rather than crashing into a wall early in the call.

"Amy," a Taiwanese woman in her early thirties, got further into an English phone call than most of my students ever did. She told me and her Oakland classmates the following story in response to my weekly Monday invitation to "tell us about something interesting that happened on your weekend." Her hand shot up immediately, before the other students had even begun rummaging around in their short-term memory banks. It was obvious that she knew I would ask about the weekend; in fact, she'd counted on it.

"Okay, Amy, let's hear your story."

"It's story and also question. But first story."

"Okay, first the story."

"Well, yesterday I had to make plane reservation. I was scared to use telephone because so difficult to understand English on telephone. But I decide to try anyway." This was in the early eighties, well before the internet revolution. Today, it's easier to book a flight since one almost always does it online, with plenty of time to consult a dictionary or a friend; Amy didn't have that luxury.

"Good for you, Amy. I'm proud of you."

"Thank you, Teacher. I also proud of me, but then not so proud."

"What happened?"

"Well, I call number for American Airlines, and a woman say hello. She ask me how are you. I tell her I am fine. I ask *her* how is *she* and she tell me she fine too. So. We both fine. Like you say, 'so far so good.' I tell her what I want to do and about number of flight I want and she ask me many question. I pay attention like never before. My head hurt I pay attention so hard. I scared but also excited at same time because I can understand her. It was amazing. I was so happy."

"That's great. I *know* how difficult it is to understand someone on the phone. Sometimes it's even hard for native English speakers. You were brave even to *try* to do it."

"Thank you, Teacher. But let me tell you what happened."

"Of course. Please go on."

"Well, as I said, she ask me so many question. About spelling my name. About how many bags I check. About how many bags I bring on airplane. About what kind seat I want: front of plane, back of plane, window seat, aisle seat. And many many many more. It was long conversation. Seem like no end. So many question. And I understand everything! I couldn't believe it. It was very special experience for me."

"That's just great. Then what happened?"

"Then she say that we almost finished, only a few more final thing to do. I tell her okay. But that's when everything change. That's when everything get crazy." Amy looked troubled as she approached this next part of her story, ashamed.

"Uh huh. What happened? What changed?" I encouraged her to go on, for I could see she had become hesitant, even afraid—she looked somehow *physically* smaller, and was still shrinking.

"We was just finishing everything, almost all done. And then, suddenly, she change subject. Change conversation to something completely different. She start talking about onions. Onions!" She was just shy of screaming it.

"Onions?"

"Yes, onions. It make no sense to me. Earlier in conversation, she already ask me about meal on plane, if I have 'special request' about food, like if I am vegetarian, and I tell her about that, no special request. So that why it so confusing when so close to end of phone conversation she talk about onions. Onions, Teacher! I not sure if I hear her right, so I ask her, 'Onions?' and she answer, 'Yes, onions.' I want to make sure, so I ask her, 'You mean the kind of onions we can cook with?' Again she say yes, the kind of onions we cook with. I feel embarrassed about what happen next because I do something very bad. I feel like lost little girl. Totally lost. Why she speaking about onions? I give up right there. I think I go crazy, real crazy, bad crazy. Like I can't breathe. I just give up. I hang up phone in middle of her next sentence, which I couldn't understand anyway. I couldn't understand nothing after she say onions. It was like I forget all my English. Maybe I forget Chinese too. I forget everything. Just because of onions. Like beginner again. After I hang up on that nice lady, I cry and cry and cry. I still so confused. I can't understand why she talk about onions. What do you think, Teacher? Why onions?"

"Hmm, that *is* confusing. Onions. Why onions?"

"Yes, that is *my* question. Why onions?"

"Well, okay, let's see. Let's investigate this mystery. Do you remember what you and the American Airlines woman were talking about just before those onions ruined your day?"

"Um, as I say, we just finishing whole thing. I think we were at maybe last step."

"Okay. Usually the last step is to give you a special code which has a lot of letters or numbers, or letters *and* numbers. It's called a confirmation code or sometimes a reservation code. I think American Airlines uses a series of capital letters and calls it a "Record Locator," or something like that. Do you think maybe that was what she was talking about?"

"Maybe, Teacher. Yes, I think she did say something about confirmation. I know confirmation. I learn that word before. I know code. I ready to write it down. But then she talking about onions!"

Suddenly I thought I knew what had come crashing down on my poor student's head.

"Ah, I think now I know what happened, Amy."

"What, Teacher, what? Please tell me."

"The woman tried to make it easier for you to understand the letters in the code, so she did what operators often do, even to native English speakers. For each letter in the code she gave as an example a word that begins with that letter." I made up a code and wrote it on the board. Pointing to it, I continued, "So, for example, imagine that the American Airlines Record Locator was OTLDPSK. She might have said, "O as in onions, T as in tomato, L as in love, D as in dollar, P as in pillow, S as in Superman, K as in kitten. You see what I mean? O as in onions . . ."

"She think that make it easier? To talk about onions?"

"Yes, I guess so."

"But she wrong. It not easier. It impossible. She make me crazy. She make me cry. Like little girl."

"Well, as you know, onions are famous for making people cry."

Amy smiled, just a small one, for the first time that day, and nodded. "I know, I know."

"So will you call them again? Will you try again to make that reservation?"

"I guess so. But I embarrassed to speak to that lady again. I was so bad."

"Don't worry, you'll almost certainly talk to a different person. American Airlines has thousands of people answering the phones, and none of those other operators know anything about your phone call, or the onions, or the hanging up, or the crying."

"Can you do it for me, Teacher? I'm a little afraid now."

"Do you really want me to?"

Amy looked down for a few seconds before looking back up and into my eyes: "No, I guess not."

"Good. Let me know what happens."

She did try again, that afternoon, and after making it through the bulk of the transaction, she and the male operator she dealt with this time had gotten to the previously baffling Record Locator recitation. The guy threw tigers, kings, newspapers, babies, elephants, potatoes, hurricanes, seemingly everything in the universe *except* onions, at Amy, but now she was invincible. Humiliation and despair, those master teachers, had given her a lesson she'd never forget: people's attempts to make things clearer often make them incomprehensible.

Wild is the Wind

At professional conferences, teachers can attend workshops that address the pedagogical, sociological, cultural, and psychological challenges of conducting a class. I have never, however, seen a syllabus listing which acknowledged the various physiological needs that can beset an instructor during a lesson: allergies, excretory needs (number 1 and/or number 2), indigestion, runny noses, and a legion of others, including the occasional but universal need to fart (perhaps they'd call it "The Challenge of Flatulence: Suggested Approaches").

Just as it does outside the classroom, the need to fart usually arrives meekly; then it can grow, gradually or with unsettling speed, into a formidable challenge to one's sphincter muscles. In the midst of a lesson, one's question is always the same: *can I contain the growing gale?* It's not unusual for things to get to a point where a teacher has to make a categorical choice: 1. Do I excuse myself for a few seconds, step briskly out of the room, and release the fart in the hallway? 2. Do I wait for the break and blow that trumpet after the last student has left the room? 3. Do I remain in front of the class and opt for the immediate surreptitious relief that only an SBD (silent but deadly) can provide?

The experience of one of my former colleagues in Oakland exemplifies a potential pitfall of that third option. Lounging in the staff room with me and a few others, Ann, a tall, blond, witty, and fashionable woman, told the story of sensing that increasing pressure in her nether region about halfway through her lesson. (What did you think teachers chatted about in that room . . . participial modifiers? Well, sometimes.) She felt confident that she could secretly sculpt that incipient fart into SBD form. Additionally, the distance between where she was standing and where her students were sitting was probably sufficient to prevent any ensuing "deadly" odors from reaching their noses, and even if they did catch a whiff, there was no way anyone could identify her as the perpetrator. She was, after all, only one of about fifteen suspects, and stylish Ann, professional Ann, was an unlikely one indeed.

So, considering all these positive factors, Ann let loose with what she confidently expected to be a low-decibel hiss, well below the threshold of human hearing. She was mortified as a big blubbery fully formed fart issued forth, and so loudly that there could be no doubt about its provenance. Oops. Her students broke up: clearly, this was the funniest thing they had ever seen or heard. Actually, Ann won a lot of points with them as she surrendered to the fact of the fait accompli (fart accompli?) and joined their hysterical chorus. Option 3 had, in a backdoor way, so to speak, worked out well for Ann (what a pro!) after all. Thinking about Ann's story can perhaps give us some insight into one of the reasons why "asshole" is such a pejorative epithet: a person whose actions typically resemble those of that body part simply can't be trusted to do the right thing.

Not to brag, but I've been consistently successful in the SBD approach to public gas buildup in the classroom. Probably I was simply less daring than Ann: whenever I felt that there was even the slightest chance of audibility, I usually resorted to option 1, the quick split from the room, or option 2, waiting for the break. Of course, those options are not without their pitfalls either.

One occasion stands out in my memory. I was showing a movie to my class, "Witness," the Peter Weir film with Harrison Ford. The blinds were closed and the lights out; I could just make out the pad on which I jotted down quotations, fodder for the next day's lesson on the film's vocabulary, idioms, themes, etc. I sat at my desk, watching the video on a TV in back of one of our more capacious rooms; my students had turned their seat-desks around to view it, so I was in back of them. About a half hour before the film's exciting climax, I felt the arrival of a fart-to-be, just a little pressure down there, not much more than the suggestion of a fart, more like the *idea* of one, a fart wannabe. It grew quickly, however, into a genuine threat, clearly too big to be containable for very long, already well beyond the border of SBD feasibility. I quickly rejected option 1 since this was the first time I was seeing this film and didn't want to run out and miss a second of it. I even considered a fourth option, a cinematic one, which was to wait and take a chance on synchronizing my fart with gunshots or loud music, but I didn't have the guts to risk that.

Option 2, I decided, was my only hope: I would do my best to tough it out until the blessed solitude of the break. This option had an inherent minor risk too. There was always the possibility of someone walking into the room right after the release and sniffing the result. I remember the time when, as a relatively new teacher at the school, I went to my colleague Misha's room during a break to ask him a question. As soon as I got near enough to ask, I was engulfed in a strong-smelling cloud. It was obvious that he had, only seconds before, executed Option 2, and my untimely entry was the flaw in his plan, if he'd had one. We had just recently met, so neither of us said a word about the polluted ecosystem we were sharing. Later, after we'd become friends, I probably would have joked about his "cutting the cheese," but, on that earlier day, we simply took care of business, and, as inconspicuously as possible, I fled. I didn't even think of that potential downside as I sat watching "Witness" in the relative darkness of the classroom-qua-cinema: I was confident that Option 2 was my best bet.

The suspense of my private drama easily matched that of John Book, beleaguered Philadelphia police detective, the character played by Ford. I watched the film with one eye and the clock with the other. During the last five minutes of the film *and* the class, I thought I wasn't going to make it, but through a Herculean effort, I *did* last until the end, said farewell to my students, watched the last one leave, and, before I even turned the lights back on, blasted a fart that seemed to rattle the windows. Sweet sweet relief!

My savoring of that relief lasted about a second. From out of the darkness, from my right, several rows away, came loud laughter, big honking guffaws. Clearly, I had miscalculated; I wasn't alone at all. Tsuyoshi, one of my Japanese students, had taken longer than his classmates to pack up his things, and was still at his desk in the dark. I turned on the lights, and the harsh fluorescent glare confirmed that Tsuyoshi was no hallucination. He was barely able to form his words he was laughing so hard.

"Whatchoo call that, Phil-san? That sound? What you did. What is word for that?"

What a shock to have a whole person suddenly appear out of nowhere, this Japanese guy who was laughing so hard he was gasping for air. Like Ann's students, he found the anomaly of a farting teacher to be the funniest thing he'd ever witnessed. His reaction was maybe the funniest thing *I'd* ever witnessed, even without reflecting on the suddenly ironic title of the movie we'd just watched; there was no not joining him in his hysteria. So many things that we assiduously avoid, whole categories of events, turn out to be harmless nothings, less-than-nothings, even comical, maybe extra-comical, when they inevitably do occur.

"Oho, Tsuyoshi, I thought I was alone! You caught me. Now you know I'm human! My teaching career is over! I'm ruined! Finished!"

Though we were both still shaking with laughter, Tsuyoshi, always on the lookout for a new vocabulary word, again implored me:

"Please, Phil-san, tell me word for that?"

"Okay, Tsuyoshi, okay, but only if you promise not to tell anyone that Phil-san is human."

"I promise, Phil-san. Is secret. Our secret. You not human."

"Fine, very good. I trust you. The word is 'fart.' F-a-r-t. Fart."

I wrote "fart" on the board, and, good student that he was, Tsuyoshi dutifully entered it in his spiral notebook, speaking it aloud a few times to make sure he had the pronunciation down: "Fart. Fart. Fart. Fart."

"Perfect."

We exchanged silly grins.

"I think I never forget this vocabulary, Phil-san."

"I'm sure you won't."

I opened all the windows wider to air out the room, and switched off the light. Tsuyoshi and I, still smiling, entered the hallway together and, human to the core, headed toward our next classes.

REALIA

Tsuyoshi will always remember the meaning of the word "fart" because he directly experienced the physical phenomenon, not merely read or heard a dictionary definition of it. Writers of ESL pedagogy textbooks have labeled this approach "realia," the use of real objects to give vividness to a lesson. Teachers who are really into this approach can often be seen hauling knives, forks, teapots, brooms, candlesticks, plungers, corkscrews, ladles, screwdrivers, mops, whatever, into their classrooms to make vocabulary literally palpable (admittedly, in Tsuyoshi's case, the "object" was, technically, not palpable, but it was both audible and, at least to my nose, smellable). It's an approach that works.

There was an essay that I had my Masters' class students read from time to time, and the gist of it involved the writer's fondness for an old mortar and pestle that had been passed down through several generations of his native-American family; on the mornings that I'd teach it, I would try to remember to put my own heavy green marble version of that ancient kitchenware into my briefcase, which seemed to double its already considerable weight. But it was worth it. My students could hold it, feel its heft, run their fingers over the marble's smooth and coarse surfaces, admire the frozen riverflow of its multi-green swirls, and grind imaginary seeds and spices into a fine powder. But probably even more effective than those planned realia-based presentations are the times, as with Tsuyoshi, that "realia" barge into one's classroom uninvited; in those cases, they are not merely part of one's "lesson," but, much more compellingly and memorably, the shared experience of several lives.

Take, for instance, the time I was teaching an intermediate-level grammar class on the Holy Names campus on an autumn morning in the mid-eighties. Since our ESL school was basically a tenant on that campus, we often found ourselves teaching English in whatever space was available; sometimes we'd set up chalkboards in dorm lounges and have our classes there, and sometimes, as in this little story, in a chemistry laboratory.

When I did have the relative luxury of teaching in a real classroom, I always preferred to arrange the students' seat-desks in an approximation of a circle and to be part of that ring, a small way of diminishing the sense of barrier between teacher and students. In the chem lab, however, that friendlier configuration was not possible. The teacher's "desk" was an enormous (maybe ten feet wide) concrete-topped assemblage, replete with a sink, goose-neck faucet, and gas taps for Bunsen burners. The students' seat-desks were bolted to the floor in four seriously academic rows, parallel to the teacher's bulwark up front. Sitting behind that mass of concrete and plumbing, I felt like my students were on the other side of the Berlin Wall. The best I could do to feel a little more intimate with them was to get off my stool, also bolted to the floor, step to the front of that imposing structure, and, with a bit of a backward leap, land on top of it. That felt much better; we were now, at least, all sitting on the same side of the wall.

As most people know, the San Francisco Bay Area is earthquake country, with several significant faults lacing each of its sections; Holy Names College, perched on one of the Oakland Hills, was, I was told, directly above the much-feared Hayward Fault. A major quake on that fault would decimate that hill and bring the college (and much more) to a crushing halt; for many of the people who worked and studied there, massive injury and death would be unavoidable. Most of our students knew about the possibility of earthquakes, but probably not about the particularly vulnerable position they were in as they went about the business of learning English (it certainly was not in our school's promotional material); those of us who did know were somehow able to put it out of our minds. Never underestimate the power of repression and self-delusion.

Well, back to that morning in the chem lab. There were about fifteen students in that group, and they had distributed themselves pretty evenly among the four rows. I was, as usual, sitting atop the "wall," feeling quite relaxed as I went over the lesson du jour. I had gotten somewhat accustomed to the idiosyncrasies of that unorthodox teaching venue, and so had my students. It was just another day in the lab.

As I was going over whatever I was going over, I saw the students in the fourth row rise gracefully above their classmates in the first three rows; then, as they sank back to their normal level, the third row bobbed up before it too gently fell; then the second did the same, and then the first. Finally, that concrete monolith, with me, probably cross-legged, upon it, was lifted like driftwood on a rolling ocean wave. It was the loveliest earthquake I've ever partaken of, not at all threatening, a day at the beach.

The faces of my students ranged from shock to delight. Hans, who, I suspect, was eager to tell all his friends and relatives back in Berlin that he had lived to feel an actual earthquake in California, couldn't, in his excitement, quite remember that all-important vocabulary word. Smiling and laughing, he asked, "Phil, was that . . . ?"

"Yes, it was," I answered, laughing along with him, sharing the rush of adrenaline that everyone in that lab was feeling, that people everywhere feel whenever the planet suddenly switches from passive to active.

Once again, the plan of the day was shelved in order to deal with an event which was unexpected and, for most of them, unprecedented. An earthquake can come in many different forms, and my students were lucky to experience one of its gentler, amusement-park modes. "Earthquake" was a word they would remember. A more frightening, devastating, quake, centered in Loma Prieta, would hit Northern California a few years later, in 1989, but, for now, for that addition to their vocabulary list to stick, that playful wave was enough.

More than twenty years later, in Berkeley, I was teaching a conversation class one very hot summer afternoon. Our school was near, but not on, the campus of that city's famous university. Sitting at the north end of a long oblong room on the second floor, I was part of an oval ring of about twenty students in their seat-desks. On my left was a wall of bookcases, and, on my right, a row of French doors opening onto a terrace overlooking tree-lined Prospect Street. The sun was so bright that day that the students sitting in front of those open doors were almost completely silhouetted.

I had spent enough years teaching to have developed a pretty reliable internal antenna for detecting whether or not I had snared every student's attention. Early on in that day's lesson, it became apparent to me that I had not accomplished that very basic goal. To be more specific, four or five twenty-something guys seated along the bookcase wall seemed somewhat distracted, each with an impish little smile on his face. Everyone else seemed sufficiently plugged in. I had no idea what was pulling that little group away. Their foci seemed to shuttle between my lesson and something outside, on the street. I looked out there for a second or two but saw nothing unusual. Well, I figured, it's just not one of my better days. So I tried cranking up the voltage of my presentation, really pouring it on, hamming it up, which only momentarily lured some of them back to the lesson before they drifted away again, their eyes returning to those open French doors and beyond.

I wondered what was going on out there. In addition to coveting their attention, there was a part of me that wondered what *I* was missing out on.

I was just about to ask them outright what was so riveting when, as if suddenly jolted by an electric shock, they all jumped in their seats at the same time, their little grins morphing into open-mouthed astonishment, ecstatic smiles, gasping oohs, ahs, and wows; laughing and squirming, they had stopped trying to be cool or secretive about the object of their attraction. And distraction. Which freed me from pretending that I hadn't been noticing.

"Hey guys, what's so interesting?"

As if stricken with temporary aphasia, they could only point at the apartment building on the other side of the street. From where I stood, I still couldn't see anything unusual, so I took a few steps toward them and again looked outside, this time from their viewpoint. There it was, or I should say, there *she* was: on that building's flat black roof, next to what might have been a small utility shed, which had fully shielded her from my previous perspective, was a young blond woman lying prone on a blue blanket, soaking up the hot rays of the sun: she was wearing only the bottom half of a lemon-yellow bikini. Its matching bra lay near what was probably a bottle of sunscreen beside her gleaming right shoulder.

Thomas, a Swiss student, was the first of the wall guys to regain composure enough to actually use a little English to explain part of what, by this point, needed little explanation. They had been enjoying the free show since the beginning of the class; in fact, this was not the first time they'd seen the bikini woman from those choice seats, which was why they rushed each day, full of hope, to snag them. The development that had caused them to instantly and totally lose their cool, Thomas explained, was the unexpected and unprecedented bonus of her momentarily propping up her bronzed torso in order to remove her tan-line-inducing top, a move which enabled them to see her breasts fully for just a breathtaking moment, temporarily upgrading the show from PG-13 to R, before she settled back down on the blue blanket.

As she lay there, it was easy to imagine her mentally visiting some tropical paradise, perhaps Hawaii, maybe

Tahiti. Those guys were right there with her. And, in a flash, so, it seemed, was everyone else, some craning their necks to see, and others even turning their seats around to view the display in unabashed comfort. No teacher could expect to compete against that sun-flooded tableau; clearly, my "lesson plan" had never had a chance. How futile to insist on proceeding with my original idea for that afternoon, whatever it was, to pretend that the roof across the street was empty. That woman had shaken this class up as much as the earthquake had rattled the group in the chem lab. Shielding their view of my competition by closing the floor-to-ceiling vertical blinds *was* an option, but not an attractive one since that would effectively cut off our already-meager air flow on that sweltering day; besides, I thought it would seem rather priggish—after all, she had chosen to join the trees, squirrels, and pedestrians as part of the potentially viewable landscape. Returning to my place in front of the room, I wasn't sure where we were all heading, but I *was* sure that there was a new rapport in there, a unifying giddiness, a new energy not to be wasted.

As I perched atop my desk, Guan-Ting Lin, nicknamed Eddie, one of several Taiwanese guys in the class, raised his hand to ask a question. He solved my problem by providing the perfect springboard to what would turn out to be that afternoon's new direction:

"Phil, what you call that kind of swimming costume that girl on the ceiling is wearing?"

"Well, when she had all of it on, both parts, it was a bikini. But when she almost gave those guys a heart attack by taking off the top, she was then wearing what some people call a 'monokini.' It's kind of a joke word." I wrote the two words on the white board and went a bit into the meanings of "mono" and "bi."

"Thank you, Phil."

"You're welcome, Eddie. By the way, you should also know that we don't say 'swimming costume' in this country; that's more common in England. Here, we usually say 'swimsuit' or, sometimes, 'bathing suit.'" I added those terms to the board's little list.

"Ah. Swimsuit. Bathing suit. Aha. Okay." He and several of his classmates entered these new vocabulary words in their notebooks.

"And one more thing, Eddie. She's not on the 'ceiling.' She's on the 'roof,'" I explained while writing those words on the board too. "A roof is *out*side, the top of a building, and a ceiling is *in*side, the top of a room." Pointing up at our own room's ceiling, I added, "If she were on the ceiling, she'd be hovering up there, right above us, like a giant hummingbird." I explained "hover" and "hummingbird," words which joined the board's growing list. Eddie and quite a few of the others smiled and tittered as their heads tilted up, and I imagined them visualizing that near-naked monokini woman floating above us, almost within reach, that surreal image perhaps even more compelling than the actual person across the street.

"Ha! Okay! Got it! Thank you, Phil," said Eddie, still laughing.

"Sure, Eddie," I answered, laughing with him, as my imagined imaginings faded away.

We finished up the remainder of the class by going over definitions of several other related words, such as "sunscreen," "suntan," and "sunburn," and then trading stories about tropical vacations and summer romances. Every student was now plugged in; incredibly, through some mysterious alchemy, most of them, even the original oglers, were actually looking more at me than at that woman on the roof, who, mercifully, kept the playing field relatively level by staying prone on her blue blanket through the rest of that class. Little did she know, as she basked in her idyllic solitude, that she had provided the realia for one of the best lessons of that month.

DONY AND CONY

In the spring of 1982, Donato and Concetta Cona, a Swiss couple in their thirties, were in my 104 grammar class in Oakland and were a consistently charming addition to that group's chemistry. Their Swiss predecessors at the school had all been from the German or French parts of that country. Dony and Cony, as they called each other, were my first students from Ticino, the Italian part of Switzerland. Dony was a banker at Credito Svizzero in Lugano, and Cony sometimes did volunteer work teaching blind people to ski in Japan (!); how she accomplished that I don't know, since, as far as I know, she spoke little or no Japanese.

Their accent was unique in my ear's experience; it was mostly Italian but had a touch of something else, perhaps German. Both Conas had a funny fixation: to describe almost any positive experience or anything they liked, Dony or Cony would comment, "Vehdy intehdesting," the "r" of both "very" and "interesting" produced by the faintest tap of the tongue on the palate; conversely, something they disapproved of or simply disliked was "*not* vehdy intehdesting." No matter how many new words they learned for expressing likes and dislikes, they almost always fell back on their trademark responses. For example, we often had variations of the following conversation:

"Hi, Phil. How was your lunch?" Cony might ask.

"Oh, it was very good. Delicious actually. I ate at the Chinese restaurant near the school. You know, the one in the Safeway shopping mall?"

"Ah, I think you eat better than us today," Dony might add.

"Oh, I'm sorry to hear that. Bad lunch? Where did you eat, Dony?"

"In the cafeteria (which he pronounced 'cafetehdeeya,' the "r," again, that alveolar tap). The food was not vehdy intehdesting."

"Actually, in English, the word for that place has the accent on a different syllable. It's cafe*teer*ia, not cafeteh*dee*ya. Try it, Dony."

"Cafe*teer*ia. Oh, it sound wrong. You know it is originally Italian word, and in Italian is the way I say it."

"Yes, I know, but in English, it's cafe*teer*ia. You try it now, Cony."

"Okay, I try. Cafe*teer*ia."

"Excellent. That was perfect. How about you, Dony? One more time?"

"Cafe*teer*ia."

"Very very good."

"But," Cony repeated with conviction, "still I must

say food in cafeteh*dee*ya was not vehdy intehdesting today."

"Cony?"

"Oh, sorry Phil. Is cafe*teer*ia."

"*Perfetto!*"

In one of that class's discussions, near the end of the session, the talk turned, as it typically does, toward plans for the future. Dony and Cony informed us with great excitement that they were planning a vacation trip to Maui; they'd be celebrating the completion of their ESL course by taking advantage of being so close, relatively, to that island. By an unlikely but happy coincidence, Joan and I had almost exactly the same plans and had already booked our plane reservations and hotel. Without hesitation, being sure that Joan would love that friendly Swiss couple, I suggested that we try to coordinate our itineraries in order to enjoy our vacations together, a proposition which they both found "vehdy *vehdy* intehdesting" indeed.

Maui with the Conas was as much fun as I had expected it to be, lots of sunsets and island food. We all enjoyed hiking, so we did a lot of that together, on mountains, in craters, on beaches, in jungles. Despite the fact that we had had a couple of days of almost nonstop rain, which Donato, grim-faced, declared "not vehdy intehdesting," our vacation was one of the best any of us had ever had.

We said our farewells on a Lahaina beach as the day was making its daily dramatic segue into evening.

Dony, the sky and ocean on fire behind him, extended an invitation:

"If you ever come to Switzerland, you must stay with us in our house in Medeglia."

"We will be so glad to have you in our little village," added Cony. "I really hope some day it is going to happen."

"Okay," I joked, "next year, Europe! See you then." Tanned and happy, we all laughed and hugged before parting.

The following year, in fact, we did take the Conas up on their offer. We visited them in Medeglia after a few weeks of traveling around that continent in the early spring of 1983. Just before driving north to visit the Conas, we spent a few days in Milan at the home of a former colleague of mine, Jean, who had fallen in love with one of her Italian students, Simon, married him, and moved to *bella Italia*.

Those were restful days. We especially enjoyed going for evening walks with Jean and Simon after eating and drinking royally at their table (oh, the carpaccio!). On our first day in Milan, Simon told us about a shop within strolling distance that had "absolutely the best gelato in Milano, maybe the best in Italy, maybe the best in the world!" Of course, we went directly there after the first dinner at our friends' apartment, and after one or two licks, were convinced that he was right. Surely, this was the ice cream they served in heaven. Invariably, on each of our post-dinner promenades, we'd wind up there; I'd buy a big enough portion to last the whole trip back to the apartment.

When the time came to leave Milan, we thanked our hosts for their splendid hospitality and headed toward the road that would bring us to Switzerland and the Conas. Approaching the on-ramp, about to begin the insane experience of white-knuckle driving on an Italian highway, I had the thought that it might have been nice to spend a few more days in Milan: there were so many gelato flavors I hadn't yet tasted. Ah well, that's life—one trade-off after another.

It felt impossible to sweep through the magnificent Lake Como region without stopping. We were a bit ahead of schedule for our estimated arrival time at the Conas', so we decided to unwind from our drive by renting a pedal boat and taking it out on the lake for an hour despite the high rental fee. It was one of those two-person four-pedal affairs, and the lake was quite placid, so, with little effort, we made good progress during our outward-bound half hour. I kept a close eye on my watch to be sure we'd get back to shore before our hour was up; even a minute late would cost us an extra hour's rental fee.

When it was time to turn around, we were quite far out; in fact, we could hardly see the dock, a black speck in the mass of water, mountains, trees, and blue sky. No problem. We'd just zip right back, jump in the car, and continue northward to Ticino and the Conas.

As we headed toward that speck, some late afternoon clouds blew in, merged, and began to turn that blue sky gray. A breeze blew in so suddenly it seemed as if someone had thrown a switch; it quickly grew into a wind which churned up the surface of that lake into wavelets that slapped against the prow of our tiny vessel, turning and shoving us—away from shore. Getting to our reunion with my old students was, apparently, not going to be the leisurely excursion we'd envisioned. We cranked up our pedaling, but we still kept moving backward; at our best, we looked like people on stationary bikes in a gym. That wind got bolder and colder; the sun was now thoroughly hidden behind a charcoal curtain, vast, covering the whole sky. How did that happen so fast? Still pedaling, our legs beginning to ache, underdressed and shivering with cold, losing sight of the dock completely, we were now less concerned about paying an extra hour's rental fee than we were about being swept away into the middle of that enormous lake as the Alpine night was falling. The Conas would learn the reason for our non-arrival through a headline in their local newspaper: "*Coppia americana muore di ipotermia nel disastro del Lago di Como*" ("American Couple Die of Hypothermia in Lake Como Disaster").

Somehow, despite the fact that our thigh muscles were screaming with the pain of our mad pedaling and the icy wind seemed to be blowing not just at but through us, we found some hidden reserves of strength (desperation can do that) and were, against all apparent odds, able to get back to the dock only about ten minutes late. The people at the boat concession did not villainously twirl virtual mustachio ends at the prospect of collecting a double fee from us, but, factoring in the sudden change in weather and current, smiled kindly and told us that we just had to pay for one hour.

After thawing out, we drove to the nearest hotel and slept like the dead. In the morning, we got back on the *autostrada*, and, before any more currents could hold us back, drove as fast as the Italians, crossed the Swiss border, and arrived at the Conas' tiny village of Medeglia. It seemed to have only a few houses, so it was easy to find my students' address. Dony was still at work at the bank in Lugano, but Cony was there to greet us with hugs and to welcome us to their world. After surviving our dramatic journey, how good it was to be in their house, in the home of our friends. While the three of us were sipping tea in the living room, we asked Cony to recommend a place we might drive to in order to find some good hiking trails. She laughed as if she'd never heard a more ridiculous request, and said, "Come."

She led us to the back door of their little house and opened it. Stepping outside, we were astonished. All of nature seemed to be out there: fields, rocks, hills, towering mountains. Laughing some more, at us, Cony said, "You say 'drive' to hiking place? I think you no need drive. Hiking place begin right here."

I thought, *This started in that classroom in Oakland.*

"You want to go hiking *now*?" Cony asked. We did. It was just the thing after hours of being folded into our little rental car.

So we set out right then, following Cony up and down those hills in the shadow of the Alps, greeting mountain goats and thinking she might be part mountain goat herself as she bounded through that ancient landscape with no apparent effort. After about two hours, we returned to the Conas' house. We thanked Cony for taking us on that memorable hike, and, once again, she laughed at us.

"Hike? You call that 'hike'?"

"Well," I said, "yes. For us it was certainly a hike. You call it something *else*?"

"Yes, we call it 'passeggiata.' Is no hike. Only little passeggiata."

"Passeggiata?"

"In English you say maybe 'stroll,' a little walk. Like promenade? For us 'hike' mean much bigger walk. Not so short one. Not so easy one."

Easy? The mountain-goat-ancestry theory was gaining credibility. Not wanting to seem like an old fart (or, worse, an old *goat*), I thanked her for taking us on that unforgettable passeggiata.

"You're welcome, Phil," said the smiling Cony. Once again, as had happened so often in classrooms, this teacher had become the student.

When we entered the house, there was Donato. He had just returned from work and looked hot and out of place in his business suit and tie. We had some more hugs before he went to his bedroom to change into something more comfortable.

Dinner that night was superb, and it didn't hurt that we were ravenous after that two-hour "passeggiata." After the last dishes were cleared from the table, we moved to the living room, where Dony served delicious homemade *limoncello*, a cold Italian dessert drink made with lemons, vodka, sugar, and water. As we sank into their comfortable easy chairs and couches, Dony asked us about our visit to Milan.

"So Phil, in Milan, did you go to Il Duomo?"

"Yes, very impressive."

"Good. And La Scala?"

"Indeed. Beautiful. We didn't catch a performance there, but it was good just to appreciate that amazing building, the incredible architecture. Wow."

"Oh yes, yes, yes. And tell me, Phil, what was your favorite thing about Milano? What was the best thing that you did there?"

"The best thing in Milano? For me? I think you'll laugh if I tell you."

"Why I laugh?" Dony said, now looking more eager to hear my answer."

"Well, it's not a famous place like Il Duomo or La Scala."

"So? That's okay. What is it?"

"Well, my nicest memory of Milano is taking a lovely walk with our friends every evening after dinner to a little place that made the best gelato I've ever eaten."

"Ha. That's funny. Do you remember the name of this special shop? Maybe the next time Cony and I will go to Milano, we will go to there to eat this magnificent gelato."

"The funny thing is, Dony, I don't think that place *had* a name. They just had a big sign that said "Gelateria."

Suddenly, our hosts, who were sitting side by side, turned their eyes away from me and toward each other, and broke into hysterical laughter, rocking back and forth, holding their sides. Clearly, something I'd said was hilarious to them.

Not giving us a chance to ask what was so funny, Dony, grinning broadly, clued us in: "Well, well, well, Teacher. I tell you something so important: it's not 'Gela*teer*ia.' The correct way to say this place name is 'Gelateh*dee*ya.' You must to practice! We are not in Oakland now." Now we were all laughing.

"Ouch! You got me. I think I just paid for our Medeglia bed and breakfast. You got your revenge on your old teacher."

"Yes, we did," Dony agreed, nodding his head and smiling triumphantly. "It's vehdy intehdesting."

His Highness

Tariq, a soft-spoken Saudi man in his early thirties, was in my 104 writing class in Berkeley in the summer of 2009; he had been at the school for several sessions, but his progress with English was so slow that it was almost imperceptible. For many Saudi students, studying English, especially writing, is a daunting project. Of course, this is partly because our alphabets are different; but probably more significant is the fact that repetition and memorization play a larger part than critical analysis in most Saudi schools, including universities. Of course, there are always students like Zaheen who, through exceptional ability and determination, break through institutional and traditional barriers.

Along with the general burdens that Saudi students brought with them to our classes, Tariq had his own additional load. He came up to my desk during a break and revealed that, back home in Ryadh, tests had determined that he was severely learning-disabled; incorporating new data, whether it was in Arabic or English, took much longer than it did with most other students. And once he did get something, the likelihood of his retaining it until the next day, or even the next hour, was low. I very much appreciated his confiding in me about that since it put my struggles with *his* struggles in a clearer context. Often, in class, he'd demonstrate beyond question that he'd finally understood a point of the language, only to show up the next day appearing never to have heard of it. Of course, Tariq's low-retention problem had disastrous consequences on exams, and that resulted in his having to repeat every level one or more times. His humiliation was compounded by the fact that his wife was also studying at the school and rose to each successive level as if she were leisurely ascending a staircase.

In that writing class one Wednesday morning, I handed out a "menu" of a dozen essay topics from which the students would choose one to write about; it would be due two days later, on Friday. Tariq chose one that I had assigned many times before: "Write a four- or five-paragraph essay about an interesting person that you have met. Use very specific details to show why this person is interesting." Straightforward, sure, but with Tariq, I always felt that I had to put in a bit more time and energy to make sure he really got it.

"So, Tariq, remember, this person can be 'interesting' for good reasons or bad reasons."

"I understand, Teacher."

"Good. It's a good idea to include a little anecdote, a little story, to show something about the personality of your subject."

"I understand, Teacher."

"Very good. And don't forget, Tariq, that this is a *real* person in your life, someone you've actually met. I don't want you or any of the students to go on the internet to do research about a famous person and then just pass that information on to me. I can find that stuff out myself if I want to. Remember, this is not a research project; it's a *personal* essay, something only *you* can write about."

"Yes, Teacher, I think I really understand. I write personal essay."

"Great. I'm looking forward to reading your essay on Friday." Well, that wasn't exactly true; Tariq's writing was consistently a thicket of badly spelled, sometimes unrecognizable, words thrown into chaotic ungrammatical sequences devoid of proper punctuation or capitalization. The time it took to read, decipher, and correct Tariq's writing routinely exceeded the limits of my patience, propelling me repeatedly to the refrigerator for snacks, or to the phone to call a friend, *any* friend, or to Tilden Park for a hike in the textless woods. The truth was that what I actually looked forward to was the completion of that brain-strangling chore. Ah well, all in a day's (or night's) work.

Friday arrived. I collected my students' essays, stashed them in my briefcase, and didn't look at them again until Saturday morning. Though I would have preferred hunkering down with a good novel, I fished those papers out of my bag and, fueled by a couple of mugs of strong Costa Rican coffee, got down to the business of facing my students' sometimes baffling versions of the language.

I was already pretty tired by the time I had worked my way down the stack of papers to Tariq's contribution, which I had intentionally buried at the bottom so it wouldn't sap all my strength before I had even begun to deal with the other students' less challenging work. Just reading his title was enough to let me know that, true to form, simple ideas he had seemed to grasp on Wednesday had vanished without a trace by Friday. He had entitled his essay, simply, "King Abdullah." Reading through the two-page typed description of the Saudi monarch, there was almost nothing to correct. The syntax, spelling, vocabulary, punctuation, and style were clearly those of a native English speaker, one who'd probably had academic training. No way was this Tariq's writing.

I turned on my computer and googled "King Abdullah of Saudi Arabia." As usual, the Wikipedia entry was at or near the top of the page. I clicked on it, and the relevant article appeared on the screen. With Tariq's essay in hand, I read what Wikipedia had to say about my student's leader. Bingo. I'd hit a hole-in-one. There they were: the same sentences, the same words, aside from several typos on Tariq's pages.

I confess that the time-greedy part of me was grateful to Tariq for plagiarizing, since "correcting" stolen writing takes almost no time, unlike performing surgery on honestly generated errors. Nevertheless, I wasn't looking forward to Monday morning's class, when I would have to give Tariq the standard plagiarism-is-a-crime sermon. I would also need to point out, of course, that he had failed to follow the simple directive to write only about someone he'd met. Here was another confirmation that this poor guy was unable to retain a few simple details from one day to the next.

Monday rolled around, as Mondays always do, and, back in that writing class, I handed out the graded essays to my fifteen students. Most of those papers were so covered with my blood-red comments and corrections that they looked like pages retrieved from a murder scene. Tariq's, however, was almost free of red ink, except for a note that I'd squeezed into the space at the top of page one, something like, "Tariq, these are not your words. I haven't given you a grade because I can't evaluate your writing in this assignment since your writing is not here, and it's not my job to evaluate the writing of the Wikipedia person. Also, remember, you were not supposed to do research about a *famous* person; you were expected to write about a person in your *life*, a person you had actually *met*. I'll speak to you after class." That was more ominous-sounding than I'd intended it to be, but I figured I'd do the necessary editing of tone when we had our talk.

I had decided to wait until the break to speak with Tariq because I wanted to spare him the public embarrassment; he was already ashamed enough of his ongoing failures. But Tariq didn't want to wait; he insisted on knowing what the problem was right away, in class. Okay, so be it.

"First of all, Tariq. You have copied the words exactly from Wikipedia. That's called 'plagiarism.' It's a crime. It's stealing words. In a university, you might get expelled, forced to leave the school, or you might simply get an F in the class, or, at best, an F on that paper. It's taken very seriously. You can steal money, you can steal a car, or you can steal words. It's all the same. Stealing is stealing."

"Oh."

"Do you see? Is it clear?"

"Yes. Clear. But when I read that beautiful writing, I am sure that I cannot write so good. I will *never* write so good. Never in million billion billion year. So I think: why I should give my teacher my terrible writing when this writing so beautiful? It's nicer for you to read this. Right, Phil?"

"Well, I admit it's easier for me because there's almost nothing to correct. But if you don't do your own writing, I can't help you to get better. And that's what I want to do."

"Oh."

"Okay?"

"Yes. Okay. I think I see, Phil. I'm sorry. Can you give me other chance? This time I will write *my* words. Please, Phil."

"Well, Tariq. There's another problem."

"Oh?"

"Yes. You see, you didn't follow the directions. You wrote about King Abdullah, but you were supposed to write about someone you have actually *met*, someone who is part of your life."

"Oh, but I did. I did that."

"No, Tariq, you just copied parts of the Wikipedia article about King Abdullah. You should have chosen a different person because you have never met the king of Saudi Arabia. Remember the assignment?"

"But, Phil, I *did* met him. Many time. He is friend of my family. *Old* friend. Our families visit each other family for lot of years. Of course, I met him. He is my father's good good friend."

His classmates seemed as surprised as I was by Tariq's rather matter-of-fact explanation. I'd work out the details of this sticky situation later, but, for the moment, all I could do was echo Tariq's response to almost any attempt at clarification:

"Oh."

Yukiko's Ears

Yukiko, a very pretty Japanese woman in her early twenties, arrived on the Holy Names campus on a Monday morning in March. Her black hair was pulled back and cinched into a small pony tail. She had a slightly shocked look on her face and a careful way of stepping about which were not uncommon among our new students on the first day of a session, or even during the first week: she seemed lost, scared, floating alone in space, *outer* space. I was to be her interviewer. I checked her name on the info sheet and began.

"Welcome, Yukiko. My name is Phil."

Yukiko gave me just a hint of a smile and nodded, but remained silent. I proceeded with one of my standard opening remarks, explaining why we were about to do what we were about to do:

"So, Yukiko, I'm going to ask you some questions, just to get to know you a little. And also to see how well you understand me when I speak English. Of course, I also want to listen to *you* speak English. Okay?"

Again, that shy little smile, just the subtlest widening of her lips, and another almost imperceptible nod. I took that minimal body language as a yes.

"So, Yukiko, which city in Japan do you live in?"

"Yes, my name Yukiko. Good morning. I'm happy to meet you."

Okay, clearly we were not yet connected. I tried my question again, this time much more slowly, with hyper-clear enunciation: "Which. Ci-ty. In. Ja-pan. Do. You. Live. In? What. Is. Your. Ci-ty?"

"Oh, city?"

"That's right. What. City?"

"Oakland."

"No. Not. In. California. But. In. Japan."

Red-faced, she seemed to get it at that point but was already so shaken that she slipped into a mix of Japanese and English: "*Ah so desukah* ('Oh, now I see'), city in Japam. *Gomenasai* ('I'm sorry')." (It was not unusual to hear "Sorry sorry" from my Japanese students after they'd made a mistake in English. Some students explained that it was a habit that had dug its roots into many of them at a very early age: some teachers in Japan, they told me, would strictly reprimand their students for any mistake in class, sometimes punctuating that scolding with a slap. I had to repeatedly assure them that they had nothing to apologize for, and certainly nothing to fear. In fact, I'd often wisecrack that I was happy when my students made mistakes, because, if they didn't, I'd be out of a job.)

Still looking scared, and seriously disconcerted, Yukiko ventured, "My city? My city in my country?"

"Yes yes yes yes," I tried to assure her, nodding away like a person who'd lost control of his head.

"Osaka city. Osaka my city."

"Good. Osaka. Okay, my next question is . . ."

I went on with my usual bag of queries: hobbies, job, university plans, professional plans, family, etc., and it seemed obvious very quickly from her non-responses or mistaken ones that Yukiko belonged in one of the school's beginning levels.

On the next day, she started her classes, and, by the end of that first week, all her teachers reported that she was struggling to keep up with the pace of the lessons. She was falling behind her fellow students. As was to be expected, she was visibly upset, deeply embarrassed, by those very public displays of her difficulties. She never volunteered to give an answer, and whenever her teachers called on her, she would stare fearfully at her questioner, remain silent, or, on rare occasions, hazard an answer in a voice just above a whisper. It was usually wrong.

The scary sense of displacement and disorientation that typically vanishes a few days into the session with most students seemed to be a permanent component of Yukiko's makeup, and it seemed to be directly linked to her Sisyphean task of learning English. Yukiko's teachers were unanimous in their assessments. She had a severe problem with "listening comprehension"; it seemed nearly impossible for her to extract meaning from the English word sounds that flew at her like bullets. We could all see that teaching this frightened doe would be no small challenge.

Yukiko repeated each level at least once as she struggled to make it through the school's program. She wasn't in any of my classes for the first few months, but we'd wave to each other and smile as we'd pass each other on campus during breaks: easy non-threatening nonverbal exchanges, perfect prep for someone planning to become a nun who'd take a vow of silence—or a mime—but, of course, life is not so neatly arranged.

Several sessions later, Yukiko wound up in one of my intermediate writing classes. She seemed slightly more connected to the goings-on there, but only slightly. I did everything I could to try to make things clear to her, but her comprehension was still excruciatingly limited. She always seemed a sob away from breaking down about it, which of course exacerbated her learning difficulties, which brought her closer and closer to that breaking point. She seemed caught in a classic vicious cycle which perpetuated her exile in outer space. I felt sorry for her, but I was running out of ideas. I was running out of tricks.

Years later, I became an avid fan of the writings of Haruki Murakami. Many of his novels and stories have a mysterious beautiful woman at the heart of the plot. Often, she'd disappear, and the forlorn protagonist would spend a good portion of the rest of the novel searching for her. Sometimes, reading about these vanishing women would make me think of Yukiko: she hadn't physically disappeared, she was sitting right in front of me, but was gone anyway. There was also a physical characteristic which linked Yukiko to Murakami's women. They often had beautiful ears, as did Yukiko, and hers were thoroughly exposed because of her tautly pulled-back hairdo. In each lobe, every day, was a little silver stud in the shape of a treble clef. I know Murakami would have appreciated Yukiko's ears, with their perfect musical accompaniment.

Yukiko wrote several essays for me, and, not surprisingly, her writing was better than her listening comprehension or her speaking. Her subjects were typical ones: accounts of vacations, family members, "comparison/contrasts" of cities, cuisines, schools, etc. One day, she chose the topic, "A Difficult Situation in My Life." In that essay, she revealed how, in Osaka, she had gone to several doctors because it was hard for her to hear what people were saying to her. When she listened to people speaking on TV or the radio, it was no easier. She felt spending money on movies was a waste because following the dialogue was too difficult, in fact impossible. The problem was not only with *voices* in her life: *nothing* seemed loud enough.

The world Yukiko inhabited was a muffled, distant, alien one. Her parents sent her for a battery of tests, and the doctors determined that she had profound hearing loss in both ears. They strongly advised her to get hearing aids, a suggestion which she fiercely opposed. She reasoned that those devices would mark her as a freak in her neighborhood and in her school, an object of ridicule, a target for bullies. The Japanese have a saying: "The nail that sticks up is quickly hammered down," a phenomenon which, sadly, exists everywhere, but which seems to be especially dominant in Yukiko's culture. She would, she proclaimed, live with her problem without advertising it to the world by walking around with ugly chunks of plastic in her ears. It just wasn't stylish. It wasn't cool.

I wondered if Yukiko's writing on this topic indicated a rethinking of her opposition to her Japanese doctors' advice. Was she sending out a veiled plea for help? If she was, did she even know she was doing it? Were her difficulties in class actually not a result of poor "listening comprehension," but of hearing itself, a physical disability, *not* a cognitive one? One can't comprehend what one can't hear. Yukiko, in her essay, lamented that her Japanese friends, teachers, and even some people in her family, thought she was "stupid" because she could rarely understand them. Of course, she simply couldn't *hear* them. The teachers at our school, always striving to sound professional, didn't use words like "stupid," but our evaluation of "low listening comprehension" was perhaps simply a handy euphemism for the same thing. Whatever the cause, it had locked Yukiko into a very lonely isolation chamber. Would she consider doing here what she adamantly refused to do in Japan? I decided to find out.

I checked her records in the school office after my last class. After digging through that pile of papers for a couple of minutes, I came to her medical record form. Sure enough, about three-quarters down the page, there it was: "profound hearing loss." Profound! None of us had suspected that. Like so much else about our students and ourselves, it was buried, hidden.

On the next morning, after going over some technical problems in her essay, I told Yukiko that I had had no idea that she had a physiological problem. Her cheeks reddened, and she gave me one of her trademark nods, just one little one. I remember that blush reaching her ears too, a bright little red flame on each side of her head, but I suspect I've imagined that part.

I made sure I was squarely facing her before I said another word. As I spoke, I could now see that her eyes were fixed on every movement of my mouth, "reading" my lips. I now understood why she always sat so close to me and all her other teachers.

"I was wondering, Yukiko, how you now feel about what your doctors in Japan said." She looked a bit scared by that reference, so I backed off a bit and tried to put a positive spin on it. Hyper-enunciating, I went on: "It seems to me that your problems with understanding your teachers are mostly a result of your physiological, your *physical*, your *hearing* problem. I *know* you're intelligent, so I really think you're having so much difficulty, so many problems with learning, because of the hearing problem you wrote about in your excellent essay. What do you think?"

I could see that, this time, she had understood me completely. Still red-faced, she replied, "I think maybe yes, maybe you right, Teacher. Yes I think so. I think so. Yes. Maybe."

We were on our way.

"You wrote in your essay, Yukiko, that you were embarrassed to wear hearing aids in Japan because you thought your friends would make fun of you, but what do you think about trying them here? I think the students here would be understanding. I think they would be kind. I don't think anyone would make you feel bad. But if you wanted to, you could even change your hair style so your hair could cover up the hearing aids, and no one would even know about it. I think they would really help you to hear everybody, and help you to understand things so much better. It might be a wonderful change in your life. What do you think?"

Again I could see that she'd gotten it. For the several seconds that it took her to form an answer, I thought I saw some of her fear slowly dissolving. *Re*solving.

"Maybe I try, Teacher."

"I think it could be a very good thing, Yukiko. My wife is a speech-language pathologist. Part of her job is to help people to speak better. And she knows people who can help you with your hearing. They're called audiologists. I'll talk to her tonight and see what she thinks about this. Okay? Would you like me to do that? Then you and I can talk about this some more tomorrow."

"Thank you, Teacher. I like that."

That night I did talk to Joan, and she was quite fascinated by this wrongly assessed "listening comprehension" problem. There was an audiologist for whom she had a special respect, so she contacted her right away and explained Yukiko's problem to her. After hearing Joan's account, she was eager to meet my student.

The next day, when I told Yukiko about the audiologist, I could see that she had moved on from her tentative and embarrassed consideration of this step to an enthusiastic anticipation of it. Clearly, she had had enough. If there was a way to break out of her isolation, she was ready to take it. To hell with the collateral consequences! Yukiko told me when she was available, and I called and made the appointment.

A few mornings later, Yukiko missed her classes to meet with the audiologist; her office was at Children's Hospital in Oakland, but her patients were both children and adults. She was very gentle with Yukiko and made her feel as at ease as could be hoped for. After running the standard audiological tests, she confirmed the findings of the Japanese doctors. Yukiko's hearing problem *was* profound. She too was confident that good hearing aids would make a huge difference. Like her counterparts across the Pacific, she encouraged Yukiko to go for a fitting. Joan and I had informed her of Yukiko's self-consciousness about the appearance of those devices; armed with that knowledge, she had brought photos of various hearing-aid-concealing hair styles to their meeting. There was one that Yukiko especially liked, and the audiologist told her, woman to woman, that she heartily agreed; she gushed that it was a splendid choice, quite a glamorous one, which seemed to cinch it. They set up two appointments for Monday of the next week, the first, in the morning, with a hearing-aid technician, and the second, in the afternoon, with the audiologist's hairdresser.

On Tuesday, Yukiko arrived in class looking kind of Italo-Asian, with highly permed ear-covering hair. Her treble-clef studs had been replaced by large dramatic silver hoops, which dangled just below her many new curls.

"Ah, Yukiko, what a beautiful new hairdo. You look like a movie star."

She laughed immediately at my quip. Absent was the usual time lag between utterance and comprehension. And gone was the wince that seemed to accompany her every attempt at making out words, English or Japanese. Her smile was now broad, amazed, stress-free. She laughed again, not only at my comment, but, I suspect, at the shock of hearing, at the shock of having arrived on this planet. *Sayonara*, outer space. Yukiko continued at our school for another three months and made very rapid progress. Her listening comprehension was actually well above average now that hearing was not such a challenge. She made several new friends, and I often saw her rejoicing in what so many of us take for granted, the simple pleasure of having a conversation, of speaking, and of hearing. Murakami would probably have missed those lovely little ears, now hiding under that pile of curls, and maybe I did too a little, but that new smile, that never-before-heard laugh, were enough, most of the time, to make me forget them.

Cheers?

It's inevitable: spoken words, which, physically, are simply sounds, often have homonyms or near-homonyms in other languages, with entirely different meanings. For example, *una casita* in Spanish means "a little house," and *onaka suita* in Japanese is one of several ways of saying "I'm hungry." In the typical pronunciation of the latter, the *u* is virtually silent, so what Spanish speakers hear is *ona casita*; they might wonder why a hungry Japanese classmate has suddenly started talking about a cottage. The confusion in this case is harmless, unembarrassing, and short-lived, but once in a while, the collision of meanings of bicultural sound-forms packs a stronger punch.

One memorable instance of this occurred during the mid-eighties, at a party with some of the students from the Oakland branch of the school. We were celebrating something or other, or perhaps nothing; I had just filled the glasses of the five students I was hanging out with, two Brazilians and three Japanese. We raised our glasses for the toast, and I said, "Cheers." The Japanese students responded with "*Kanpai*," and the Brazilians finished with "*Chin-chin*," at which point the Japanese students began tittering in a way which reminded me of the Marla-testicle incident; there was a kind of raunchy delight, the relishing of an inside joke.

"What's so funny, guys?"

They looked at each other, and the level of their giggling went up a few decibels.

"Oh, can't say, Teacher," said Koji.

"Why not? Is it embarrassing?"

"Oh yes," said Ryo in a mischievous tone. "Oh, yes. Embarrassing." The giggling got louder yet.

"You don't have to be embarrassed with me. Nothing embarrasses me." That was a bit of an overstatement, but mostly true.

"Okay. I tell you. '*Chin-chin*' is slang word in Japanese. It's mean, you know, what man have. What woman not have."

It was a déjà vu of Hiroshi's explanation of the meaning of Marla.

"Yes, okay. Could you be more specific, Ryo?"

"More specific, Teacher? You no understand?" He looked at me, apparently amazed that I needed more specificity in order to be certain. Could I really be that dense?

"I think I *do* understand, Ryo, but I'd like to be sure. I can think of at least two things that a man has that a woman doesn't."

Ryo laughed loudly. "Oh, I see. I know what you mean, Phil-san. I be more specific. '*Chin-chin*' mean 'prick.'"

Now I was the one laughing. "I thought that was

probably it. Do you know the non-slang word for 'prick'? The scientific word?"

"Ah, I think maybe I know, Phil-san. Is other word 'dick'?"

"No, Ryo," I said through my now near-hysterical laughing, "good try. But 'dick' is another slang word. But, of course, there really *is* a scientific word, a word which is in every English dictionary."

"Sorry, Phil-san, I don't remember. Maybe I never know. What is real word? Scientific one."

"Penis."

"Penis." He was laughing harder now. Ah, the joys of learning. "Penis, penis, penis. I think I going to remember that now. Penis." He wrote it down quickly in the notebook he pulled out of his back pocket. "But I think *'chin-chin'* mean more 'prick' or 'dick' than 'penis' because is slang. I think so. You agree, Phil-san?"

"Yes, I do agree. Absolutely. You've got it."

"Thank you, Phil-san. I think you can see why is so funny to hear this when we drink something together. 'Cheers! *Kanpai!* Prick!'" Now the Brazilians were laughing harder than any of us. They said that, in the future, if they were having a drink with Japanese friends, they would stick to English when it was time for the toast. Or Japanese. We toasted each other again, this time chanting the safe but relatively boring "Cheers!"

As I walked back to my car after receiving that surprise lesson in safe toasting, I couldn't help thinking about another student party, one I had organized a few years earlier. That summer, I was the site coordinator for a large study/vacation program, a couple of hundred international students who both lived and had classes in one of the enormous residence halls at U.C. Berkeley. Back then, our school had a relatively hefty budget, so I was given a pretty free hand in putting together a farewell party on the last night of the program. I ordered lots of food and drinks and hired The Real Band, a local Berkeley blues group that I had enjoyed on several occasions. When my Brazilian students heard about the upcoming party, a few of them approached me and excitedly volunteered to make a giant batch of a drink which is wildly popular in Brazil and which I had never tasted: caipirinha. They assured me that it was the perfect party drink, refreshing, delicious, and, yes, of course, rather intoxicating. Even after factoring in the typical Brazilian penchant for exuberant hyperbole, it seemed like an excellent idea, an ideal way of mixing festivity with "intercultural exploration."

Caipirinha is a very simple drink made with muddled lime, raw sugar, and cachaça (a sugar-cane rum which is typically between 38% and 48% alcohol). At that time it was more difficult to find cachaça in the States than it is today; my Brazilian students searched for it in several stores, but struck out in each of them. One of them called his São Paulo home and spoke to his father, an authority on Brazilian mixology, who assured him that it was perfectly okay to substitute tequila for cachaça, especially since no one at that huge gathering except his fellow *brasileiros* had ever tasted the classic recipe, so there would be no basis for comparison or disappointment. It was decided. Tequila it would be. Lots of it.

The Saturday night of the grand event arrived. It took place in an enormous room, spacious enough to accommodate the big crowd that we were, more than two hundred bodies. The live music was hot, and the tables were covered with yakitori, guacamole, nachos, samosas, salads, hummus, sushi, kim chee, dolmas, cheese and crackers, cookies, a huge chocolate cake with "Farewell Students" inscribed in white icing, and, of course, a good variety of drinks, both alcoholic and not, to wash it all down. At a separate table, near a window, the Brazilians had set up what quickly came to be called "the caipirinha table." Surrounded by a ring of limes and little clear plastic glasses was a tureen of caipirinha that looked big enough to bathe in. The Brazilians looked ecstatic as they ladled that sweet drink into the cups and handed those cups to the many outstretched hands; after all, they were sharing an important part of their culture and everybody loved it, and said so. Liquid Brazil!

The party was going splendidly. The students were dancing with increasing abandon, wolfing down the food as soon as it was brought out of the kitchen, and returning, again and again, to the caipirinha table. "*Chin-chin*," the *brasileiros* sang as they served their now wildly successful concoction. "*Chin-chin*," the non-*brasileiros* echoed back as they downed yet more of that innocent-tasting lime drink. Now that I know the Japanese meaning of "*chin-chin*," I think I understand why the Japanese students were laughing so hysterically as they chanted "*Chin-chin! Chin-chin! Chin-chin!*" to their fellow drinkers at that table. At the time, I must have figured that it was simply the tequila that had fueled all their guffawing, and of course, it partially *was* that, but it must have also given them a sense of cockeyed (pun intended) freedom to bellow, "Prick! Prick! Prick!" in a public place where everyone else was doing it too, just for the hell of it. The Brazilians had a reputation for being crazily funny, but, to Japanese ears, this was a custom that must have seemed off any known scale.

"Prick!"

"Prick!"

"Prick to you!"

And on and on. The *brasileiros* kept ladling, the other students kept drinking, the *brasileiros* kept mixing up new batches in the grand tureen, and it was looking like we had put together the party of the century. That is, until I looked over at Sumiko, a Japanese woman who was holding one of the caipirinha glasses and chatting with her friends, just a few feet from where I was standing. Her eyelids had drooped to half-mast, and she seemed to sway a bit from port to starboard on the heaving ship which that room had become. I strolled over to her. I was probably swaying a little myself since I'd been enjoying fair quantities of the Brazilian national drink too.

"Hey everybody, are you enjoying the party?"

They all assured me that they were. Sumiko raised her glass for a toast. I raised mine too, and we clicked our plastic glasses.

"*Chin-chin*," she laughed.

"*Chin-chin*," I answered.

She laughed even harder. Little did I know how bawdy this toast must have sounded to my tipsy student.

And then her eyelids lowered a bit more, so that I couldn't see her pupils. I got a little worried then and asked her, "Sumiko, are you all right?"

"Yes, Phil-san, I'm . . ."

And then she sank. One of her friends, Tai, a Japanese guy, lunged, caught her, and, cradling her head, laid her gently on the brown linoleum floor. I crouched down next to her.

"Sumiko?"

Nothing.

"Sumiko, it's Phil-san. Are you okay?"

Still nothing.

Tai took a bottle of spring water and sprinkled a little on her face. That roused her just enough for her to slur "*Chin-chin*" before passing out again. It was mercifully convenient that we were holding the party in the community room of the dormitory where she and most of the other students had their beds. I took her feet, Tai slipped his hands under her armpits, and we carried the sleeping Sumiko down a longish corridor to and into the elevator. Gilberto, one of the caipirinha servers, pushed the button for her floor, and the four of us began our ascent, only three of us conscious of it. Fortunately, Tai knew her room number. So, after I had dug out her key from her small sequined evening bag, we entered her room and laid her out on the bed.

Tai then went to the sink in her bathroom and filled a glass with water, which he again sprinkled on Sumiko's sleeping face. Again, she stirred a bit, slowly opened her eyes, and smiled at me. I was relieved.

"Are you okay, Sumiko? I was worried about you."

"Yes, okay, Phil-san. Okay. *Oyasuminasai* (Good night)."

"*Oyasuminasai.*"

She then fell back to sleep and immediately started snoring, quietly, like the purring of a kitten. I was convinced that, aside from the probable arrival of a fierce morning hangover, nothing dreadful was lying in wait for her. Tai, Gilberto, and I went back down to the party, which was in full swing.

The pulse of the music sent Gilberto dancing back to the caipirinha table, which was still swarming with partiers chugging down that drink like it was

Mountain Dew. I hit the food tables again since I had worked up an appetite during the Sumiko rescue operation. I was feeling quite festive myself, dancing a bit as I filled my mouth with one delicacy after another. Suddenly I felt a tugging on my sleeve, and someone was screaming my name, trying to be heard over the wails of the blues band's lead electric guitar solo. It was Emilie, one of my Swiss students.

"Pheel, please come weef me. We 'ave a problem. It's Louis . . . 'e fall down. Maybe 'e 'ave too much Brazilian drink. Please come 'elp us."

I ran across the room with her to where a few students huddled around Louis, who was indeed lying supine, eyes closed, on the hard floor. I knelt and took hold of his shoulders and shook him gently.

"Louis. Louis. Wake up. Louis. It's Phil."

He opened his eyes and saw me peering down at him. My eyes were distracted by a bright green smear on the collar of his yellow shirt; my guess was that it was an errant gob of wasabi. Or was it guacamole? But, of course, what did it matter?

"*Oh la la*, zat is some very funny lemonade, Phil."

Then he closed his eyes again and curled up as if he were lying comfortably on a pillowtop mattress. I shook him again and he briefly opened his eyes and groaned before re-closing them. I motioned to Tai and Gilberto and, faithful souls that they were, they again helped me out. As we had done with Sumiko, we hoisted Louis up and deposited him safely in his room.

As we left and entered the corridor, we saw another group of students shuffling towards us. They were carrying Aditya, an Indonesian student, to *his* room. I knew before they explained that he too had toppled after swigging way too much of that innocent-tasting punch. I did an about-face and joined them. It was 11:30, and the party would soon be over, since we were approaching the midnight curfew. I found myself looking forward to that. After assuring myself that Aditya was okay, I headed back to the party, now somewhat apprehensively. For good reason.

My memory is not totally clear about the remainder of that evening, but I *do* remember making several more shuttles between the party and the dorm rooms, either carrying or steering caipirinha-walloped students to their beds. Even before the revels had officially ended, I was envisioning multiple parental lawsuits, general disgrace, and, at the very least, getting canned. I was already preparing my defense, but everything I came up with sounded pathetically lame: *It was so sweet. It tasted almost like a soft drink. Who knew it was so potent? By the time we realized what a kick it had, it was too late. The damage had been done. It was all in the spirit of innocent fun. Everyone's all right. Right? No one got hurt. Right? No one died . . .*

Ah well, there was nothing I could do but deal with the repercussions of this disaster when Monday stomped back into my life. I asked the caipirinha servers to bottle up the dregs of remaining caipirinha and take it home with them. Impish smiles on their faces, they nodded as they ladled for the last few times. Midnight finally arrived, and after cleaning up, it was time for me to guide my own tired carcass toward my house and *my* bed.

Well, Monday arrived, and nothing was said about all the students who had keeled over like so many felled trees. In fact, nothing ever came of it. I guess I was lucky. No lawsuits. No warnings. No firing. No self-righteous finger wagging. No damning insinuations that I'd been a *chin-chin* to allow all that to happen on my watch.

The *chin-chin* revelation is also linked in my mind to a more recent, seemingly unrelated, incident, but related it is. You'll see.

In June, 2010, I had asked each of the dozen or so students in my Berkeley Masters' class to speak on the following topic: "Does your name have a meaning? How do you feel about it? Can you tell a story or two about it?" Each student had complied, and, as was typical, I was asked to do the same. Fair is fair.

So. I explained that my name "Phil" is a nickname for "Philip," derived from the Greek *Philippides*, which means "lover of horses." (In checking the spelling of that Greek name while writing this chapter, I discovered that I've been making a mistake about this for most of my life; the Greek origin of "Philip" does, in fact, mean "lover of horses," but it's *Philippos*, not *Philippides*. I picked up that wrong form when I graduated from elementary school, P.S. 230, in 1956 Brooklyn. There was a long-standing tradition at that school: each graduate would visit Mr. Healy, the school's "superintendent," or "super," essentially the head janitor, in his "office," a cleaning supply closet with a desk. Mr. Healy had an ancient-looking book of names with their derivations and meanings, and copied the appropriate one into each student's little blue leatherette-covered autograph book. In mine, he wrote, "Philip, from the Greek *Philippides*: lover of horses." I don't mean to hang the rap on the now probably deceased Mr. Healy; he was a kind, intelligent man, and, anyway, it was the book's error, not his. But I'm digressing from my digression.)

I explained to my class that, in fact, I had never felt that the meaning of my name was appropriate for me, since the truth was that, until a recent trip to Costa Rica, I had been astride a horse only two times, the first time not especially pleasant and the second downright annoying. My first "ride," as a Brooklyn kid, was actually not a ride, but, to be accurate, more of a "sit." There was an old Italian man, Tony, who sauntered into our neighborhood from time to time. Behind him, at the end of the reins he held, was a smallish palomino pony, rather pretty to look at, with big chocolaty brown splotches on a vanilla-white field. The pony carried saddle bags filled with photographic equipment and kid-sized cowboy duds. For a price which most of the mothers on the block were willing to pay, he'd dress their kids up in cowboy hat, denim overalls, chaps, bandana, and boots. Then he'd set up his tripod and affix an enormous black camera to it before hoisting the kid to the top of the pony and depositing him or her onto the too-slippery-for-comfort saddle.

When I was about four, I sat up there. My mother stood just far enough away to stay out of the picture but close enough to lunge and catch me if I started to slip off the saddle. She was beaming, obviously enjoying the experience more than I was. Tony then virtually disappeared under a large black cape that was attached to the camera. It covered his head and hung to his knees. From under that cape he said to me, "Now, Filippo, when I counta to tree, you give me big smile and we make a beautiful picture for your mamma." Obliging boy that I was, I fully intended to give Tony my best photo-ready grin, but he took so long to coordinate all his moves that my smile muscles got tired and gave up. Right at that moment, a flashbulb exploded atop a metal rod which Tony held a couple of feet over that cape. I still have the five-by-seven black-and-white photo, which somehow is out of focus despite the tripod, the "professional" photographer, and the stationary horse: the pony is looking down, and the little boy is staring at the lens with deadly seriousness, a fake cowboy on a horse that just stood there. In Brooklyn.

I then told my students about my second chance to see if I truly was a "lover of horses." It came about twenty-five years after the cowboy photo shoot. Joan and I had signed up for a ranger-led horse ride in Yosemite National Park. There were about twenty horses walking in a single long line on a loop trail that went on for about fifteen butt-bumping miles. My horse was at the very end of that line. That meant that I got to hear zero percent of the ranger's talk, and I couldn't even enjoy the beauty of the un-narrated landscape because I was totally obsessed with my bloody horse, who was impervious to my experimental tugging on its reins, as if the whole rein-horse connection were irrelevant; as if *I* were. I assume the ranger offered horse-managing tips along with his nature commentary, but, of course, everything he said was drowned out by the noise of eighty clopping hooves. I was on my own, astride a demon who, at will, would speed up, slow down almost to a stop, suddenly veer left or right for reasons of its own, and generally act as if my sole raison d'être was to be on the receiving end of a ride so punishing that it would be painful to sit down for the next two weeks. Lover of horses? Hardly.

Then, just a month before I told these stories to that Masters' class, I vacationed in Costa Rica, where I met Pinto, the horse that finally gave truth to the ancient meaning of my name. Joan and I were staying at a relaxing place called Termales del Bosque in Aguas Zarcas. We had spent our short time there bathing in its natural jungle hot springs (where one can get the best margarita in Costa Rica), getting massages in the spa, and enjoying excellent food. By our final morning there, we felt relatively tranquil and happy. However, the plan for that morning held a threat: we had signed up for a horseback ride, Joan enthusiastically, I reluctantly. I still remembered Yosemite.

We were joined by a Hispanic couple who lived in Miami, Hernan from Cuba and Julia from Guatemala. Their English was excellent, and, of course, so was their Spanish, so they were ideal translators. Carlos, the caballero who tended the horses, was *muy simpático*, and, in response to my request to supply me with a horse that would be appropriate for a "beginner" (my euphemism for "reluctant coward"), brought me Pinto, a caramel-colored horse with a white spot in the center of his forehead and white hair from his hooves to his knees, which made him look like he was wearing boots. He didn't seem jumpy, which helped me to feel a bit less so myself. Carlos placed a short wooden platform next to Pinto. I stepped up on it, and Carlos helped me to mount that horse in one surprisingly fluid motion. He then explained the very simple technique of using the reins to have the horse do what you want it to do. Hernan and Julia provided expert translation, so everything was *clarissimo*. Then Carlos opened a gate to a vast prairie which led to a jungle trail, and the five of us set out.

I extolled Pinto to my students:

"It was fantastic. I felt as if I had cracked a fundamental code. I could do whatever I wanted with Pinto. When I wanted to go left, we went left; when I wanted to go right, we went right. If I wanted Pinto to speed up, he sped up. If he was going too fast, I could slow him down in a second. We penetrated all that greenness of the jungle with a feeling of power and freedom that I had never felt before. It was exhilarating! The longer we rode, the more I felt that we were one organism. It felt more and more natural. It seemed like we could go on forever. I know it sounds crazy, but I think I had actually fallen in love with my horse, my Pinto."

As I was carrying on about my equine romance, the two Brazilian students in the class, Marco and Renata, burst into hysterical laughter, completely out of control. They had obviously been trying to suppress it for a while, but had lost that fight as I continued rhapsodizing. I couldn't imagine what element of my horse story had set them off. I didn't think it was particularly funny. Over the top, yes; even perhaps a tad inspiring, in the mode of "you're never too old . . ." But hysterically funny? Not that I could see.

"Hey, what's so funny, Renata? Marco?"

Marco spoke first. "Is only funny if you are from *Brasil*. But if you *are* from *Brasil*, is very very *very* funny." Renata's broad grin and cigarette-roughened laugh confirmed the truth of Marco's statement. She was still doubled over in her seat.

"Renata? Marco? You have to tell me."

They clearly had none of the reluctance or shyness that my Japanese students had shown about "Marla" and "*chin-chin.*" Renata, with delight, matter-of-factly proclaimed to the class, "In *Brasil, pinto* is a slang word for 'penis.'" Whoa, there it was again: it seemed there was just no way to discreetly keep that unruly organ in its place. Marco then added, still on the verge of hysteria, "So, Phil, you can see how funny it was when you were talking about how you love your *pinto*, how you can make your *pinto* do anything you want, go slow go fast go left go right. And you can do it forever! Ha! It was like, WOW, Phil has a Super*Pinto*!"

"What do you mean 'like,' Marco? Did you think I was talking about a horse?"

Now almost everyone was laughing. A few had to look up 'penis' in their dictionaries, and one confused Argentinean guy had thought it meant "pine trees" (*pinos* in Spanish). But soon enough we were all on the same page. Then Wichai, the one Thai student in the class, happily added that the name of one of his favorite Thai restaurants, on Shattuck Avenue in downtown Berkeley, is Pintoh. Once again, my students and I were drowning in a flood of laughter, that great unifier.

Marco and Renata had shown that they were worthy ambassadors of their Brazilian culture, which, among other things, is famous for being able to transform almost any situation into a good semblance of a party, with or without caipirinha.

Twister

On a summer morning in the nineties, I brought some tongue twisters to my Masters' class in Oakland. The ten students, sitting around a rectangular oak seminar table, tried their hands, or rather tongues, at reciting some of them; for example, my favorite:

> Betty Botter bought a bit of butter,
> but, she said, this butter's bitter;
> if I put it in my batter,
> it will make my batter bitter,
> so Betty Botter bought a bit of better butter
> and put it in her batter,
> and it made her batter better.

Or, six times fast:

> She stood on the balcony hiccupping
> And amicably welcoming him in.

And so on. These were good challenges, and there was no shame in getting them wrong, since, if most native English speakers didn't have much success with them, who could expect ESL students to nail them right away?

Before handing out the "scripts," I'd show off a bit by speeding through an initial recitation, enjoying the looks of zero comprehension on every face. Again, there was no shame since they were all in it together. Then I'd slow it down to a crawl, and watch it progressively dawn on them that these were not just nonsensical elocution exercises; the words had meaning, and sometimes even told a little story (albeit one without much character development), as in Betty Botter. We went over the definitions of words like "bitter," "batter," "balcony," "hiccup," and "amicable." I also invited them to share tongue twisters from *their* languages (fair is fair). And then to translate them into English, which might yield a few more useful bits of vocabulary.

Of the two Italian women in that class, Serafina and Chiara, only the former was present for our stint of twisting tongues. When I took roll, Serafina, seated just to my left, told me that Chiara, after returning late from a party the previous night, had had considerable trouble getting out of bed that morning but would probably arrive in time to join us for the second half of that two-hour class, after we'd taken our ten-minute break.

Break time arrived, but Chiara still hadn't. I left the room to take my ten minutes, and, when I returned, there, in fact, was Chiara, seated on the other side of her friend. Serafina was, it seemed, going over, in Italian, what Chiara had missed during that first hour. (In the following transliteration the "ch" has the usual English pronunciation, as in the initial sound of "chair," not the "k" sound at the beginning of "Chianti," or, for that matter, "Chiara.")

"*Aka EE chee cheeoo PEE*," she explained.

"Ah," Chiara said, smiling and nodding with comprehension.

I was curious: which part of the lesson was she explaining? Or was she perhaps reciting another Italian tongue twister? Whatever it was, I loved the sound of it and wanted to learn its meaning.

"Serafina, I love your language. For example, what you were just saying to Chiara. It was beautiful, like poetry, like music. Could you repeat it?

"Sure, of course, Phil," she readily agreed, but was laughing at the same time. As was Chiara. She repeated, "*Aka EE chee cheeoo PEE.*"

"One more time, Serafina, so I can try to say it too. I'd like to learn it." Again the Italian women laughed.

This time, Serafina sang it, quasi-operatically: "*Aka EE chee cheeoo PEE. Aka EE chee cheeoo PEE.*" She was no Cecilia Bartoli but was actually a pretty good mezzo-soprano, which only added to the allure of the phrase. Trying to be the model of a good student, I jotted it down in my notebook.

"Okay, I think I've got it. *Aka EE chee cheeoo PEE.* Okay? Is that it? "A*ka EE chee cheeoo PEE?*"

"Yes, Phil. That's it. Exactly. *Perfetto*!"

"Great, so now tell me. What does it mean?"

Now they laughed even harder.

"What's so funny? Does it even *have* a meaning?"

"Well, yes and no," Chiara laughed.

"Yes and no? What do you mean, yes and no? Tell me, tell me. Now I'm even more curious."

"Well," explained Serafina, still chuckling, "I was only telling Chiara how to spell 'hiccup.' *Aka* is 'h.' *Ee* is 'i.' *Chee* is 'c.' *Oo* is 'u.' And *pee* is exactly the same as English: *pee* is 'p.' So, *aka EE chee cheeoo PEE* is h-i-c-c-u-p. Hiccup!" She then punctuated her explanation with a good imitation of the real thing, an Italian hiccup that could only be spelled with those Italian letters.

"*Grazie, Maestra Serafina*!" The three of us had a good laugh, break-time ended, and it was again time for me to teach *my* language, which seemed rather flat compared to Italian, which could transform the simple spelling of a word into an aria. *Che bella lingua!* Learning how to spell hiccup in Italian has been of no practical value in my life, but twenty years later, I still enjoy intoning it, even when I'm not telling this little story, feeling its staccato-legato syllables play with palate, tongue, and lips. You should try it.

Aka EE chee cheeoo PEE.

It's No Joke

Most people are not good joke tellers. Delivery and timing are often as important as the material itself. And when you seek to export a gag across cultural/linguistic borders, the bar is raised significantly higher; very few jokes make that journey with the punch of the punch line intact. It can get lost in mispronunciations, untranslatable idioms, an unfluent limping delivery, culturally different ideas of what's funny, or fundamental differences in the cultures themselves. However, some people are intrinsically funny; they can make us laugh regardless of the meaning of their words, or even when we're clueless about what that meaning might be. In fact, they can make us laugh without opening their mouths; the humor is in their genes, in their bones.

Mr. Chiba was the kind of student no teacher can ever forget. He entered my life and Oakland classroom in the late seventies. A stocky guy in, probably, his mid-fifties, Mr. Chiba gave one the sense that he was a successful businessman. With his gun-metal grey hair sculpted into the same shape every day with some Brylcreem-like fixative, his dress pants and shiny black patent-leather loafers, and his seniority, he was a sharp contrast to the young twenty-somethings in their jeans, tee shirts, and sneakers.

There were other qualities that distinguished him from his classmates: an impish look in his eyes and a jester's wink-wink tone of voice that could make you laugh even when you had no idea what he was talking about; you felt like you had been invited into a conspiracy of mirth where comprehension was not necessarily a prerequisite for membership. Laughing with Mr. Chiba was its own reward.

When my students introduced themselves to their classmates on the first day of class, I would ask them to come up to the front board, one by one, write their names on it, and then tell the class something about their lives. In Mr. Chiba's debut in my class, after he had written the English transliteration of his name on the board, I asked him to add its renditions in the characters of each of the Japanese alphabets, hiragana, katakana, and kanji. No problem. The non-Asian students were, as usual, impressed by the intricacy of those characters, which had the additional effect of enhancing the exotic mystique of their unusual classmate. After he had finished writing the four versions of his name, Mr. Chiba turned around to face the class. I nodded to him and smiled, his cue to start speaking.

"Hello. My name Mr. Chiba," he began, his voice

gravelly from, I assumed, decades of smoking. When a sly grin spread slowly across his face, I knew what was coming: I had heard from several of my colleagues that Mr. Chiba had a stock joke that he loved to tell at the beginning of every four-week session. I was eager to hear it in person for the first time.

"Chiba. You know, sound *exactly* like Chibas Regal."

He then winked mischievously at us all and laughed rather maniacally at his own joke, clearly assuming that everyone had gotten it. It did break me up the first time I heard it: it was mostly his wacky oddball delivery, but it was also how his conspicuous fondness for the referenced whiskey came through, and his complete certainty that "Chibas" and "Chivas" had "exactly" the same pronunciation. (It was not surprising that Mr. Chiba had this pronunciation confusion; distinguishing between "v" and "b" sounds is a common difficulty among Japanese students of English, a problem they, oddly enough, share with Spanish speakers.)

Most, if not all, of the younger students had never heard of Chivas Regal Scotch, but it didn't matter; everyone laughed anyway because it was impossible not to if you were in the room when Mr. Chiba started losing control. Or was he, perhaps, gaining it?

He clearly enjoyed sculpting his persona, month by month, as the "crazy" but benign eccentric in our midst. Here's an example. As I have mentioned, our school had twelve levels, 101 through 112. Mr. Chiba had decided, for reasons he alone knew, that he would take 101 once, 102 twice, 103 thrice, 104 four times, and so on, until he had taken 112 twelve times. If you add all that up on your calculator, you'll come up with a total of seventy-eight sessions, or, in standard time, six-and-a-half years. Although he didn't actually make it that far, he may have been the most unheralded performance artist of the latter twentieth century. His initial entry into one of my classes was in the first of the four months he would spend in Level 104. I had him again for his second month in 105 and for his final session at the school, his fifth month in 105. That's a total of fifteen consecutive sessions, or one-and-a-quarter years. Every session, he told the Chivas Regal joke in exactly the same way, and I found it funny every time, maybe f*unnier* with each repetition, the identical deliveries somehow adding to its surreal punch. I know I would have been disappointed had he skipped it. It was like hearing his theme song: "Hello. My name Mr. Chiba. Chiba. You know, sound *exactly* like Chibas Regal . . ."

Who knows why Mr. Chiba decided to call it quits after completing his fifth and final month of 105? For all we knew, maybe he had never planned to go longer than that and was simply enjoying our growing amazement as month by month slipped by, and there he still was. By then, every teacher in the school had had him in class at least once, and most of us multiple times, and we were all quite fond of him. As were all his classmates. And, clearly, it was mutual. Before he said *sayonara*, he gave each of his teachers an identical-looking present: wrapped in delicate blue rice paper sprinkled with silver stars was a small rectangular box with a good heft to it. When we unwrapped our presents, we saw that we each had the same gift. It was (what else?) a calculator.

Years later, in Berkeley, Abdulkareem, nicknamed Kareem, a soft-spoken Saudi man in his twenties, was in my intermediate writing class. This tall milk-chocolate-skinned bespectacled man seemed shy at first, a bit self-conscious. He didn't say much, and when he did, it was *sotto voce*, with an occasional stutter which didn't seem to daunt him in the least, a mere bump in the road. When this "shy" man spoke, there was often a glint in his eyes and an incipient smile which hinted at something different, something more. Of course, there's *always* something more.

Our class was in a tiny room, a space that had recently been converted from an office to accommodate the school's growing student population. My ten students and I just about fit, I at a small rickety desk in front, and they in a u-shaped formation against the three remaining walls. On the second day of class, after taking roll, I was about to start that day's lesson when Kareem, seated roughly in the center of the back row (which was also the front row), raised his right hand, index finger pointing at the ceiling.

"Yes, Kareem?"

"I have a question, Teacher. Is that okay?"

"Sure. Of course. It's always okay. Go on, Kareem."

His question, about a fine point of grammar, was an interesting one, one that showed that Kareem had a probing intelligence. We took about five minutes to discuss and clarify, and then went on to the lesson of the day.

On the next morning, near the beginning of the class, Kareem held up his right forefinger again, as if that single digit were saying, "This will take just one minute."

"Yes, Kareem?"

"I have a question."

"Uh huh?"

We then spent a few minutes to clear up another troubling point of this troubling language.

By the next day, when Kareem's finger slowly rose again, I think everybody in that little room knew what was coming.

"Yes, Kareem?"

"I have a question."

I laughed, Kareem laughed, and so did all the others. Clearly, a riff was born.

"Of course you do."

"Is it okay?"

"Is that your question?"

He laughed again, asked his question of the day, and we all discussed its answer.

So began a daily ritual. Sometimes with a subtle smile and sometimes with a deadpan delivery that rivaled Jack Benny's, Kareem would raise that finger and repeat his I-have-a-question routine. By the end of the second week, Abdulkareem's shortened form, "Kareem," was supplanted by a second nickname, at least in *my* class: Question Man.

It's funny how comedy routines work. Often, as with Question Man, they don't start out as jokes, but, with just the right delivery, especially with judiciously spaced repetitions, they become sure-fire shticks.

One day near the end of that session, I was in the school's cafeteria at lunchtime, famished as usual. (In fact, typically, the thought of eating became a formidable distraction at least an hour before we could actually do it. Class discussions in the late morning often gravitated toward topics like "What's your favorite food?") The food line was especially long and slow-moving that day. It took about ten minutes before I even arrived at the counter where I could make my selections: then, dish by dish, like a person working a jigsaw puzzle, I filled my tray with salad, soup, spaghetti Bolognese, garlic bread, iced tea, and cookies. By the time I made it to the end of that maddeningly slow line, I was ravenous. Eager to whisk my tray away to an empty classroom before my food got cold, I made a beeline toward the doorway to the nearest staircase. I had just reached it and was about to spring up to the second floor when I heard a familiar voice.

"Phil?"

I turned and there was Kareem with one of his Saudi friends.

"Hi Kareem. What's up?"

Taking his time, he flashed a rascally grin and slowly raised his now-famous index finger, pointing at the cafeteria ceiling: "I have a question."

It was one of those moments when I became disconcertingly aware of the limits of my patience. Yes, he was just being his friendly self, as usual, and his question was probably a good one, as usual, but this was absolutely *not* the time to get into this: he had come up against the raw selfishness of hunger.

"Can't it wait for class, Kareem? I'd like to eat my lunch now. I promise I'll answer your question when we get back to class."

Kareem and his friend started laughing.

"Just kidding, Phil. Enjoy your lunch. I don't really have a question."

"You don't?" I laughed too, as much from relief as amusement. "Oh, Question Man, you got me!"

"I did, didn't I?"

"Oh yeah. You're a bad man!" At the risk of dropping my entire lunch on the floor, I propped up the tray with my left hand and left hip, freeing my right hand to high-five Kareem before making my escape. I could still hear the reverb of his laughter as I fled up the stairs to a questionless classroom.

Luke Pham, a theology student from Vietnam, had, like Mr. Chiba before him and Kareem after, a comedian's spirit. Luke was short and had such a delicately framed body that when I first saw him, in 1998, on the opposite side of the rather large reception room at Holy Names, I thought he was a boy, perhaps eleven or twelve years old. Only upon approaching him and seeing his face did I realize that he was probably in his early thirties. He was extremely friendly, smiled a lot, and was clearly eager to practice speaking English, which he did quite fluently. There was a problem, however: his thick Vietnamese accent often made it almost impossible to understand him. In my initial interview with him, I interrupted him several times to ask him to repeat sentences more slowly, which he was happy to do. He knew he had a problem and was undefensive about it, but, as he excitedly raced through whatever he had to say, he tended to forget an important fact: when he spoke at his normal speed, his listeners often had no idea what he was talking about.

As fate would have it, Luke wound up in my 107 grammar class. On the first day of class, after all the students had introduced themselves, Luke, with a big grin on his small face, raised his hand.

"Yes, Luke?"

"I have very funny joke, Teacher. May I tell to class?"

"Yes, yes, of course, Luke. That's great. I love jokes. Lay it on us."

"Okay. Here we go." He then proceeded to deliver

his monologue at breakneck speed with most of the vowels and consonants so bent out of shape that it was almost entirely incomprehensible. I had no choice but to stop him before he got too far. If *I* was getting *next* to nothing, my other students were getting *less* than nothing.

"Whoa, Luke, please slow down. I'd like to help you with your pronunciation, so we can enjoy your joke better."

"Oh, okay. Sorry teacher. I go too fast. I know. I always go too fast. I make problem. I make more work for teacher."

"That's okay, Luke. That's my job."

"Thank you, teacher."

"Okay, please start again from the beginning. And remember, there's no need to hurry. Take your time."

And so he did. Syllable by syllable, word by word, phrase by phrase, sentence by sentence. After ten or fifteen minutes of dissecting, deciphering, and correcting, we finally arrived at the now essentially punchless punch line. Everyone chuckled politely, and we were free to begin that day's official lesson. I silently vowed to avoid getting snagged by Luke's jokes in future classes. I meant it, but . . .

On the next day, Luke was the last to arrive, and he burst into the room, out of breath and with a huge smile that looked nothing less than beatific.

"I have another joke. It even better than yesterday joke."

I hadn't forgotten my resolution, but I didn't have

the heart to squelch his zeal; it would have felt almost blasphemous. So much for vows.

"Great, Luke. Let's hear it!"

And once again the process took up another quarter of an hour. Despite everyone's fondness for Luke, I could see some of his classmates squirming with impatience; clearly, this could not go on indefinitely. At the same time, I could sense that the students shared my concern about not hurting Luke's feelings. Out of this unspoken empathy grew a collusion that I'm not particularly proud of.

When Luke arrived on the next day, he was laughing at that day's joke even before he started telling it. His narrative was as hard to understand as ever, but I mostly hung back, giving a few token corrections from time to time, and chuckling appreciatively at the points where Luke himself laughed. Just as *I* was taking my cues from Luke, his classmates were mimicking both of us as they joined this expedient and, I hoped, benevolent ruse; in no time, we were caught up in Luke's whitewater surge of mostly unidentifiable words. By the time Luke reached the punch line, he and the rest of us were laughing hysterically, not faking it, he at the punch line that only he was privy to, and we as the willing "victims" of Luke's contagious guffawing—and at the surreal phenomenon of the virtually contentless joke. And yet, somehow, it felt like we and Luke were fully in it together. By allowing the benign madness of raw laughter to possess us, we found ourselves in a rollicking sub-verbal (or maybe meta-verbal) communion with the joke teller. It was not unlike the wacky rapport that the students had had with Mr. Chiba when he told his trademark joke, which was incomprehensible to many of them for different reasons. The whole process took no longer than a couple of minutes, like most uninterrupted jokes.

Like Kareem's questions, Luke's jokes and our mass hysteria became a daily ritual, one that all of us actually looked forward to. Luke never arrived without a new joke to share. Occasionally, some of us could even "get" it, but usually not. We consistently enjoyed the teller, if not the tale. One day, he was quite late, and we wondered if he was absent. I felt a bit like I had lost the key to the ignition of the vehicle that was my class. I couldn't quite get started. When Luke finally arrived, again out of breath but, as usual, with a giant smile, we knew that, after we'd had our daily cathartic outburst, we would be ready to take on the challenges of the future perfect progressive tense.

Before Luke finished his studies at the school, I had a private chat with him about his pronunciation problems. I know I did it out of a nagging certainty that I had failed to help him as much as I should have; to boot, I had a lingering sense of guilt from breaking my own private rule against feigning comprehension. I confessed as much to him, and, of course, model Christian that he was, he forgave me. I mentioned to him that my wife was a speech pathologist who sometimes helped patients with "accent reduction," and that she would be able to take the necessary time to focus on his pronunciation. When I asked him if he'd be interested in working with her, he said that he would; first, however, he had to ask the governing board of the monastery where he lived if they would fund that therapy. They readily agreed. Hey, what's a brother for?

Luke worked with Joan for about six months. She said that he had the thickest accent she had ever worked with. It was slow going. His thicket of mysterious sounds seemed to require a therapeutic machete. Of course, she had a luxury that I hadn't had: there were no other students waiting for the seemingly endless process to end, so she could substitute a scalpel for that machete and meticulously attend to Luke's problems, one by one.

He made some progress with his pronunciation over that half year, but not enough to fully escape from his private woods; he was concerned about that, of course, and at times disheartened, but, I suspect, never so much so that he ever missed a chance to delight in the incomparable release of a good laugh. I would think that that priest-in-training's list of what he was most thankful for probably included, near the top, his ultra-sensitive funny bone. It's not hard to imagine him, from time to time, turning to Joan during a therapy session or to whomever whenever, and, with a boyish smile, inquiring, "Would you like to hear a very funny joke?"

After Luke had left the school, it occurred to me that joke telling might actually be a useful activity in conversation classes. Instead of being something extraneous to the lesson, stealing precious time, delaying the main event, it could be the focus of the lesson itself. I'd sometimes ask the students to return to class on the following day, ready to tell jokes from their countries. I was well aware that, translated from their original languages and exported from their native cultures, these jokes would probably not resemble jokes as we know them, would fall utterly flat. It also occurred to me that, perhaps, I could exploit this probability. There's something intrinsically funny, maybe funnier, about a *failed* joke, if it's handled right; some of Johnny Carson's best moments occurred when a joke from his opening monologue bombed. He would replace his usual Howdy-Doody smile with a deadpan acknowledgment that the worst had just happened. Taking advantage of the fact that he was still breathing, he would then improvise about that dud in a way that got more laughs than the original joke ever could have. The ritual of the bombed joke became one of his trademarks, a much-anticipated leitmotif.

The telling of the first few student jokes confirmed and re-confirmed that, as a rule, jokes just don't travel well. It seemed as if no one could make one work as it was supposed to; there was no embarrassment in that because nearly everyone was in the same boat, so to speak. We shared a growing appreciation of the almost universal unfeasibility of what each attempted, with little hope, to do. Having the content of the joke itself provoke laughter was no longer the only goal of telling it.

I developed a routine which, in its absurdist slapstick way, managed to smuggle in the hilarity that the joke itself could not provoke. Often, I'd have to ask the joke teller if the line that she or he had just delivered was, in fact, the finale. That's because, in most cases, that last sentence bore no resemblance to punch lines as we know them, especially after I had picked its preceding lines dry by correcting their technical errors. Upon being told that, in fact, it *was* the "punch line," I would turn to the "audience," already broadly smiling, and say, "Are you ready?"

Oh yes they were, they would loudly assure me, they were ready indeed.

Like Toscanini with pen-qua-baton, I'd raise both arms in the air and proclaim: "Okay, here we go. One! Two! *Three!*" And, at that point, madly waving my arms, I would lead them in a chorus of maniacal laughter, a voluntary insanity that fed upon itself. The more I roared like a lunatic, the more they did, and vice versa, on and on, all of us berserk, until suddenly I'd wipe the smile off my face and shout, "Stop!" They would try to regain their composure immediately, which was the slapstick goal, but it was like attempting to stop a speeding car on a dime. Then it would be another student's turn to lead us through another home-grown joke before we all engaged in teacher-sanctioned psychosis yet again.

It was rare that a joke succeeded on its own terms, and when it did, it was almost a letdown, since, although soberly considered chuckles of appreciation were satisfying on an intellectual level and gave the students the sense of having made progress in their listening comprehension, they did not provide the catharsis of that unbridled animal roar. Yet, I sometimes had to remind myself, this *was* a classroom, and communication and comprehension of this language called English was still my primary goal. So, I couldn't lose: we laughed when they got it, and we laughed when they didn't.

I don't remember many of the jokes that actually succeeded on their own terms, but I do clearly remember one that did so resoundingly. I've repeated it many times myself since the day that my Italian student Giuseppe told it in our Oakland classroom.

When Giuseppe's turn to tell a joke came around, he was clearly pumped up, determined to bowl us over with what he informed us was a quintessentially Italian gag. In Italy, there is a clear number-one butt of ridicule, the carabinieri, the Italian military police, whose uniformed representatives one can see guarding the public buildings of Rome and other major cities. They are famous for one quality alone: stupidity. It's not fair, of course, but fairness is not the goal. It's akin to Polish jokes in America, Portuguese jokes in Brazil, and Spanish jokes in the rest of Latin America. For these jokes to work, there can be no mitigating factors of intelligence or noble humanity to cloud the monolithic portrait of a moron; political correctness must be assiduously avoided. After Giuseppe explained this sub-genre of modern Italian folklore, he launched into his carabinieri joke.

"There is two carabinieri, Renato and Mario. They are in their police car, and Mario is driving. Renato is sitting in the passenger seat."

As he spoke, Giuseppe arranged four of the seat-desks to resemble a small car, two seats in front, two in back. Then, with the commitment, delight, and madness of a Roberto Benigni, he proceeded to play both parts.

Sitting first in the "driver's seat," as Mario, he turned to the seat beside him and said, "Excoose-a me Renato, but can you do for me a favor?"

Hopping into the "passenger seat," he had Renato respond agreeably, "Sure, Mario. What I can do for you?"

Again, more and more Benigni-like, he jumped back into the driver's seat and explained, "Renato, I tink dat my righta turn-a signal in back no worka right. Is maybe a problem. Maybe is no okay."

"Uh-huh," answered Renato after a super-quick seat transfer. (In fact, every time the dialogue shuttled back and forth between these two Italian cops, Giuseppe made sure that he was in the appropriate seat as he delivered each line, a maniacal performance that had everyone riveted to each word and move.)

Giuseppe-qua-Mario continued his explanation:

"Okay, so, Renato, dis is what I wanta for you to do. Please-a, when I park-a da car, please-a get out and go to da back. Den, I turn onna signal, you look at light, and you tell me if is okay or is not okay. Okay?"

"Okay."

Then Mario, after driving down one of the streets of Rome while singing a few bars of "*O Sole Mio*," went through the motions of pulling the car over to a curb.

"Okay, Renato, please go to da back and wait-a for me to turn onna da signal."

"Okay."

Then, Giuseppe-qua-Renato mimed opening the invisible door, exiting, closing the door, and going to stand behind the car.

"Okay, Mario, I'm ready."

This next part entailed even wilder running back and forth, between the driver's seat and the right rear tail light, as the dialogue progressed.

"Okay, I'm-a gonna turn it on, okay?"

"Okay."

"Here goes, okay?"

"Okay, turn it on. I'm-a gonna tell you if is okay or no okay."

"Okay."

"Okay!"

Then Mario mimed flicking the directional lever up to activate the right turn signal. He then made appropriately timed clicking sounds with his tongue to replicate the click that accompanies each flash of light. Click . . . click . . . click . . . click . . .

"Well, Renato, is okay or no okay?"

"Is okay, Mario. Oh, wait, is *no* okay. Oh, just a minute . . . *is* okay. Actually, *no* okay. Okay. No okay. Okay. No okay. Okay. No okay . . ."

You get the idea.

As Giuseppe continued his rant as the overwhelmed and befuddled Renato, I think everyone in the room could *see* that turn signal flashing on and off: okay . . . no okay . . . okay . . . no okay . . . Giuseppe had us all in the palm of his hyper-gesticulating hand. Benigni could not have done it better. We'd been expertly tickled and had, once again, become a community of laughers.

That was more than okay.

Teacher First

After telling our little conversation class about various Argentinean traditions, Sonia smiled sweetly (or was it slyly?) and said that she had a special surprise for us. The nine or ten of us were sitting around the oblong seminar table in the same room at Holy Names where Dorje had mimed "watching the fish." If you stood by that room's windows and looked off to your right, following the bay and the western hills as they stretched north, you could see the Bay Bridge cutting across the water from Oakland to San Francisco; further north and further west, if the day was clear, you could also see about half of the Golden Gate Bridge, that elegant orange "gateway" to the Pacific and unseen lands, an excellent reminder of our little global community's global context. It was a good angle to have when encountering unfamiliar customs. As it turned out, it was a good angle to have on that day.

"Okay, Sonia. Let's have it. Surprise us."

She then reached into her book bag and extracted a clear round plastic container of what looked like small chocolate-covered candies, quite similar in appearance to Raisinets, one of my favorite movie-theater noshes during my Brooklyn youth.

"Ah, chocolate candy. Mmm."

"Yes, Teacher, this is very popular, very special candy from my country." She then grandly held the little box above her head and extended her gracious invitation. "There is sufficient candies for all of you."

Still in thrall to the Raisinets association, I asked, "Is there a raisin inside, under the chocolate?"

"What is raisin, teacher?"

"You know grape?"

"Si. Yes. Is fruit. Small fruit."

"That's right. And raisins are dried grapes."

"Ah, yes, I see. I know raisins. Delicious!"

"Yes, they are. And are there raisins inside your special snack? Inside this chocolate candy?"

"No," she laughed, "not raisins."

"Nuts?"

She laughed harder. "No, no. Not nuts neither."

"Either."

"Either?"

"It's 'Not nuts either,' not 'Not nuts neither.'"

"Oh, my terrible grammar. Okay. It's not nuts either."

"Okay. Is it just chocolate?'

"No, no, Teacher. I told you it's surprise. Raisins, nuts, chocolate no are surprises, right? This is *real* surprise. A good one."

"I'm almost ready to give up. Anybody? Anybody else want to guess what's under that chocolate?"

The other students joined the guessing game and came up with mints, caramels, cherries, booze, coffee, various creams, as well as several less likely centers, none of them particularly surprising, all of them wrong. It seemed that we had come to the limits of Forrest Gump's proverbial box of chocolates. Finally, we all conceded defeat and looked to Sonia to finally satisfy our curiosity. And, of course, to surprise us.

"Okay, Sonia, we give up. What *is* this special Argentinean treat? What's inside the chocolate?"

"It's what we call in Spanish '*hormiga*.'"

"Sounds very exotic. I don't know if we have '*hormiga*' in this country. Is it only in South America?"

"Oh no. You have many here too. I seen them here. They look same as Argentine ones."

"Oh, I see. But I don't know this Spanish word. Do you know the English word for '*hormiga*'?"

"Yes, I do. I look it up in my *diccionario*. I mean my dictionary. English word is very different. '*Hormiga*' in English is 'ant.'"

"Ant?"

"Yes, you know. Small black insect. Well, usually black, the ones we eat. You know?"

"Yes, of course. I know ants. But I have never eaten any."

"Great! This will be first time. Special experience, yes Teacher? Maybe first time for everyone here, no?"

"Yes, Sonia, I think so."

After I'd written "ant" on the board, the other students dove into their bilingual dictionaries and, with an array of reactions ranging from fascination to disgust and horror, everybody affirmed, not surprisingly, that ants had never been a part of their diets, even on special occasions. We were all about to lose our ant-eating virginity together. Sonia carefully tore off the clear outer seal on that round box and opened the lid. Those smooth little brown morsels were shiny under the ceiling's fluorescent tubes. Observing one of the unwritten rules of classroom etiquette, Sonia held the open box out to me and said with the utmost decorum,

"Teacher first."

Trying to look unfazed, I smiled and quickly scanned the candies in search of the smallest one. Apparently there *was* no smallest one. They all seemed uniformly huge. I thanked her and lifted one out. Just one. Holding it aloft, I examined it for a possible protruding leg or proboscis. Nothing. It continued to look like the most innocent of Raisinets. Now everyone's eyes were glued to me, waiting for me to finally pop that little corpse into my mouth. Which, of course, I did.

So far so good. The chocolate coating did, in fact, taste and feel exactly like the outside of a Raisinet, and I sucked it contentedly for a few ordinary seconds before chomping down for the moment of truth. There was a crisp cracking, like the breaking of tiny bones (do ants have bones?), and then an explosion of saltiness, a stark counterpoint to the sweet chocolate. Was the saltiness, I wondered, from salt that the candy maker had added to the "filling," or were ants naturally salty, or was it actually ant blood that provided that zing? I have never found out. Chewing my mouthful as thoroughly as I could—while trying to appear nonchalant—I was finally able to cajole myself into swallowing it. I found myself craving, somewhat desperately, a glass of cold water. Or maybe a quart.

Sonia looked hopeful, proud, and eager to hear my assessment. "Do you like it, Teacher?"

In my relief and elation that I had actually accomplished the feat, I was probably overly effusive: "Wow! I've never eaten anything like that in my life! Sweet and salty! Soft and crunchy! Amazing! Thank you, Sonia. It's very generous of you to share these special treats with everybody. You are right. This is very special indeed. Wow!" I then handed the box to the student seated on my left, a Japanese woman who looked a little freaked out by what she now held in her hand; she seemed to be turning a few interesting shades of green. Before she could try one, however, Sonia popped in again and, temporarily, saved her:

"Oh Teacher, I'm so glad you like our *hormigas*, our chocolate ants. Since you loved it so much, you *must* have another one."

"Oh, thank you, Sonia, but I want there to be enough for everyone."

"Oh, don't worry, there is more than enough. Enjoy another one. Enjoy, enjoy. I insist!"

Obviously, I wasn't going to squirm out of this so easily. The other students were more than happy to delay their entry into the insect-eating world and laughingly (sadistically?) insisted that I have that second one before they tried their first, which I did.

And a third, which I also did. And a fourth, which I was able to refuse without looking rude or dishonest (I hoped), and the box finally made its circuit around that table, stopping at each tremulous student before winding up back with Sonia, who popped a few into her mouth with gusto. She offered to send the box on another lap around the table, but we all said no thank you: we wouldn't dream of wiping out her only supply of that rare delicacy.

That was years ago, and public awareness of insect cuisine, and its ecological benefits, has slightly changed (*very* slightly). I recently discovered that there's a place in San Francisco, Don Bugito, a "pre-Hispanic snackeria," that specializes in many gourmet variations on this theme. Of course, in Argentina, Mexico, and many other Latin American places, it never *was* considered a particularly odd choice for a bite.

Once in a while, when I taste a sweet/salty snack, like yogurt-covered pretzels, I think of Sonia and her ants. I'd probably think of them too if I re-enjoyed some Raisinets—if I could find them. Of course, the associative link doesn't have to be so overtly Proustian: just seeing a line of those tiny black invaders marching silently at a picnic, or, on a morning after, carrying off the crumbs of the previous night's dinner, can bring me back to that Oakland classroom . . . and Sonia's sweet (sly?) smile.

Sneak Previews

My memory of teaching in the seventies has a distinctly Iranian flavor, partly because, for a while, our student body in Oakland had more people from that country than from anywhere else. So many relationships: fulfilling and frustrating, endearing and maddening, simple and complicated, and, by the end of 1978, historically portentous. I've chosen just a few of them to write about in this chapter, because of their personal impact, historical significance, or a hybrid of both.

From time to time, I still see one of my Iranian students from those days, a gentleman named Moe, who studied hard, sometimes helped out in the office, did well in his classes, and stuck around. After he left our school, he worked for others for a couple of years before deciding to try to make it on his own by selling flowers on the street in the famous Telegraph Avenue area of Berkeley. After successfully developing that little enterprise, he expanded into his own storefront, where he still conducts a thriving business today. Whenever I drop into his shop, Moe, surrounded by the colors and shapes of a thousand flowers, greets me with a soulful warmth that brings back that long-gone

Iranian period, and some of the people who were part of it. It all ended so abruptly.

By no means do I intend the men in the following anecdotes to somehow collectively symbolize a general "Iranian personality"; if I've learned anything about people in my long stint of teaching English to them, it's that it's always both inaccurate and unfair to construct a single national character for *any* culture. It's not only unfair to them: we cheat ourselves as well, ignoring the complex fascination of each tree by focusing on an imaginary forest.

There were some very good times with my Iranian students, but there were a few that were almost pure frustration. In that category, one stands out: Harry.

Harry lived as if everything in life were subject to negotiation. When he first arrived at the school during the mid-seventies, looking studious in his horn-rimmed glasses and dark brown corduroy sport jacket, he made sure to tell us all, emphatically, that he belonged in an advanced level. Because of his fluency and certainty, we pretty much believed him . . . until we saw the results of his placement test and the state of his written English. He placed in level 105, squarely intermediate. After his first hour in that class, he told his teacher that it was too easy for him, and gave her a long list of reasons why he really belonged in 106. Or 107. Or 108. She didn't budge. Harry barely made it through that level, living right on the borderline of each exam's passing grade; sometimes, when he was just below the border, he would cajole his teacher into fattening that line until it was wide enough to include his grade. The campaign continued until the end of the session, which was when Harry leaned just hard enough on his teacher to receive a "mercy pass." He basically repeated the same pattern with his next teacher, in 106.

Then, in the following session, Harry entered my 107 class. Two weeks later, he failed my midterm exam and vigorously protested that the test was "unfair," which took supreme *chutzpah*, since all of the other students had passed it handily. I told him that he shouldn't fret, since he could still pass my class if he performed well in class and passed the *final* exam. It would please me greatly to pass him, I added; that was true, not only because I generally prefer passing students to flunking them, but, also, because, selfishly, passing him would save me from his inevitable end-of-session barrage. He reluctantly backed off.

The day for the final arrived, and I kicked back with a novel while my students went through the stressful business of dealing with the test. Every few minutes, I'd look up from my book and do a cursory monitoring of the group. On one of these checks, as my eyes did their little sweep of the room, I saw Harry, plain as day, bending toward the desk of his neighbor, a Venezuelan woman named Elena. He was methodically copying her answers; there could be no doubt about it. It was done so openly that it was as if he had forgotten that his teacher was still in the room. I didn't want to embarrass him, and I also wanted to give him a chance to pass the test honestly, so I simply cleared my throat in a ridiculously loud and histrionic way.

"Ahem! Ahem!"

Harry, along with several other students, looked up at me. I glared directly at Harry in a way that I hoped sent him the message that I had caught him stealing Elena's answers. I continued "speaking" to him with my eyes: *You're busted, Harry. Your only hope for saving your neck is to finish this test on your own. You know that I saw you copying from Elena. I'll overlook it if you stop doing it. Don't be a schmuck, Harry. Stop! Right! Now!* His face gave no indication that my message had been received, and my eyes had run out of vocabulary.

A few minutes later, he resumed his project of brazenly stealing Elena's answers. Again, I did my throat-clearing routine, and again Harry, as well as a few other students, looked over at me. My eyes repeated their warning, and, this time, Harry looked back at me with some apprehension, but he still—incredibly—went on with his copying. When time was up and the students turned in their papers, I asked Harry to stay a bit later. He looked as if he knew why but didn't say a word. The other students left. Alone now with Harry, we both remained silent for several seconds, a "silence" which hummed with the electricity of all that remained unspoken between us—or perhaps that was just the sound of the fluorescent lights. Feeling a little like a traffic cop, I spoke first:

"Harry, do you know why I want to speak to you?"

"No, Teacher, I don't."

"It's because you were copying answers from Elena."

"But, no, Teacher, I was not copying."

"Harry, I saw you. You *know* I saw you."

"No, Teacher, it is not possible. I didn't copy. I didn't cheat. I am not cheater. It is not possible for you to see me copy because I did *not* copy. And why would I copy from Elena? I am better student."

"Harry, I *saw* you. I can't really pass you on this test because what you've done on it you haven't done alone."

"Please, Teacher. Please check test, and then we talk more, okay?"

Having to get to my next class, I reluctantly agreed to hold off on my final decision. Feeling pressured and a bit conned, I said, "Okay, Harry. We'll talk about it tomorrow."

"Thank you, Teacher." Stone-faced, I nodded. He half-bowed and walked backwards out of the room, looking into my eyes with what felt like both an imploration and a threat.

That night, after dinner, I took the folder with the exams out of my briefcase and, one by one, went through the routine of correction and grading. When I came to Harry's test, I hesitated, as a soldier might as he stood at the edge of a known mine field. Whether his answers were mostly right or mostly wrong, the odds of crossing that field without getting blown up seemed small. There were so many other ways of spending an evening; I think I considered most of them.

But I couldn't put it off forever, so I forced myself to begin. Question by question, I proceeded through Harry's paper; pretty quickly, it became clear that, despite his attempts to reproduce Elena's (passing) paper, he was not even adept at copying. His test was an unambiguous failure and was not even in the same neighborhood as the passing grade. In a way, I was relieved; here was an objective basis for Harry repeating the level. Never enjoying the role of disciplinarian, I hadn't looked forward to flunking him on purely punitive grounds. Any reasonable person would acknowledge the rightness, the logic, of a student with such a low grade taking that level one more time. Of course, Harry was not quite reasonable.

After a night in which I had lost sleep contemplating the coming confrontation, the sun rose as usual, as if there were nothing foreboding about this morning. After tooling through the streets of Berkeley, I drove leisurely up the Warren Freeway, through the rolling green of the Oakland Hills, music blaring, windows rolled down to fill the car with cool morning air, toward Holy Names College, my classroom, and Harry. I was in no hurry to get there.

I handed out "Final Reports," our version of report

cards, and then went over the test with my students, fielding questions about its contents. I could see that Harry was, not surprisingly, upset, but he was obviously waiting for the optimal moment to launch his missiles at me. That moment came after the other students had left. The ongoing melodrama of Harry's campaign was about to revisit me. I had braced for it, but, as I would soon discover, not sufficiently.

Harry rose from his seat and approached my desk.

"Teacher. Please."

"Yes?"

"Please."

"Please what?"

"Please."

Of course, I was, to a large extent, playing dumb. There could only be one thing that Harry was pleading for in his nonspecific way, but I wanted him to come right out and say it.

"Harry, please tell me what you want me to do for you."

"Teacher, you know."

"Yes, I think I do. But tell me anyway, so I can be sure."

"Please. Please, Teacher. You must pass me. You must!"

"I can't do that, Harry, and you know why."

Harry's face had turned a dangerous-looking shade of red.

"Why? I *don't* know why. Why?"

Okay, I could now see that there would be no shortcuts that morning. We would not be skipping any steps on the way to who-knew-where.

"Well, there are two good reasons. First, I clearly saw you copying answers from Elena during the final exam." At that point, Harry took a deep breath and, I'm sure, was about to repeat his emphatic denial, but I again turned into a traffic cop and held up my right hand in the international street signal for "Stop." Amazingly, it worked, so I was able to continue: "And, second, Harry, even though you copied from Elena, your grade was *still* too low anyway. *Way* too low. You simply haven't mastered the work in this level, Harry. If you study well next session, I'm sure you can pass. I'm sure you can pass without copying." I wasn't *really* sure but was trying, and failing, to put a positive spin on a conversation I didn't want to be having. I was in no mood for preaching, mine or anyone else's. *Feh*. Was there any way to stop hearing my own voice?

"I am honest man, Teacher. And good student. I don't know why my grade is not better. But please. Please pass me to next level. It is very important to me."

"I'm sorry, Harry, but I can't do that. I'm afraid that's final."

"But it can not be. You don't understand. You don't understand how so important is this for me."

"I know it's important, Harry. And I don't enjoy making you unhappy, but I feel this is the right thing to do."

Feh.

"You don't understand that if you fail me in your class, you are destroying my life!"

I had a sudden flashback of my Brazilian student, Thais, pointing that knife at me in the restaurant, accusing me of essentially the same crime.

"No, Harry, I don't think so."

"You don't know! If I don't pass your class, my family will insist that I immediately go back Iran. They will punish me in very bad ways. It is very dangerous. Maybe even it can kill me. You can save me from this. Only you!"

Only me? Who *needed* this?

"Please, Harry. This is way too dramatic."

"Too what?"

"It's too emotional. I'm just doing what I think is best for your English, best for your life."

"Then pass me. That is what is best for my life. I know what is best for me. I know what is best for my life."

I got up from my seat and moved to the front of my desk. I put my right hand on Harry's left shoulder and said, "I'm truly sorry, Harry, but this is my decision." That's when things got crazy.

Harry wailed desolately and dropped down to his knees.

"Harry, get up! What are you doing?"

"I'm begging you. That's what I'm doing. I'm begging you."

"Harry, you must get up this instant!"

"You don't understand, Phil. You really don't understand!"

Harry then grabbed my pants legs, just above the knees. He couldn't have known that, along with the thin denim of my jeans, he had taken hold of many of the hairs on both my thighs and was painfully tugging at them, pulling at them with such force that it felt as if he were going to yank them out by their roots; it was excruciating. Anyone witnessing this bizarre scene would have seen a classic tableau of submission and supplication, but they would have gotten the roles wrong. They would not realize that *I* was the one feeling subjugated, oppressed, beaten up. *I* was the one who needed mercy.

"Harry! Let! Go! You're pulling my leg hairs! That hurts! Let go!"

"Please, please, please, Teacher. Have mercy!" He maintained his iron grasp.

"Ow! Harry, *you* have mercy. Let go of my pants! You're hurting me!"

"Please!"

The pain was intense, and I was now beside myself. We had moved beyond teacher and student roles and had become, in a primal way, two men in weird intense combat. I completely forgot my principles of pacifism, my beloved self-image as the endlessly patient instructor, looked down into his eyes, and screamed, "Harry, if you don't let go of my pants right now, I am going to kick you to the other side of this room! I mean it!"

He got the message and, miraculously, released me from his double grip.

"Now, please, Harry, get up." He did, slowly, apparently accepting his fate, finally acknowledging that this negotiation was over; he had done what he could. Somehow regaining a semblance of composure, I had one more thing to say to him:

"Harry, let me just give you a bit of advice. I think you're a smart enough guy to pass this level. Next session, when you take 107 with another teacher (I hoped), you should put your time and energy into studying the material instead of trying so hard to persuade your teacher to have mercy on you. Try to create a situation in which you won't *need* mercy. And won't need to peek at another student's test. Study hard and you will be okay. Do you understand me? Is my meaning clear?" (*Feh.*)

"Yes, Teacher, it's clear, but it doesn't matter. Because I won't be taking 107 again when my family finds out about this."

"I hope you're wrong about that."

"I am not wrong. I know. There is no hope for me. I am finished here."

"Good luck, Harry."

He nodded and walked out. I sat back down, the roots of my leg hairs still smarting, and wondered if, against all my suspicions and expectations, his story of imminent banishment, and worse, could actually be true.

That question was answered on the first day of the following session when I peered into the classroom of one of my colleagues, and there was Harry, sitting at attention, far from home, ready to start his new class, and probably his new campaign. He saw me seeing him there. I waved hello to him from the safe distance of the hall, and he, looking a tad sheepish, smiled (contritely?) and waved back.

Ramin, another of my Iranian students during that period, mostly kept to himself, only speaking when spoken to, a quality which didn't add much to the conversation-based class that he was in. He wore the same olive green military field jacket every day, regardless of the weather. His five o'clock shadow never seemed to darken or lighten. I wondered if he worked at achieving that uniformity of shade. Was this a studied approach to sporting an unstudied look? Revolutionary chic?

I don't recall ever seeing him smile. He didn't seem to have any close friends at the school, and kept his distance and his silence, even with other Iranians. Most Iranians loved a lively conversation and a good laugh, and were almost always eager to give you their opinions on everything from politics to food, but I hadn't ever heard Ramin voluntarily string more than two sentences together, in English or Farsi. Until one day in October 1978, in that class . . .

The focus of the day was: "Speak about a person from your country whom you admire." Ramin was one of the last to address the class. He walked with uncharacteristic briskness to the front of the room. Observing him from my temporary seat at the back, I noticed that he had a look of passionate engagement on his face, almost a smile, not his usual frown. His voice, likewise, was fervent.

"Today I will tell you about a great Iranian man. He is greatest man in Iran, but he is not *in* Iran. He is in village near Paris. In France. He cannot be in my country right now because is not safe for him. But he *will* return. And he will be Great Leader of magnificent revolution, revolution that will bring God back to Iranian people. And it will bring Iranian people back to God!" His voice had grown gradually louder as he went on, as if a volume knob were being slowly turned.

I jumped in where I could: "Ramin, you have not told us the name of this man."

"I will, Teacher, but first I tell you more about why is he great."

"Okay. Sorry to interrupt. Please go on."

"Well, this great man is surrounded by other Iranian patriots in France. And they are getting ready for day when they will be victorious over Shah who tears his people from God and steals their freedom. The Shah is enemy of his own people, so he is also enemy of this great man in France. My great leader name is Khomeini, the Grand Ayatollah Ruhollah Khomeini." He wrote all four words on the blackboard in dense white chalk strokes. This was the first time I had ever heard or read that name. I was surprised to hear Ramin speak so boldly, so fearlessly, against the Shah. In fact, it was the first time I had heard any Iranian say anything negative about that monarch.

I couldn't help but think about a brief but chilling demonstration of an opposite mentality in another of my conversation classes a year or two earlier. The question of the day was, "What is your opinion of your country's government?" The students in that group gave a variety of assessments, both positive and not, and then one of the Iranian students in the class reached into his pocket and withdrew an old well-worn brown leather wallet. From the wallet he extracted a small slightly wrinkled color photo of Shah Mohammad Reza Pahlavi and held it up as if in front of an invisible camera.

"This is my Shah," he proclaimed. "I love my Shah."

He then moved among us in order to give us a better look at his king. It felt embarrassingly staged, awkward, like watching an amateur theatrical production in which the acting is unconvincing and self-conscious. This, it's important to point out, was during a period in which it was suspected that the SAVAK, the Shah's infamous secret police, were allegedly everywhere, watching and listening. Did my student suspect that one of his Iranian classmates was a member of that group which could send him to an Iranian prison for even the slightest of suspicions about his loyalty to the regime? Was this groundless paranoia, or was the Iranian political drama, in fact, being played out in far-reaching places like this classroom in Oakland? The two interpretations seemed equally feasible. And equally farfetched. We all nodded politely, and I sensed my other students' uneasiness with the stilted patriotic proclamation we'd all just witnessed.

And now, a couple of years later, here was Ramin openly slamming the Shah in front of the whole world, so to speak, and in the presence of several other Iranians. Where was the caution, the crippling fear? It was as if the Shah had already been deposed, as if danger did not lie in being *against* him, but in being *for* him.

In early January 1979, about three weeks into a session, two of my Iranian students, Kourosh and Naveed, brothers in their early twenties, came up to me during a break.

"Phil," Kourosh, the older brother, began, "You are Jewish, aren't you?" Ah, that big nose of mine, I thought. There's no hiding it. Subtle it's not.

Cautiously, remembering the skirmish with my Saudi student Yaqub, I said that, yes, I was.

"We thought so. Naveed and I want to tell you something. But it's a secret. Do you promise you will not tell nobody?" This was clearly not the time for a mini-lecture on double negatives.

"Yes. Sure, I promise. You can trust me."

Naveed then said, "Kourosh and I are Jewish too."

"Good," I said, simultaneously patting Naveed's left shoulder with my right hand and Kourosh's right shoulder with my left, a gesture which I hoped was received as an acknowledgment of kinship.

Naveed's dense black eyebrows rose. "Well, maybe not so good. In Iran."

"Go on."

Kourush then explained that although the Shah still seemed to be in control, his power was virtually gone. They then echoed the prediction that I had already heard from Ramin a few months earlier: a man named Ayatollah Khomeini, in exile near Paris, would lead a successful revolution and would supplant the Shah as the leader of Iran. This was not speculation, they assured me. All the pieces were already in place. However, unlike Ramin, they did not view this as a good thing.

"What does this have to do with your being Jewish, Kourush?"

"Well, Khomeini said many times that he hates Israel. My family is sure that life will be very difficult for the Jews, in fact dangerous, when Khomeini takes over government. There are many things everybody can criticize about Shah. He has been guilty for many very bad actions. But, for some reason that we do not understand, he has protected the Jewish people against anti-semitism of religious fanatics, protected them against dangerous fanatics like Khomeini."

"So what will you do?" I asked, already anticipating their answer.

Naveed continued, "We are not going back. We are happy to study English here, but is not main reason that we come. Our parents send us here to rescue us from the trouble that will be coming. It will be new time in history of Iran, bad time for Jewish people."

"Will your parents join you?"

"If God wills it. Somehow. Some day."

I shook hands with them and expressed my wishes for a safe reunion with their family. Again, I assured them that they could trust me to keep their secret ("Kourush" and "Naveed" are not their real names). We then exchanged firm handshakes before parting.

It's odd: surely one of the components of my self-image is being Jewish, but it doesn't usually predominate; however, in some situations, like relating to my Saudi student Yaqub, or to Kourush and Naveed, my Jewishness expands and seems to become my prime characteristic, covering everything else with the history, the plight, of the Jews. Growing up in Brooklyn, surrounded by Goldbergs, Bernsteins, and Cohens, it had never made sense to my young mind when people referred to Jews as a "minority group." It wasn't until I moved to Madison, Wisconsin to attend graduate school at its university that I started to see the bigger picture. As I walked down State Street one afternoon, a guy I could hardly get a look at screamed at me through the window of a passing car, "Jew bastard!" That gave me an odd sense of satisfaction, of resolution: I had officially attained minority-group membership. I felt as if I had become my nose.

The brothers left the school a week later, and I never heard from them again. A week or two after that, on January 16, the front pages of newspapers around the world reported that Shah Mohammad Reza Pahlavi, with his wife, had fled Iran for Egypt after the Iranian military forces and, it seemed, most of the people, had turned against him. His sons escaped to the United States. On February 1, after fifteen years of exile, Khomeini returned, triumphantly, to Iran. America was declared to be "Satan," which effectively ended the flow of Iranian students to this country and, of course, to our schools. Since the revolution, we've had only a handful of Iranians study at our school; they have arrived one at a time, quietly, sometimes via India or Mexico, but never directly and openly from their own land.

Whenever I need to buy flowers for a birthday or anniversary, I go to Moe's store. You can believe me or not, but I don't return again and again simply to get the steep discount he insists on giving his old teacher.

We always reminisce about the old days and gossip

about some of the other teachers. He is sure to introduce me to any other customers who happen to be in the store and inform them, “This man was my English teacher when I first came here.” Occasionally, he would turn to me and affirm, loudly enough for everyone to hear, “You were my favorite teacher. You always showed respect.” (I’m not sure that Harry would agree.) It’s an assessment that means at least as much to me as hearing that I taught the language well. When a current student compliments a teacher in a similar way, there’s always room for silent, not-so-respectful, doubt: “Is he saying that to butter me up? To crank up his grade?” When a former student says it decades later, that sneaking suspicion is blessedly absent.

Before I leave the shop with my flowers, we do a kind of reverse negotiation about the price: if he lets me pay at all, he talks *me* down. I usually feel just a little guilty not paying the current market price at Moe’s (but not so guilty that I insist on paying it). Clearly, Moe enjoys our “transaction” at least as much as I do. Respect, simple but sometimes elusive, goes both ways. I never walk away from his store without remembering what the most valuable currency is in this business of being human. Not money. Not even English.

Love's Labors

Kyoko was a good, responsible student in my 106 grammar class in Oakland, but she had a curious quirk: she was absent every Friday. When she'd return to class on the following Monday, she seemed exhausted, distracted, moody. Well, I reasoned, everyone has a private life, endless personal considerations outside the classroom. Learning English certainly didn't exist in a vacuum. It was none of my business. She basically kept up with the course work, so, academically, I was not particularly concerned.

On Monday morning of the fourth and final week of that session, I was in the mood to start things off with a conversation, so I trotted out my old war horse, that time-tested topic: "What did you do on your weekend?" When we got around to the droopy-eyed Kyoko, her answer surprised everyone except Midori, her closest friend.

"I went Japan."

"You went to Japan?" I responded, not sure if I'd heard her correctly.

"Yes, Phil-san."

"For the weekend?"

"Yes. Weekend. Friday, Saturday, Sunday. Weekend. Yes, Phil-san. Weekend."

"That's amazing, Kyoko. That's a lot of flying to do in one weekend."

"Yes, it is. Too much flying. Too much airplane."

"Was there an emergency this weekend?"

"No. No emergency. I go Japan *every* weekend."

"Every weekend? You fly to Japan every weekend?" I definitely needed a little extra time to process this data.

"Yes, every weekend. That right, Phil-San." Kyoko, shrugging her thin shoulders, didn't seem to find this pattern quite so unusual.

"Ah, so now I see why you're absent every Friday and why you're so tired every Monday. But, if I may ask, if it's not too personal, not too private, why do you take this big trip every weekend? Is there a problem in your family?"

"No. My family don't know about it."

"Hmm. This is getting even more interesting. Do you feel okay about telling *us* about it?"

"Yes. I do. Actually, yes. I feel okay to tell you. I want to."

"Okay. Thank you, Kyoko."

She really had me now. Along with everyone else.

"Well, actually, is very simple. I visit my boyfriend. Every weekend I visit him because I miss him so much. He miss me too. We meet in hotel in Tokyo. Same room every time. It's secret. Big big secret. My parents doesn't like him. Maybe they hate him." Kyoko paused at that point, as if wondering if "hate" was too strong, and then concluding that it wasn't. After a decisive nod, she continued, "Yes, *hate* him. Maybe they go crazy if they know about my visit him. We are like Juliet and Romeo. They have similar problem, yes?"

"Yes, they did." I avoided the details of how all that Montague-and-Capulet business ended. It was common enough knowledge internationally, so why dwell on it?

"He cannot come here because of job. So I must go to there."

"But you are only here for one month. That's not so long to wait to see him again, is it?"

"Is very long to wait. We cannot. We crazy, *crazy* about each others. Even one week too hard. Impossible. That hotel room is so special place for us. I love all about it. Blue walls. Giant picture of Mount Fuji on one wall. Hokusai wave of ocean on other wall. Tree outside window have little green leaves. I watch them moving in breeze for long time. Many time. I look up English word for that tree. I think it maybe 'maple.' Maple tree. I not sure, but tree is most beautiful tree in world maybe. The bed . . ." Kyoko's face reddened a bit as she arrived at this most significant piece of furniture. "Very comfortable."

It was clear that, when judged beside Shakespeare's young lovers, Kyoko and her paramour lacked nothing in ardor or, apparently, budget. She finished the session and returned to Japan, to a future I will probably never know about. I hoped that, once home, the reasons for her Juliet-identification would evaporate, and that the fate of her great romance would be as remote from that of those "star-cross'd lovers" as Tokyo is from Verona.

It was not unusual for infatuations and more to thrive in the naturally exotic soil of our multicultural groups. I've seen it happen right in class many times, the stirring of fresh hot feelings competing unfairly with my lesson for the attentions of the newly smitten. Such was the case, in an intermediate grammar class, one autumn morning in early-eighties Oakland, when Carlo Spadaccini first laid eyes on Hiromi Kobayashi . . . laid eyes on her and seemingly never laid off.

Hiromi was indeed striking: when she first entered the room, a little late, I don't think there was a single pair of eyes that didn't glom onto her and follow her all the way to her seat. This woman, in her mid-twenties, had hair like polished ebony, high-arching cheekbones, full red lips, and eyes that gave off a heady mix of innocence and sensuality; her tight red tee shirt and blue denim mini-skirt did nothing to make her softly sculpted body less conspicuous. Carlo looked like a cartoon depiction of the conquered male: mouth agape, tongue tip just visible as it rested on his bottom lip, eyes widened to a degree that seemed anatomically impossible, about double their previous size.

It took Hiromi about five minutes to notice Carlo staring at her. (I should mention that he was as handsome as she was pretty. There was a classic southern Italian ruggedness about him: abundant black curly hair, large brown eyes that looked perpetually surprised and delighted by what they saw, a large friendly face, and a stocky muscular body that was just about a couple of inches taller than Hiromi's.) At first, she turned away from him and returned her gaze to me and the blackboard at the front of the room as I continued to present the grammar point of the day. But, seconds later, she turned her head back to her left and met Carlo's eyes; this time she gave him a smile which was like a billboard with one large word stamped across it: WELCOME. I don't think either of them heard another word I said that day.

From that day on, Carlo and Hiromi were seen everywhere together. It was obvious to everyone that this was no casual attraction, no weekend fling; as the weeks passed, things only got more intense for them. What on earth were they to do with the inescapable fact that there was a time limit on their romance? If events followed their usual course, Carlo would be returning to Rome and Hiromi to Tokyo, the natural end to so many international liaisons in ESL classes. But Carlo was determined to break with this sad tradition.

He proclaimed to Hiromi that she was the one true love of his life and that he would rather die than say goodbye to her. She felt exactly the same way. When

Carlo told me about his proclamation to Hiromi, I imagined a scene that was grandly, wildly, operatic, an Italian aria for the ages by that world-class tenor, The Great Spadaccini.

At the end of our session, after they had completed the secondary business of taking English classes, Carlo announced to Hiromi that he would not be returning to Rome empty-handed. He implored her to join him and meet his family. No begging or persuasive arguments were necessary. When Hiromi contemplated a life without Carlo, she agreed to his plan with little or no hesitation. The stage was set. Both of them were full of hope that this unconventional pairing would have a happy ending; after all, they were not going to sixteenth-century Verona, but to modern open-minded Rome.

On a weekend shortly before Christmas, the lovers boarded a Rome-bound plane. They took the next session off and were very busy all month visiting relatives in Italy and Japan. They returned in early February, glowing, ecstatic. Carlo's family was crazy about Hiromi. They treated her like a contessa: dinners, parties, and adoration as only the Italians can dish it out. Hiromi's family was equally accepting: despite their more reserved way of expressing themselves, they gave Carlo full assurance that they couldn't be happier about the treasure their daughter had found in Oakland. Montagues and Capulets be damned.

As with Kyoko and her boyfriend, I didn't expect to

discover anything more about the future of these lovers after their last session at the school had ended. After all, that *is* the usual pattern for ESL teachers: learning about the fates of our ex-students is, with few exceptions, not part of the package. We learn to live with the curtain coming down at the end of Act I, maybe Act II, but rarely beyond. In this case, there *would* be more to come, but I didn't know it yet.

A few years later, Joan and I took a trip to Europe. She had to get back to her job in California before I had to get back to mine, so I traveled alone to Rome and was graciously put up in the Campo dei Fiori section of Rome by an old student of mine, Francesco de Conno, an attorney who, at that time, was studying to become a diplomat, an ambitious project which, eventually, he successfully completed. (He began his diplomatic career in 1984 and worked in Australia, Prague, Malta, Argentina, Denmark, Australia again, and Canada before retiring in 2011.) Francesco gave me a palpable demonstration of Roman hospitality by giving me his apartment to stay in while he stayed with his mamma in another section of the city. It had an excellent collection of Miles Davis LPs and a bathroom that was essentially a big shower stall with a drain in the center of its floor. At the time I stayed there, there was a problem with the hot water—there wasn't any. Of course, I was young, and, as you can see, that ice-cold water didn't kill me.

Of course, Francesco and I got together several times

and chatted about old times and new developments. In those streams of conversation, he brought up the remarkable fact that he had been in touch with Carlo Spadaccini, also now a lawyer, who was working for a small firm in that city and, amazingly, was living just a few blocks away from Francesco's mother's apartment with his wife, none other than Hiromi, and their baby boy, Tadashi. I was very excited about the prospect of surprising them with a visit from their old teacher in that very un-Oaklandish context. With Hiromi there from Tokyo and me from Berkeley, it was starting to feel like perhaps all roads really *did* lead to Rome.

Francesco gave me Carlo's phone number. I called him, and he sounded shocked when I told him who I was. Shocked, but also delighted. When I told him that I was in Rome, he immediately insisted that I come over for dinner, an invitation which I, of course, accepted. The day and time were set, six o'clock on a Wednesday, and I was jazzed to think about visiting my old students, now married, now parents of a little bambino.

When that Wednesday rolled around, Francesco kindly offered to walk me over to their place; he was a little worried that I'd get lost on the way, a valid concern. We strolled down their very modern, very busy street toward the address Carlo had given me. As we were walking, I noticed that Francesco was about to step into a sizeable mound of dog shit. Having just visited Paris, where it's typical to sound the warning

"*Attention!*" when *un ami* is about to step in it, I instinctively bellowed out the Italian equivalent: "*Attenzione! Attenzione!*"

Francesco chuckled. "It's okay, Phil," he said calmly, coolly. "In Rome, we are, how you say, philosophical about this. We have a saying: 'If you step in shit, it's good luck. Because, right after that, life will almost surely get better.'"

"That's very different from Paris. They shout '*Attention!*' as if stepping in *merde* were the greatest possible calamity, the ruination of a life."

"Yes, of course. But that is Paris. This is Rome. But thank you anyway, Phil."

"*Prego*. Actually, I prefer the 'philosophical' approach of you Romans to the somewhat hysterical reaction of the French, but still, I'd appreciate a warning if you see me about to step in it."

"It's a deal, Phil. If you wish, I will steal that good fortune from you."

A few minutes later, we arrived at my destination, a charmless apartment building, about a half-dozen gray plaster stories. I thanked Francesco for accompanying me, and he went on his way. Upon entering the vestibule, I scanned the directory and quickly found Spadaccini near the bottom of the residents' name list. Apartment 3E.

Each apartment had a button associated with it. I pushed the one for 3E and waited a few seconds for a response. When it came, it was difficult to understand the words because of the fierce screaming of a baby dominating every syllable. It didn't help that the sound from that tiny speaker in the wall was crackling with static.

"*Pronto*." It was Carlo, I was pretty sure.

"Hello. *Pronto*. It's your teacher. It's Phil. Hello. Carlo?"

"Ah, Phil. Hello!" I still could barely make out his words, which were almost completely drowned out by the continuing cries of the baby and the now even louder static of the probably-ancient intercom.

"Hey Carlo. Hello to you!"

"Phil, we will be down there in few minutes. Our baby is having a problem. Sorry for the delaying."

"It's totally okay, Carlo. I understand. Take your time."

"Thank you, Phil. I'll be down very very soon."

For the next several minutes, I waited in the vestibule for Carlo to square away the problems of his little family. After a few minutes, I heard Carlo's voice on the intercom, still accompanied by the frantic crying: "Hello, Phil. I'm sorry. Our son is not easy baby. He cry a lot. Very a lot."

"It's okay, Carlo. I understand. It's the same all over the world. Being a parent is not easy."

"Thank you, Phil."

"Of course, Carlo."

"I'll be down in few minutes. Tadashi will be sleeping. He cry a lot, but then he fall asleep very fast. When he sleep, he no cry."

"It's okay. I can wait. I'm not in a hurry. Take your time, Carlo."

"Okay, *grazie*, Phil. Just few minutes."

The intercom flipped off with a loud electronic snap, leaving me in the church-like silence of the marble-walled lobby. About five minutes went by, and I started wondering if this Italian reunion would ever actually happen. Then, finally, I heard Carlo's voice again through the static: "Hello, Phil? You are still there?"

"Hello, Carlo. Yes, I'm here."

"It's okay now. Tadashi will be sleeping very soon. I'm sure." He didn't sound sure.

"Okay."

"Okay. I will see you in one minute. I am so sorry make you wait, Phil."

"It's no problem. I'm on vacation. I'm very happy that I'll see you and Hiromi again, and meet Tadashi." I realized that I was screaming all this.

"One minute, one minute." Again the intercom snapped off.

I leaned against a white and gray marble wall and waited for Carlo to arrive. A few seconds later, it seemed that they had moved into their corridor because, even from two floors away, I could hear the baby's cries. I could also clearly hear my two former students screaming at each other. After another minute or so, the whirring of the elevator cables joined the mix of Tadashi's squeals and her parents' yelling, growing louder as the cubicle descended to my floor. Then, like theatrical curtains, the elevator doors opened to reveal a little family. Standing there was a frazzled older version of Carlo, standing next to an exhausted-looking vague approximation of Hiromi, who was holding a little Japanese-Italian baby, red-faced and insanely crying. Carlo's formerly full head of black curls had thinned considerably, and his hairline had receded a couple of inches. He had grown a little paunch which sat atop his black leather belt. Hiromi no longer radiated the youthful sensuality that had driven Carlo so crazy in Oakland. She too had gained a bit of weight, her hair had lost its sheen, and a gray sweatshirt hung loosely from her slightly slumping shoulders to about midway down her thighs; one of the knees of her baggy plaid slacks had a whitish splotch on it, which was more likely the result of Tadashi cheesing up than a rogue splash of Alfredo sauce; that youthful body, every curve of which she had been proud to exhibit in Tokyo and Oakland, was nowhere to be seen. A nun's habit could not have cloaked her more effectively. Had I seen her walking alone on the street, I probably would not have recognized her. Both husband and wife had sizeable gray bags under their matching bloodshot eyes. As their baby kept shrieking, I imagined lots of sleepless nights, lots of tears. As they exited the elevator, they appeared almost apologetic about the sad tableau they now presented.

Bear hugs. Warm greetings. Continued bawling, embarrassment, and apologies.

"We make very delicious Italian dinner for you,

Phil," Hiromi shouted above the racket of her crying bambino.

"Fantastic! I'm very hungry. I hope you made enough for me," I joked, but nobody laughed. It was painfully obvious that I had stumbled into a domestic minefield. I felt like leaving, but, technically, I hadn't arrived yet.

"I think there is enough lasagna, even for a big American appetite, Phil," Carlo responded, forcing a smile.

Through it all, Tadashi kept screaming, piercing cries that were so amplified by those marble walls that I feared permanent ear damage. Hiromi rocked him back and forth, left and right, singing to him in Japanese, singing, singing, singing . . . It seemed like Tadashi's screaming would never stop, but, after several minutes of Hiromi's sweet ministrations, the cries grew gradually weaker, Tadashi's eyelids started lowering, and he finally succumbed; gurgling peacefully, Tadashi fell into a deep-looking sleep. Hallelujah. He was a picture of angelic peace. We three non-babies looked at each other and exchanged sighs of relief.

We were now finally ready to enter the elevator and take our trip to the third floor. Before we got in, Hiromi cautiously handed Tadashi to her husband, who looked eager to re-establish a modicum of *Pax Romana*. Hiromi smiled sweetly at me and gracefully swept her right hand toward the empty elevator, an invitation to her old teacher to enter first. I did. Then Hiromi joined me. Last to enter was Carlo, cooperative compliant husband, holding his sleeping silent seraph. Careful with their baby, so careful, so careful, he tiptoed toward the little chamber. With a thankful and tentative little grin, he was nodding at Hiromi and me at the rear of the elevator. As he took his initial baby steps, so to speak, into that compartment, he misjudged the width of the elevator's doorway. With something akin to horror, I saw that the right side of that soft little head was about to slam into the steel frame. Before there was a chance to even call out the first syllable of "*Attenzione!*" it happened. The thud of that collision was sickening. Tadashi's return to the world of the conscious was immediate and frightening. Piercing the hard-won silence, his shrieks, other-worldly, deafening, maddening, returned with twice the force of his original crying marathon. I wouldn't have thought such volume could issue from such a tiny source. His mother was furious. Hiromi had found the Italian language almost impossible to learn, and Carlo spoke virtually no Japanese, so they tended to communicate with each other in broken English. Pushed to her limit, Hiromi bellowed out one of the only Italian phrases she knew: "*MAMMA MIA!*"

Carlo looked whipped, hopeless.

What the hell was *I* doing there?

Hiromi was anything but a picture of patient forbearance; yet, somehow, with a measure of divine patience, after ascending to the third floor and entering the Spadaccinis' modest apartment, she resumed her rocking and Japanese lullabying, and, within five or ten more minutes, Tadashi again stopped his deafening protests, and fell back to sleep. Hiromi deposited him in a bassinet in the corner of the living room, under an unframed print of one of Modigliani's long-necked reclining nudes, a cruel reminder of an ostensibly easier life.

We ate lasagna and drank Chianti Classico, both delicious. Clearly, Hiromi's problems with the language did not extend to reading Italian recipes. But it was hard to enjoy the dinner. Resentment hung in the air like melted mozzarella; the couple would still have to go through the ritual of apology and forgiveness to repair the damage of the evening, but my presence was making it more difficult, if not impossible. Of course, there was no guarantee that they'd be able to pull that off even after I'd left. They put all their energies into pretending that everything was okay, into showing their old teacher that the romance that had started in our 105 grammar class had endured, but it was an unconvincing performance. I longed to get back to my refuge in Campo dei Fiori, to put on one of Francesco's Miles Davis records, and savor the solitude. And I suspected that my hosts were even more eager than I was to call it a night. So, after a cannoli-and-espresso finale, I gave them each another hug, scurried down the three flights of stairs, avoiding the angst-ridden elevator, and escaped into the cool Roman night.

After returning to California, I continued to be in touch with Francesco for a while, exchanging letters every few months. Several years after that Roman visit, Francesco wrote me that Carlo and Hiromi had gotten divorced. That, of course, was sad but not surprising; yet I had held out hope, however faint, that they might overcome their problems and return to the freshness of an earlier time. Of course, that's always more easily said than done. Carlo, whom Francesco saw from time to time, was devastated. No other details.

I wondered who had gotten custody of Tadashi and how they dealt with the difficult issues of visitation rights, alimony, and all the rest of that mess. I also wondered whether Hiromi had returned to Japan or stayed in Italy. I wonder how they are today, and what kind of man Tadashi has grown up to be. Questions never to be answered. Probably never. Of course, I had already learned more about the futures of my students than I usually do.

Sometimes I think about what Francesco said to me on that Roman street, about good luck and bad. Sure, it was just an old adage, but causality being the mystery it is, who can be sure that things wouldn't have turned out better if, years before, Carlo had stepped in dog shit somewhere along the way?

The Tale of the Magical Lampshade

One autumn session in 2010, the module-of-the-month that was laid in the laps of Masters' class teachers by a central curriculum committee was "Folk Objects," a subject that I'd had to deal with several times before. It could be mildly engaging for a day or two for the lay folklorist, but trying to stretch it out for a month-long session seemed like a very bad idea. Some teachers who'd attempted to do so had watched their students slip into a collective coma. I decided to emphasize a variation of that theme: physical objects which had attained special significance for personal reasons. What's personal is generally more interesting to students, who are, without exception, persons. For one of their main projects, I asked the students to give a short talk about how a physical object had made a difference in their lives, to tell the class a story about it in a way that made it, and its personal importance, real to the listeners.

Several students had said, dejectedly, in varying ways, "I can't think of anything. I don't *have* a special object in my life." We got into a discussion about how inanimate objects can sometimes acquire significance. I tried nudging them along by offering some examples: "An object can be special because someone special gave it to you, or because it was important in a specific situation, or because it reminds you of a special place, or simply because it's beautiful."

Scanning all the faces, I could see that some had already "found" their objects, some were still sifting through the artifacts of their lives, and some had no hope that they'd ever come up with anything. I tried my best to loosen that last group up with a pep talk: "Don't worry. Be creative and just tell a good story. Have fun with it. Remember, whatever you talk about, you're practicing your English." We took another five or ten minutes to hash out various ways of being "creative." I tried one angle after another to somehow persuade everyone that this was a doable project, that it didn't have to be drudgery, that it could be, against all apparent odds, meaningful, even entertaining. If nothing else, I had managed to convince myself.

As it turned out, as each of the appointed presentation days rolled around, everyone *was* ready with a little story. Here's one of them.

The Taiwanese student, Hsiu-ching Lin, better known as Susie at our Berkeley school, was in her early twenties, bright, lively, and rather fluent, if not grammatical, in English, and, hence, quite relaxed as she told us about her "object."

"When I was very young, my parents give me special object. It was old but perfect. When my mother was little girl, she enjoy it too. My grandmother give it to her. Then my mom give it to my older sister. She enjoy it too. Then my mom give it to me and I love it more than any other thing in whole life. Of course, now I make you too curiosity. You wonder what is it. So I don't torture you no more, heh, heh. I tell you. No waiting more. It is . . ." Here she smiled and paused for dramatic effect, a silent drum roll: "It is lampshade."

I briefly interrupted her to make sure that every student understood what a lampshade was; a few weren't sure, so I quickly explained it. Generally, I try not to break into the flow of my students' stories, but a central vocabulary issue is a high priority: miss that and you miss the gist of the whole tale. As I was explaining that, it struck me that Susie's tightly curled, slightly A-lined pillowy perm evoked that very object, an observation I kept to myself.

"Sorry to interrupt you, Susie. Please continue."

"Okay. So. I know all of you thinking, 'What can be so special about lampshade? Especially for little girl.' Now I show you. Listen carefully. Lampshade have many holes cut out in shape of different things (I tell you in a minute about the things). This lampshade is on very special lamp. Not ordinary lamp. It have motor. You know 'motor'?" We all nodded that we did. She continued, "So when you turn on lamp, lampshade turn around and around and around. The light from lamp shine through cut-out holes in lampshade, and the things look big on walls of room, and they go around and around. Okay? You got picture?" We assured her we did, and now she was really getting into it: "It is important describe what is things on lampshade because that is wonderful part. It have animals and trees. Beautiful friendly animals: deers, lions (of course friendly ones), tigers (*very* friendly, don't worry, heh, heh), teddy bears, giraffes, llamas, sheep, even unicorns. Then, also, as I say, many many trees. Oh, and I almost forget to tell you about the stars, many many stars. And moons too. When lamp is on in my dark bedroom at the night and the lampshade turn around and around, the animals and the trees and the stars and the moons go round and around and around and around on my walls. It is so fan*tas*tical. Whole room become magic place. And all time that this happening lamp playing music, beautiful Taiwanese folk song, like bells." Susie then sang a few bars of that song, which was lovely indeed. From her rapturous smile, it was obvious to all of us in that Berkeley classroom that, in her head, she was back in her bedroom in Taiwan and was clearly seeing the light-pictures swirling around on the walls of that unique sanctuary. As were we.

She went on: "Sometimes I have bad day, like everybody. Everybody have bad day. Bad day part of life, right?" We all nodded that, yes, bad days were an unavoidable part of life, wherever you lived, whoever you were. Like a pro, she scanned the room to make sure that all those nodding people were thoroughly tuned into her narrative, which, in fact, we were. Satisfied, she continued: "Even if I have terrible day, I can go into my bedroom and turn out lights and turn on lamp, and the animals and trees and moons and stars go around and around and around on my walls and the music is so sweet, so beautiful, that I always, *always*, feel better. More than better. I feel great! Always!

"So now you can see why this lampshade so special for me. When I get married and have baby, I will give this special thing to him or to her, to my sweet baby, and it continue be special for next and next and next generation. That is end of my story about my very special object."

The class and I clapped wildly at Susie's conclusion, and she looked very pleased and relieved that her presentation had gone so well. And that it was over. There was still another week-and-a-half left before we'd reach the end of the session, and as time tends to do with a good group, it flew.

On the last day of the session, I gave everyone their grades, went over the final exam with them, and was about to wrap things up, when Susie raised her hand.

"Yes, Susie?"

"Phil, I have to tell you something."

"Uh huh?"

"Well, it's about my presentation, about lampshade story."

"Oh, sure, fine. That was a great presentation. Everyone loved it. It was one of the best ones."

"Thank you, Phil."

"Of course. So what did you want to tell me about it?"

"Well, Phil . . ." She hesitated for a few beats, and her cheeks suddenly resembled a couple of pink-lady apples. "Well, Phil, remember when you explain the presentation topic to us, you tell us we should 'be creative'?"

"Yes, I remember. And you certainly were. Parts of your presentation were like poetry. I know *I* could imagine those animals and trees and stars on your lampshade and on your walls very clearly. I could really *see* them. It was very creative indeed."

"Thank you, Phil. But I was maybe *too* creative." Susie's smile was a composite: part sly, part triumphant, part guilty. Remembering my creativity mini-lecture, I was pretty sure I knew what she was hinting at. I could see that, once again, her classmates were captivated by Susie and her delivery of this *new* story.

"*Too* creative?"

"Uh-huh. Remember, Phil, when you talk about 'be creative,' you wink at class?" She winked at me as if I might not know the word and it needed modeling.

"Yes, I *do* remember that wink," I said. I had, in fact, used a hammy hyper-wink to punctuate my remark.

"Then I think you not sure that we understand meaning of your winking, because you explain it to us. It was surprise to me: you say it's okay for us to *lie*, to make something up. You say that if we fool everybody, teacher too, that is even better thing. Better *accomplishment* is word you use. You say we can lie in our presentation, yes?"

"Yes. You're right. I did say that." I had; it was a comment I'd made to many groups, and I'd meant it, but I usually expected no one to take me seriously.

By then, judging by the looks of delighted shock on their faces, all the other students had already guessed what Susie was about to confess.

"Well, Phil. I remembered what you say, that it was okay to lie if we *good* liar. Good enough to make you believe. And it was important to me because I really *don't* have special object. I *never* had special object. I never had magical lampshade. There *is* no magical lampshade. So I made that up. *All* of it. Nothing in my story ever really happened."

Laughing our heads off, we all clapped even harder than we had for the lampshade story itself. Yes, this was a confession, but it was also a well-earned boast. Susie's classmates and I looked at her with open admiration, awed that we had been so magnificently duped.

"Thank you for telling us your secret, Susie. I really appreciate your honesty. *And* your bravery." She was beaming. Then I asked her to show me the "Oral Presentation Evaluation" sheet I'd handed her only about forty minutes earlier; it had the grades for various aspects of her telling of the lampshade tale. For a few moments, she looked curious and maybe a bit concerned, as if she were thinking that perhaps she should have kept her mouth shut and left more-than-well-enough alone.

"These are good marks, Susie, but not high enough. I'll have to raise some of them."

"Really, Phil?"

"No, not really. I was just kidding."

"Oh, okay," she said, smiling graciously, but again looking a little insecure. "It was—how you say?—too good be true?"

"It's 'too good *to* be true,' but, actually, it's not. I was just kidding about 'just kidding.' I really *am* going to raise your grades."

Everybody was laughing again, especially Susie: "Hey, I fool you and you fool me!"

"Yep, now we're even."

"Yep, now we're even," she echoed, still laughing, and maybe not a hundred percent sure that another tricky reversal wasn't about to arrive. To remove all doubt, I immediately raised her grade on her paper *and* in my record folder, which I then showed to her.

"Wow."

"Wow, indeed. I told you it was okay to make things up, and you did it like a true master. You fooled us all! That *is* a great accomplishment. Congratulations!"

The other students broke into another round of applause. I don't think anyone begrudged Susie a few extra points; she had attained heroic stature in that class.

It was then time for us to go. Susie was the last to leave. She came over to my desk, took my hand, and thanked me, and I congratulated her again for doing such a bang-up job.

"Have great weekend, Phil."

"You too, Susie."

A final laugh emerged from under that lampshade-like perm as she realized that this bizarre interchange really had happened, and she left the classroom, closing the door gently behind her.

As happened so often, sitting alone at my desk after the crowd of students had left, I found myself mulling over the details of the previous fifty minutes. Was I encouraging this lovely young woman to lead a life of deception? Was I extolling the efficacy of lies as the key to success? Did my message to her simply boil down to "Crime pays"? I preferred to think of it as a pat on the back for wielding the language so effectively, the prodding and nurturing of a creative spirit, encouragement for a weaver of utterly believable fiction. That's what I told myself anyway.

The Green Rabbit

A couple of years after Susie's successful fiction, Fernanda, a Brazilian woman in her early twenties, told a story to a class in Berkeley that made me think of that magical lampshade. It was at least as fanciful, but, alas, far less plausible. In fact, one part of it made it especially hard to willingly suspend my disbelief.

The assignment: "Tell a story that involves a superstition, your own or that of someone you know, or one linked to your culture." I liked to have my students show me a simple outline of their presentation before they delivered it to the class, so I could nudge them in the right direction if necessary. As I sat with Fernanda at my desk, looking over her outline, I got stuck about halfway through. The problem was her introduction of a green rabbit. At first, because her handwriting was often almost illegible, I thought that maybe I was misreading part or all of the two-word phrase. I pointed to the confusing entry:

"Green rabbit? Does this say green rabbit, Fernanda?"

"Yes, teacher, that's right. Green rabbit." She told me that she and her family considered green rabbits to be extremely bad luck, sometimes fatal.

"That's surprising, Fernanda. When I was a kid, many people believed it was *good* luck to carry a rabbit's foot in your pocket. In fact I had one I used as a key chain."

"Key chain, teacher?" I took out the purely functional single-link steel hoop that held my keys.

"Oh, I see. But didn't it smell? The foot of the rabbit? The foot of the *dead* rabbit?"

"No, no smell. They did something to preserve it, I guess, so it didn't smell." Actually, sitting there with Fernanda, I wondered, maybe for the first time, why they hadn't smelled. Little kids generally don't acknowledge taxidermy as a link between the animal and the artifact. Those ubiquitous rabbits' feet, so popular in fifties Brooklyn, looked and felt so real, with their off-white fur, their little claws, and underlying bone structure, that nobody ever seemed to doubt their authenticity; if those dismembered limbs populating thousands of dungaree pockets were synthetic, what a triumph of artifice they were.

Fernanda shook her head in wonder. "I think your good-luck superstition maybe is more strange than the bad-luck one in *Brasil*."

"Maybe it is. In fact, I don't remember my luck being especially good during the time I carried that rabbit's foot in my pocket, but I liked the feel of it, and I would secretly stroke it with my finger. It was almost like a pet." Fernanda was starting to look genuinely concerned about my sanity. Who could blame her?

Getting back to *her* subject, I commented that green

rabbits shouldn't be a cause for much worrying, since, as far as I knew, there had never been any evidence of their existence.

"But, teacher, I see many of them near our house in countryside. In countryside of *Brasil* there are many many green rabbits. How can you say they no exist?"

At that point, I started to wonder if Fernanda was simply a bad liar or, more troublingly, a victim of her own delusion. Were we discussing a fabrication or a hallucination? Or was there something *I* wasn't getting? I probed a little further.

"This 'rabbit,' this 'green rabbit.' We are talking about the little animal that hops, right? It hops rather than walks, right? 'Hop' was a verb she didn't know, so I got out of my chair and hopped around the full perimeter of my desk, which, not surprisingly, made her laugh.

"Ah, *that* is hop! I see. Yes, of course, rabbit hops. All rabbits hop. Everywhere. That is what rabbits do. They hop. In your country too, yes?"

"Yes. That's right. But it's the 'green' part that's confusing. I didn't think that rabbits were *ever* green. Unless, maybe, as a joke, someone painted them—dyed them—that color." Fernanda's eyes widened, as if she couldn't believe that a teacher could actually be so ignorant. I was starting to wonder if the whole apparent misunderstanding might simply be due to my limited knowledge of the huge variety of international fauna. But I didn't think so.

As I said, these pre-presentation outline checks were for the purpose of making sure that my students were on the right track; after that was established, I usually reined them in from telling me the whole story before they told it to the class, so their presentations could be fresh for me too, free of spoilers. So, in this case too, I would wait another couple of days to hear the whole story, and then, perhaps, in context, with the help of my other students, the mystery of the green rabbit would be solved. Perhaps.

Fernanda's presentation day arrived, and I was eager, and a bit apprehensive, to hear her tale; if it turned out that the green rabbit really *was* a delusion or a poorly devised deception, there was the potential for serious public humiliation. That was the last thing I wanted; Fernanda was a fragile soul, hard on herself, easily brought down and hard to resurrect. Most of the time, she was trapped in a not uncommon vicious cycle: her fear that she was "a stupid student" distracted her from learning effectively, which confirmed her suspicion, which made it even harder for her to focus on taking in new material, which made her feel even more like an "imbecile," and so on. A couple of weeks earlier, she had told me, with tears in her eyes, that she was considering dropping out of school because it was all too hard for her. I had done my best to assure her that it was my "professional" opinion that she was *not* stupid, that I was sure that she had more than enough ability to be an excellent student, and urged her to stick it out, at least until the end of the session. Now I was concerned that, true to the Brazilian superstition she had described to me, a green rabbit might, in fact, wreck everything for her.

She was the third of three students to speak that day. Sitting among my students, I had the presenters sit at my desk in front of the room to address me and their classmates. When her time arrived, I called out her name, and with a backhand motion of my right arm, like a maître d' escorting his customer to the appointed table, I invited her to take the place of honor and, when she was ready, begin to tell her story. Looking somewhat nervous, Fernanda took a few seconds to scan her outline, and then began.

"Good morning, everybody. Today I going to tell you a story about one night in *Brasil*. It's about a night during one vacation that I have with my family at our country house. I was just a little girl, maybe with only eight or nine years. We have two houses, my family, one house in downtown São Paulo and another house in the country, very very quiet, so much nature, very very tranquil. At our country place, we have two buildings, the main house and a second building which has the only restroom, the only one. It's the country, like I say. Not luxury like São Paulo. Not so convenient.

"Well, on one night, during this vacation, I am lying in my bed late at night. It's late, after midnight, and I am in a difficulty to fall asleep because I have to, uh . . . pee. As I say before, restroom is in other house, and other house not so close to our main house, across a kind of field. But, you know, when you have to do that, when you have to pee, you have to pee, you have to do it right then or you don't sleep that night. At all.

"So I have no choosing other thing. I no want to do that, but I get out of bed and get dressed with my jacket over my pajamas. I take our, how you say . . . electric light? No, light *is* electric, but that's not right name."

"Flashlight?" I offered.

"Ah, yes, teacher, yes, flashlight. I heard that word before. Flashlight. I take with me a flashlight because it's very dark at night in the country. Sometime if there is big moon then is not so dark, but on that night there is no moon. Even though you can see so many stars in the sky, still it's very very dark. I went outside and I remember it feel a little cold. Believe it or don't, sometimes even in *Brasil* it can be cold. Remember, everybody, it is late in the night time. I shine the flashlight in front of me when I am walking on the grass to the house with the restroom. My dad was just change the batteries in the flashlight when we left São Paulo, so it is very bright and the grass look so green. You know, *Brasil* is a very very green country, especially in the country, I mean the countryside, the natural parts. I can hear a little stream making bubbling as it hurrying through our place, and I kind of was seeing a movie in my mind of the hurrying water, you know? I think maybe it make me need to pee even more than before. You know what I mean?"

We all let her know that we did. In fact, listening to

Fernanda's story, I was starting to have the same need myself, albeit, mercifully, far less intense; it could wait for the break.

Fernanda, buoyed by our solidarity, went on: "Then, in the light of the flashlight, in the green grass, I see something that make me crazy afraid. It is a green rabbit, just sitting there. Looking at me. That green rabbit in that green grass. Green and green, everything green, almost same green, so I almost don't see him, but then I *do*. It was like first he isn't there and then suddenly he *is* there. Poof! Like ghost. Right outside the door of restroom! That was crazy and it frighten me. Really frighten me. I already told Phil that me and my family are very afraid from green rabbits because we think that they cause very bad luck. Very very bad. Sometimes you can even die from green rabbit. It's maybe just superstition but we feel really afraid when we see green rabbit."

Okay, here we were. The green rabbit had finally arrived. Where would this go from here?

"I run back to the big house. It was like nightmare."

Nightmare? Ah, now I see, I thought. It's the old story-telling ploy: the narrator wakes up relieved to discover that the horrific situation was only a dream. Of course. Green rabbit, indeed. Sure, the "it-was-only-a-dream" scenario is a cliché, and probably everyone in that room had seen, heard, or read it repeatedly, but she had had us going for a while. Soon she would tell us about finally waking up.

"I am so afraid that I want my father or my mother to protect me from the rabbit. I can't just hide in main house because, you remember, I have to pee. And now, after so much time, I have to pee more than ever. You know, the longer you have to wait for peeing the more and more and more you have to pee. I had to pee so bad that I was dancing. You know?"

Again, we nodded and laughed. Of course, we knew. Who hasn't done the God-I-need-to-pee jig at one point or another?

"So I go to my parents' bedroom, crying and dancing, and maybe hopping just like the rabbit himself. I say too loud, 'Wake up, Papa! Wake up, Mama!' And they both sit up very suddenly. They look scared too. I tell them about the green rabbit in the grass between our house and toilet house and how I can't wait much longer to pee, but how I'm too afraid to go there by myself. Well, because of what I just tell them, they are also afraid to go outside. Remember, they are the ones who tell me about the dangerous green rabbits since I was even younger, the very bad luck, the maybe dying. But my dad, he get up and he put on his jacket. He is typical man of *Brasil*, you know, macho. He need to show his daughter and his wife that he is brave enough to protect me from the rabbit. He look funny, like clown, I remember, because his purple pajamas with different-colored monkeys on it and his bright red jacket was funny combination together. But I was not laugh at a clown saving me from that rabbit, because that green rabbit frighten me too much, and I am too uncomfortable with my needing to pee so bad."

I was still waiting for the little girl to wake up. Perhaps all Fernanda's classmates were expecting the same, predictable plot twist. But her nightmare continued.

"My dad pick up the flashlight with his right hand (he is right-hand man). Then he hold my hand in his left one. Maybe I imagine it, but I think my macho father's hand is then a little bit shaking, like he take my hand not only to make me less scared, but to make *him* feel more safer also.

"So, anyway, we walk into the black night and my dad puts on the flashlight and, again, it's like before; it's like the flashlight light is green, everything is green because the grass is so so *so* green. My dad move the flashlight slowly slowly. We just stand there outside the house's door. We don't take a step. We are looking for that rabbit, the green rabbit on the green grass. But only thing we see is grass, no rabbit. Meanwhile, don't forget, I still need to pee, of course more than ever. My dad say, 'Fernanda, I don't see no rabbit,' and I say, 'Dad, really it was not my imagination, I really see it before.' He was very nice (my dad is almost always very nice) and say, 'I believe you, Fernanda. Maybe the rabbit go away. Let's walk to the toilet house. Keep holding my hand.' So that's what we was doing, slowly slowly. His hand is maybe a little bit more shaking now.

"After a few steps, when we are about halfway there, we both see the green grass move and hear a sound of something moving in that grass, like whispering, like, how you say for this sound?"

"Swish?" I offered.

"Swish. I like that word. That's a very good word. It sound just like the sound in the grass."

I considered a brief interruption to give a mini-lesson on the wonders of onomatopoeia, but I decided against it. She still hadn't gotten to the part where she wakes up, and I was starting to wonder if she ever would. Like everyone else in that room, I needed to know what would happen next in that black and green Brazilian night. So I just nodded and said, "Yeah, there are lots of words in English that do what 'swish' does. It's called 'onomatopoeia.' We'll all talk about that later."

"Okay. Thank you, Phil. I continue with story?"

"Please."

"So. We hear the swishes in the grass, but we no see rabbit or anything else either. Just grass. Very carefully, so carefully, we take a few more steps toward toilet house, all the time looking with my dad's flashlight, all the time I'm thinking I'm gonna pee in my pajamas before I get there, I'm gonna pee in my pajama pants. We hear more swishes and more swishes and more swishes. And we hear the stream streaming like stream is peeing, and I'm *sure* I'm gonna pee in my pants. And then we hear the rabbit's voice. And then again. And again. We hear him making his sound, so my dad pointed the flashlight at the sound, but we don't see it. And then, suddenly, like before, like when I was alone, we do. We *do* see him, that green rabbit in the green grass. So clear. He is looking at us when we are looking at *him*. And he keep making his sound. His deep deep sound. Then my dad starts jumping up and down *hard*, fast, right foot up in the air then down hard, then left foot up and down hard, then right again then left, right left right left very very fast, like crazy dance, and I am *already* dancing with my needing to pee, so I dance harder and I'm sure we look like two people with serious mental disease dancing in the night. And my father, acting so brave like a macho man, is jumping and shouting, in Portuguese of course, 'Go away, rabbit. Go away from my girl. Right now!' And, you know what? That green rabbit so calm, so slow, just hop away to where we can't see him no more. So, finally, with my dad being like a police guard outside restroom door, I can finally *finally* use the toilet. When I come out, my dad take my hand again and he continue to shine that light on the green grass, but we no see that rabbit no more when we walk back to our house. However, we can still hear him making his deep sound, again and again and again."

I had to ask: "Deep sound? The rabbit was making a deep sound?"

"Yes, of course. Like all rabbits. It's like what you say about 'swish.' What was that big word again?"

"Onomatopoeia?"

"Yes, that one. It's like that one. The name for this green animal sound like what he say, like the sound he make . . ."

Fernanda's face suddenly lit up. "Ah, just a minute. I show you. You will see. You will understand." She excused herself for a few seconds, darted over to her desk, and rooted around in her purse for something. She then pulled out her iPhone and told me she was going to show us some green rabbits on YouTube. Expecting perhaps some animated or computer-doctored clips of green rabbits, I encouraged her to proceed.

"This is my favorite little movie of a green rabbit. Even on iPhone, he still scare me a little. But I want to show you this rabbit. He is so so similar to the one that scare me in my story. He look like it and he sound like it too. Watch. Listen."

After pushing the appropriate sequence of buttons and doing the requisite hocus-pocus finger-swiping across the little screen, Fernanda called the ten or so of us over to huddle around her in order to get a view of the YouTube page she had selected. She tapped her phone, and a movie began. It was *not* a cartoon; it was a film of a gurgling stream in a lush green jungle, almost certainly somewhere in Brazil. The music was Brazilian, a bossa nova, and the narration was in Portuguese. The camera panned right and then stopped as it came upon a fat green frog sitting on a moss-covered rock. It stayed there for a few seconds, then hopped off the rock and hopped a few more times along the stream bank. Zooming in, the camera caught several more seconds of the frog just sitting at the edge of the water. I think Fernanda was the only one who knew why we were all looking at that frog.

Then it began to croak, a rather basso profundo croaking that sounded something like "Rabbit . . . rabbit . . . rabbit . . ."

Behind the Veil

When I first started teaching English in Oakland in 1974, the great majority of my students were male, a reflection of the dominance of that gender in most cultures of the world. This imbalance was especially noticeable among my Arabic students. During the few decades preceding the horror of September 11, 2001, many young men had come to our school from Saudi Arabia, the United Arab Emirates, Qatar, Kuwait, and Libya, but only a handful of women. Of course, after 9/11, Arabic students of both sexes stopped coming, and, if they were already here, usually went home as quickly as red tape would allow.

In 2005, in response to repeated requests by Saudi King Abdullah, George W. Bush re-opened the possibility of Saudis getting student visas. Between then and the present, the Saudi female-to-male ratio has been steadily climbing. Sometimes, married couples arrive together. They often present a rather odd picture to western eyes: the men wear western-style clothes, but the women generally have far less leeway in their attire. Typically, they keep their heads covered and wear an abaya, the customary full-length robe (or an unbelted raincoat or other overcoat as a stand-in);

often, jeans and running shoes can be seen peeking out from just below its hem. Variations on and deviations from this basic theme seemed linked to the degree of each woman's orthodoxy. Sometimes, women choose not to wear the abaya but still cover their heads, and that covering might be either a traditional hijab or a more fashionable kerchief with a colorful print.

When I'd been teaching for only a year or two, in the mid-seventies, a chic blond woman placed into one of my grammar classes in Oakland. Almost Twiggy-thin and always dressed in the latest styles, this extremely attractive woman spoke in an accent that sounded vaguely French, but it had a tinge of something else. I looked on the class list and saw that her name was Arabic. During the usual first-day introductions, I discovered that this un-Arabic-looking woman was, in fact, a Saudi princess who had been living in Paris for several years. Later that day, I heard through the grapevine that her appearance, the life-style it represented, and her self-imposed Parisian exile were a great scandal back in the Kingdom. It would be bad enough for any Saudi woman to so comport herself, but for a member of the royal family, it was a sin that was off the charts. Since she was the first Saudi woman I had ever had in my classes, I had no idea how rebellious her deviation was.

In 2011, more than thirty years after the princess's visit, after having had quite a few Saudi women in my classes, another unconventional one snuck up on me. Mai, a brilliant student, was here with her husband and was planning to pursue graduate studies in public health; when she arrived in my Berkeley Masters' class, she had none of the usual trappings of Saudi women. In a snug-fitting beige sweater and jeans, ink-black wavy hair cascading to her shoulders, she took her seat on the first day of class. My guess was that she was Italian, Turkish, or Spanish. It wasn't until I took roll that I discovered that she was Saudi. She seemed to enjoy my obvious surprise. It quickly became clear that the freedom she enjoyed in her physical presentation was just one reflection of a more general mode of thinking, speaking, and living. For several sessions, she continued to surprise me with her ironic wit, sharply analytical mind, and love of life, all of which would have been impressive in a student from *any* culture. Her plan was to do advanced graduate studies here, and then return to her country to put her education to work. Mai was no exiled princess, but, still, the path she'd chosen was perhaps the more arduous one, despite the strong support and love of her family.

The physical appearances of both the princess and Mai had stood out because of their total break from the traditional Saudi dress code for women. A few years before Mai's arrival, I had been surprised by the garb of another Saudi woman, for reasons that were at the opposite end of that cultural continuum. She was in one of my advanced grammar classes in Berkeley and was married to Akram, a student in a "low-intermediate" conversation class of mine. After more than three decades of teaching, cultural surprises were rather rare for me; there weren't many firsts by that point. But Azeeza, fully swathed in an abaya, was the first of my Saudi students who had covered not only her head and body, but also her face. Except for her eyes, of course, which were almost lost among the seemingly endless windings of beige cloth. As I went through the ritual of calling out the students' names and arrived at Azeeza's, she raised her hand, said, "Yes, Teacher," and we looked at each other in a way that forever changed my sense of the term "eye contact." In a unique fashion, for me at least, we had met.

Before that day, I had never fully appreciated how much I depended on my students' facial reactions to gauge the extent to which I had gotten through to them during a lesson, or failed to do so. With Azeeza, that reliable monitoring device was reduced to just her eyes. Actually, I shouldn't say *just* her eyes. "The eyes are the portals of the soul" is a cliché, but, like most clichés, it has persisted because it's probably true.

At first, I was disconcerted by what felt like partial blindness. Things felt skewed in her favor, to say the least: it was as if I were fully exposed (facially speaking) and Azeeza were freely peeping at me from behind a curtain, which was essentially the case. Then, little by little, I became more adept at reading the subtleties that those eyes could convey. I could tell when she was smiling, analyzing, doubting, joking, frowning, teasing. On some days, she even wore black eyeliner and mascara; I remember the first morning she did that, about two weeks into the session. Her eyes seemed to triple in size, and her lashes seemed to have suddenly grown so long that I had the surreal and unsettling feeling, as she fluttered them, that they could tickle me clear across the room. It was difficult to tell her age, but I estimated that she was about as old as her husband, who was in his late twenties.

Azeeza was in my classes for the next couple of month-long sessions, and then she had other teachers for her last few sessions. Whenever I'd pass her on the stairs or in the hallway or cafeteria, we'd say or wave hi. Her eyes would always "smile" as she greeted me.

One morning, about three weeks into a session, I showed up for work a little before 8:30, as usual, and saw a new student, a young Saudi woman, standing at the front reception desk and chatting with the student advisor. She was dressed in the typical fashion of most of the Saudi women who came to our school, hijab and abaya over jeans and running shoes; yes, her head and body were covered, but unlike Azeeza, not her face. This new student appeared to be about seventeen or eighteen years old.

"Hi Phil," she said, surprising me by knowing my name. She had a shy little smile on her roundish, rather pretty, face.

"Hi, uh . . ." I was a bit spooked because the voice speaking my name was oddly familiar. And I knew those eyes too. Very well.

"Azeeza?" I said, just a tad tentatively.

"Yes, Teacher. I am Azeeza." Of course she was.

"Of course you are."

"You are surprised?"

"Of course I am."

She now looked almost apologetic, and, for the first time, I could see her blush, a rich cherry redness suffusing those oh-so-naked cheeks. She nodded, as if the surprise factor were first dawning on her. "Of course you are."

I couldn't get over how young she was. It was like the experience most of us have had of initially meeting someone on the telephone, perhaps having several repeat calls, involuntarily developing a mental image of a face to go with the voice, and then finally meeting that person in the flesh and being surprised, perhaps shocked, by the disparity between the imagined and the real. For once, I was at a loss for words with one of my students. I didn't feel free to say any of the things which were bubbling away in my brain: *Wow, I thought you were much older. Wow, you're so much younger than Akram. Wow, what made you decide to uncover your face? Wow, you're actually very pretty. Wow.*

Wow indeed. I just dumbly stood there smiling and staring. Azeeza looked both excited and embarrassed, simultaneously thrilled by an unprecedented form of freedom, and mortified, as if she were consciously living the classic nightmare in which a person suddenly discovers, to her horror, that she's naked in public.

"It's nice to meet you, Azeeza" was what I found

myself saying, hoping she'd recognize and even be amused by my stab at jocularity. Her cheeks actually turned an even darker shade of scarlet. She chuckled a little nervously, smiled sweetly, and completed the loop of our little riff:

"It's nice to meet you too, Mister Phil."

And then we ran off to our respective classes. For the next few days, the news of Azeeza's transformation was the talk of the school, for both teachers and students. I wasn't the only one who'd been astounded. But why had she done it? Why, for no apparent reason, had she chosen this time for her unveiling? I couldn't push that question out of my mind. We'd still wave and smile when we'd see each other, and each time, Azeeza looked a little more comfortable in her own skin, perhaps even happy. And, each time, my curiosity would rear up anew, seemingly unkillable. Since she wasn't in any of my classes at that point, I didn't have an opportunity to ask her directly.

Her husband, Akram, however, was in a small, actually tiny, conversation class with me, and we had a good, friendly, informal relationship. Unlike his wife, bundled up and covered up even on the hottest summer days, Akram dressed more comfortably in typical western clothes: tee shirt, jeans, running shoes. His rather large black-rimmed glasses made him look more studious than he was. The only other student in our little discussion group was another Saudi guy, Sultan, who was a close friend of Akram's. That made it easier to ask Akram about the grand surprise that Azeeza had sprung on everybody, but it didn't make it easy. I approached the topic gingerly.

"Akram, I have a question for you. And maybe it's a little personal, a little private, so if you don't feel comfortable answering it, of course I would understand. You don't have to answer. I'm just curious about something."

"What means 'curious,' Phil?"

"What does 'curious' *mean*?"

"Oh yes, that's right. What does 'curious' mean? So what *does* 'curious' means, Phil?" I decided to leave Akram's grammar problems for later. But, for now, first things first.

"Well, a person is curious when he wants to know something but doesn't *have* to know it. I mean, he has a question and wants to know the answer, but he doesn't *need* to know it in order to do something useful with it or for any other reason; he just *wants* to know it. Just finding it out *is* the reason."

"So you want to know something, but you don't *have* to know it. You don't *need* to know it. I'm not sure I understand. If you don't *have* to know it, if you don't *need* to know it for good reason, why you *want* to know it?" Curiosity was starting to sound like the stupidest of conditions, not to mention shallow and self-centered.

"Good question, Akram. The reason I want to know is simply that I'm just *curious*. I want to know because I want to know."

"Oh, maybe I think now I maybe understand. Maybe. 'Just curious' mean answer is not important."

"Well, it's important to the person who's curious, but, yes, I guess you could say it's not important in general." I was starting to feel that if we followed this line of logic much further, we would relegate his answering my question about his wife to the trashcan of total insignificance. We needed to get back on the original train. Akram took care of that.

"Oh, I almost forget. Your question. So what *is* question, Phil?"

"Remember, you don't have to answer it if it makes you embarrassed."

"Please, Phil, ask your question. I want to answer." Fine, no more pussyfooting.

"Okay, here it is. I was wondering if you would feel comfortable telling me why Azeeza has suddenly taken off her face covering, why she has decided to show her face to the world at this time."

"Oh," Akram laughed, "no problem. Sure I will tell reason for this to you, Phil." I admit I was relieved.

"Great! I'm all ears."

"All ears?"

"Oh, sorry." I told myself that I had to try harder to keep idioms from just popping out like burps, as they tend to do. If I didn't keep this little inquiry on track, I'd *never* get my answer. "'All ears' is an idiom. Remember idioms?"

"Yes, Phil, I remember meaning of 'idiom,' but I don't know *this* idiom, 'all ears.'"

"Oh, it means that I will be listening to you very carefully. That I'm going to give you *all* my attention."

"Oh, okay, that's good one, 'all ears.' I am really understanding now. I like that one."

"Yes, it *is* a good one. So. In fact, I *am* all ears."

"Okay. This is why Azeeza now show her face. You know, Phil, is unusual for woman cover face in United States."

"Yes, it *is* unusual. Very."

"Sometimes I get worry for Azeeza. I get afraid for her safety."

"Here? In Berkeley?"

"Yes, Berkeley, San Francisco, Hayward, Oakland. Everywhere in this country. Yes. Beeble get mean. Angry. Say bad things to Azeeza. On bus. On street. Very bad things."

"Like what?"

"Like when we on bus in Hayward, some man say to Azeeza, 'Hey you! You man or you woman? I cannot tell. Take off coat. Take off coat now! Show us face! You have bomb under your coat? Why you hiding from us? Go back to your country if you no show yourself to Americans! You suicide bomber going blow up bus? If you not blanning something, if you are not fucking terrorist, show us your face!'"

"Whoa, that's terrible, Akram. That must have been very scary. I'm sorry you went through that. But Hayward is kind of different from Berkeley. Aren't people in Berkeley more open-minded?"

"I thought so, but then we had bad experience in Berkeley too. On Telegraph Avenue. We was walking down street and some womans, maybe two or three womans, start shouting at Azeeza. Loud shouting. Crazy loud. Very very angry. Shouting something like 'You not free. You bondage. Men forcing you cover yourself, to be shame of yourself. Tear off your veil. Be proud woman. Don't let this *man* keep you in brison! (Here she point very angry at *me*! Her finger is like gun.) You are stopping brogress of all women in world! Break free!' Later, Azeeza explain me meaning of 'bondage' and 'brogress' and 'veil' and other words too. You know, Azeeza will go to university in Ohio before *I* will go. She going to be alone. All alone. I am afraid for her safety."

I could now see that poor Azeeza was getting it from the Right *and* the Left. It would, of course, be safest for any Saudi woman to be as inconspicuous as possible in post-9/11 America, to show she had nothing to hide, especially when what she was hiding was a lovely picture of innocence like Azeeza's face. It was 2008, seven years after the attack, but people all over this country, from New York to our city on the opposite coast, were still, to say the least, jittery in the presence of the unfamiliar, especially the Arabic unfamiliar. Fully concealed, Azeeza was virtually a walking symbol; her problem and what she and Akram hoped was its solution gave new depth to the idea that it's harder to insult a person to her face.

"I see. So you decided it was okay for Azeeza to uncover her face."

"It not so easy, Phil. This is very strong custom in my country, in my religion, in my family."

"Yes, I know. It must have been a very difficult decision for both of you."

"Yes, it *was* difficult. I didn't want me or Azeeza to sin against my religion, but, also, like I say, I was afraid for safety of Azeeza."

"So then what did you do?"

"So then I call my friend in Jeddah. Very close friend. Very *very* religious man. Very wise man. I think he will know right thing to do. And I am right. He say to me, 'Akram, here in Saudi, of course Azeeza must to wear niqab on face.' Niqab is Arabic word for the cloth that cover face, Phil." I nodded, and he went on. "Then my friend he say, 'Outside Saudi it is different, completely different. In other country where beeble doesn't understand Islam, especially America where beeble angry at Arabic beeble because 9/11, it can be dangerous for woman cover face. It make so many beeble nervous.'" I briefly interrupted to model the pronunciation of "p" and "people," and Akram imitated me, but I told him we'd work more on that later. I was determined to hear the rest of Akram's explanation before our time ran out. I motioned to him to continue. "So my friend he say 'So to be safety, Akram, to protect your wife, it is okay for Azeeza to go in street and to school in America without niqab on face. When she return here, of course, she must put it back on.' My friend he really help me, Phil." Then he reiterated that his friend back home truly *was* a pure and "very religious man," as if it were crucial that I didn't miss this point, as if it were essential to getting *my* endorsement too. As if he needed it.

"Uh huh. I understand. Thank you, Akram, for telling me all that. That's a really interesting story."

"You're welcome, Phil. You agree that it is good idea."

"Yes. Absolutely."

"And thank you too for having all the ears."

I laughed. "For *being* all ears."

He laughed at himself. "Aha, yes, right. Thank you, Phil, for *being* all ears."

"You're welcome, Akram."

The three of us did take some time to practice pronouncing the "p" and "b" sounds before the end of that class, the final one of the morning, and then Akram went off to meet his lovely young wife for lunch in the cafeteria.

The Inadvertent Collaboration of Alberto and Jürg

It's a pity that I've fallen out of touch with Alberto, a fun-loving artist from Buenos Aires, who attended the Oakland branch of our school in the late nineties. His wide almost-maniacal grin was infectious in the best way; whenever it spread across his broad thirtyish face, which was often, it made everyone in that classroom feel instantly tipsy.

I remember the day Alberto arrived on the Holy Names campus. It was a dank grey winter morning when even the folks who hadn't traveled to Oakland from super-hot places felt their bones getting chilled. Alberto stood out in the crowd of new students. His wild bush of blond curls gave him the look of a man having a perpetual brainstorm. A full shaggy beard framed the rest of his broad face. His eyes shone with a kind of tickled madness; apparently, something was hilarious, but only he was in on the joke.

There was something else that distinguished him: he was swathed in a thick wool sweater that looked like it could protect one not only against the icy air of a mid-winter Andean peak, but against all the depressing data of existence itself. It was more like a thick blanket with a zipper down its front than a conventional cardigan. Its design and colors seemed perfectly balanced to me. The background was a sober olive green expanse, like a plush field of ancient moss; about halfway up, a bit above the waist, was a horizontal broad band of deep brown, edged top and bottom with scalloped stripes of densest blue, the blue of the sky just before nightfall, or just before dawn. Dancing across that brown band were bright little orange diamonds which shone like tiny suns. Ringing round the chest and back and sitting atop the shoulders were zigzag bands and lines of burgundy, purple, red, and brilliant orange. The more I got to know my wild-eyed student, the more those bright zigzaggy lines seemed like his unique electroencephalogram, a mantle of singularity that he wore unselfconsciously. I'm not one who cares, or even thinks much, about clothing, but Alberto's sweater, against all my personal predilections and past history, fascinated me. Yet another minor mystery.

Alberto quickly became my favorite in-class playmate/student. There was no riff that was too ridiculous for him, or me, to join in on. He was a talented artist, kind of a meta-cartoonist, who was eager to illustrate vocabulary words on the board as they came up. He even drew a caricature of *me* once on a sheet of lined notebook paper: I was trapped in a cartoon jail, each hand gripping one of the vertical bars. My face was outsized, sweating, and my eyes were veined with red—bulging, deranged, desperate; one looked east, the other west. The caption was, simply, "My name is Phil. Help me. I'm crazy." It was delightfully loopy. I had to admit (only to myself) that it caught some of my real inner chaos, so it was as unsettling as it was diverting, like a lot of good art. It was the kind of elbow-in-the-ribs jesting that only good friends can get away with. (That drawing adorned a wall in the teachers' staff room until 2003, when ELS announced, momentously, somberly, that they were going to close their Oakland branch within the not-too-distant future; all the teachers were advised to salvage whatever we valued from the staff room before a final dumping would take place. I removed Alberto's Phil-the-jailed-nutcase picture from the wall a day or two later. I would have liked to include that drawing in this book, but, sadly, one of my co-workers, in a fit of over-zealous house cleaning, transferred Alberto's drawing from the cubby hole where I had stashed it for safekeeping—ha!—into the recycling bin. Gone forever.)

The session progressed through its four weeks. And, since the relatively wintry weather continued, Alberto wore his beautiful sweater to class on most days. In fact, like many of my students from hot countries, he'd bundle himself up even on days that seemed warm enough for tee shirts to most of us. Uncharacteristically, I continued to comment effusively and repeatedly about how great that sweater was, but often felt compelled to stress that I was rarely that zealous about articles of clothing, the implication being that I, a deeper creature, was above going gaga over garb. Weirdly, however, I just couldn't help myself, despite my reverse snobbism; it was as if that multi-colored blanket-with-arms had bewitched me.

That session reached the end of its four-week life, and I bade farewell to my students. As is also always the case, I knew I'd miss some of my students more than others, and Alberto topped that list. At the farewell party, Alberto and I had a heartfelt goodbye hug, and I figured that, following the usual pattern, I'd probably never hear from him again.

The weekend passed, and, on Monday morning, the first day of the new session, I was going through the usual bureaucratic routines when I was told that there was a package for me in the office. I went there immediately and found a large bundle sitting on the mail table, covering it completely. It was a lumpy looking thing, wrapped in plain brown paper: my name was scrawled on it in thick blue-markered letters. Just my first name. No return address. No postage.

I picked it up and found that it was both soft and heavy. Of course, I already knew what it was, just as you do. I laid it back on the table and ripped the paper off, liberating the woolly smell and all the colors of Alberto's sweater. There was no note, just that extraordinary garment, neatly folded and zipped up to the top. Picking it up again, my fingers sank into the thick aromatic wool; it was like cozying up to a sheep. It was such a heavy thing that it felt as if the sheep might still be in there. I unzipped it and read the label:

handspun and hand-made
by
MANOS DEL URUGUAY
100% PURE WOOL
made in Uruguay

This was way beyond a friend giving me the proverbial shirt off his back. It was more like his skin, his fur.

I'd like to think that I would have refused such an extravagant gift had Alberto proffered it to me in person. I imagine that he had had the same thought, so he didn't give me the chance, wily guy that he was. He'd gotten on a plane back to Argentina on Saturday, two days earlier. He was probably already there, perhaps shopping, hoping to snag another amazing sweater before the next cold night.

Years later, shortly after the start of this new century, when Jürg Lüthy entered my Oakland classroom one morning, my guess was that he was perhaps about forty-two years old, maybe forty-three, somewhere in that ballpark. I know now, from having recently looked at the bio on his website, that he was actually in his early fifties at that time. Maybe my miscalculation had something to do with how fit he looked. This thin neatly dressed Swiss fellow peered at the world through smallish round metal-rimmed glasses; he seemed to be analyzing, evaluating, but also savoring what he saw. Processing. Interpreting. Perhaps what made him seem younger was a sense of existential delight, a light in his eyes that seemed more like emanation than reflection.

When he gave his first-day introduction, he informed us that he was married, had two sons, and lived in Brugg, Switzerland, not far from Zurich. He also said that he was a classical pianist, a detail that immediately hooked the music lover in me. I'm afraid I gushed quite a bit. He looked pleased at how pleased *I* was to discover what he did for a living. We spoke for a few minutes about favorite composers and pieces before I reminded myself that there were fourteen other students in the class, reeled myself in, had the other people introduce themselves, and proceeded to the lesson of the day.

A few days later, Jürg approached my desk during a break and asked me if I had a couple of minutes to discuss something. I did.

"Maybe I have a gift for you," he said. *Maybe?* "I have a few copies of a CD that I recently recorded. I would like to give you one of them. As a present. A gift."

"Oh thank you, Jürg. That's great. As I told you, I love music. Thank you very much!"

"You're welcome, Phil. But I want to ask you to do something for me."

"Yes?"

"Listen to the music, and, if you like it, then please keep the CD. If you don't like it or if you feel, you know, just so-so about it, please give it back to me, okay? Please understand, I only took a few of these with me on this trip, so I only want to give it to people who actually like the music. I hope you understand."

I more than understood. I loved the way he was presenting this "gift" to me. That "maybe" now made perfect sense. In his meticulous fashion, he was seeking the same certainty that Alberto had surely possessed when he gave me that outrageous sweater, the certainty that the recipient of the gift truly adored it. Jürg's perfect logicality trumped any concern most others might have had about this unorthodox mode of gift-giving. It was an arrangement as neatly structured as a bar from a Bach partita. He, in his own way, cared as little for the petty details of social convention as my wild-eyed Latino benefactor had. Bravo!

"Yes, yes, of course. I completely agree. You shouldn't waste a single one."

"Great, Phil. I'm glad you understand."

Now satisfied that the terms of this tentative transfer were understood, he reached into his bag and pulled out a blue, yellow, and white CD case. On its cover was a composite photo of two facial profiles: the one on the left, Franz Schubert's, was partially superimposed upon the other, Jürg Lüthy's. Schubert's hair was profuse and curly, unlike Jürg's, which was shorter and straighter. The great composer's face looked chubby compared to

Jürg's quite lean one; they both gazed off toward the right through similar little round spectacles, both heads tilted slightly upward as if rapt by the same celestial attraction, perhaps the score of a Schubert sonata.

He handed the plastic square to me and I didn't have to feign enthusiasm when I saw that the music was Schubert's, the pieces two of my favorites, his piano sonatas in A Minor (D 845) and B flat (D 960). Schubert completed the latter just two months before his far-too-early death.

"Wow, Jürg, this is so great. I know these pieces very well. I love this music."

Jürg allowed himself to look, as the saying goes, "cautiously optimistic." He repeated the terms of our arrangement, confirming that I understood that the usual order of things was being reversed: the student was giving the teacher a test.

"So, Phil, I hope you enjoy this. And that you will keep it." The implication, of course, was that there was the possibility of its boomeranging back into Jürg's hand and bag.

"Oh, I'm sure I will, Jürg. Such great music. How could I not love it?" Of course, I couldn't be entirely sure. The potential for dissatisfaction certainly existed. I had never heard Jürg play; what if his performance of these difficult sonatas fell short technically, or if his interpretation somehow missed the spirit of Schubert's monumental pieces? But, even after knowing Jürg for only a few days, I was cautiously optimistic myself.

We shook hands in that efficient time-saving Swiss manner, one good tightly clenched pump. Jürg left the classroom for his next class. Holding the CD in my hand, I wanted my day of teaching to end, so I could go home, have dinner, and then, later that evening, drown myself in Schubert.

After washing the dinner dishes, I poured myself a little more wine and retired to the living room of my house in a semi-woodsy part of Orinda, just on the other side of the Berkeley hills, about halfway up one of them. After slipping Jürg's CD into my player, I sank into the couch at the other end of the room, wine glass in one hand, remote control in the other. From there, I faced a wide tri-sectioned window which was flanked by my ancient but still warm and precise speakers. It was not quite night outside, so I could still enjoy the view of other green hills, stretching north-to-south beneath the darkening blue of a cloudless sky.

I took a sip of the wine, set down the glass, and pressed the play button: from the first few contemplative oh-so-tender bars of the first movement, *Moderato*, of the A minor sonata, and through all the playfulness and thunder that followed, Jürg had me, as did, yet again, Franz. This was no close call, but a wholly faithful re-creation of a masterpiece. I knew Schubert better after listening to Jürg's performance. And, of course, I knew Jürg better too.

On the next morning, before the class had even begun, I rushed over to Jürg as he entered the room.

"Your Schubert is amazing. A revelation. I absolutely

loved it. You'll never see that disk again, Jürg. It has found its true home. Don't even *think* about taking it back." There was no way he could doubt that I meant every word. A smile spread across his face.

"That's great, Phil. Enjoy! Enjoy!"

Out shot his hand, and we had another vigorous Swiss hand pump.

As almost always happens with my students, at the end of the session, Jürg returned to his country and his family. We exchanged email addresses and said, sincerely, that it would be great to see each other again some day. The usual underlying thought is that the odds are ninety-nine to one against it ever happening. In this case, however, we actually beat those odds.

In the summer of 2002, Joan, my then fifteen-year-old son Ezra, and I took one of our several trips to Europe. Our plan was to spend two weeks in Italy, but we found an irresistible deal on a flight to Zurich, so we arranged to rent a car there before setting out for the Italian border. I emailed Jürg in advance and let him know we'd be in the vicinity of Brugg in early August on our way back to Zurich to return the car, and asked if it would be possible to get together. He promptly responded and enthusiastically told me that it was. He made a reservation for us at a very comfortable little hotel not far from his house and invited us to join his family for a barbecued dinner, Swiss-style, at their home. He signed the email "George." Of course, I accepted the invitation and looked forward to our reunion.

I don't remember the specifics of that meal with Jürg

and his friendly family, only that it was delicious and plentiful. His wife and two sons spoke English well, so, despite our almost non-existent Swiss German, the conversation at the dining room table was fluent, informative, interesting, and fun. Perhaps I don't remember that night's menu so well because of what happened *after* dinner.

After finishing our desserts, Jürg asked us if we'd like to join him upstairs, to see his studio . . . and, incidentally, be a little audience for a private concert. I can't remember a question ever sounding more rhetorical. I had, of course, been secretly hoping for that invitation all along.

We all ascended a small staircase which led to the wood-lined room in which Jürg's grand piano lived and reigned. We took our seats and faced the piano. Jürg got comfortable on his piano bench. I was no less awed than I'd been while gawking at the Alps in Dony and Cony's "backyard," and the same familiar thought revisited me: *this started in that Oakland classroom.* What other job has such fringe benefits?

And then he began to play. Each note filled that little space completely; within seconds I—once again—inhabited Schubert's universe, Jürg's universe. It was like a homecoming, a haven, after weeks of schlepping around Italy. This was yet another musical gift from Jürg—in fact, the grand finale of our trip. This time, he didn't have to ask if we had "liked" it; it was written across all of our faces as we applauded con brio after each piece.

It's December 2012 as I write this chapter in my Orinda home. It's been an unusually cold December for this area, with temperatures more common in places that have *real* winters, like New York, Wisconsin, or Switzerland. Sweater weather. On moderately cool nights, pretty much any sweater will do, but when things get really frigid, I reach for Alberto's Sweater *Grande*.

That's what I did a couple of nights ago after dinner. Joan had some work to do in the little office in the back of our house, and I decided to kick back with some Schubert and cognac in the cold living room. Rather than turn the heater on, I picked up that almost comically heavy garment, put it on, and zipped it up: I could still smell those Uruguayan sheep. I pulled Jürg's CD off the shelf, slipped it into my player, and cued it to Track 5, the first movement of the B Flat Sonata, Molto moderato. I poured some cognac into a snifter and sank into my couch. It was already dark outside. I took a sip, pressed "play," and closed my eyes.

Wrapped in Alberto's enormous sweater, I was already feeling warmer when the sacred procession of that movement's opening chords emerged from Jürg's piano and entered the room, filling it, filling me; I've rarely felt more at home in my own home. Thank you again, Alberto. Thank you again, Jürg. For having such good aim.

Duet for Cuatro and Desk

Writing and thinking about Jürg Lüthy brings to mind another music-making music-loving student, Jackeline (Jackie) Rago, from Venezuela. When Jackie first arrived in my Holy Names classroom in 1982, when she was about twenty, she appeared to have none of the first-day jitters that beset most new students. Under a profusion of black wavy hair, her eyes shone with fascinated intelligence as she took everything in: all this new stuff, all these new people. Like Jürg years later, Jackie gave me the impression that, as she sat in my classroom, she was analyzing, absorbing, interpreting, and relishing what life was now throwing her way. I somehow sensed the music in her before she told me she was a musician.

First-day introductions, despite their regularity and predictability, never got old for me. I never knew what new surprise might be lying in wait; after all, every one of these people was human. Jackie's classmates went through the routine questions and answers: name, birthplace, job, marital status, hobbies, professional plans, etc. In most cases, their plans were linked to making enough money (or more than enough, or *a lot* more than enough). Not that there's anything wrong with that, but . . .

Then it was Jackie's turn, so, like the others, she walked to the front of the room. After writing her name on the board and quickly taking care of the basic statistical information, she let us know the lovely fact that her "job," her "plan," and her "hobby" were identical: making music. Clearly, music-making was so much more than a way of earning a living; from the way she spoke, I could see that, for Jackie, music-making *was* living. Whatever revenue might come her way as a result of that joyful process was almost incidental. Gravy. Groovy.

"That's great, Jackie. What instrument do you play?"

With a little smile, she answered, "Maybe you never heard of my instrument. They don't play it much up here in North America. It's called a cuatro. It's like . . ."

I got so excited that I did something I usually try to avoid, on principle: I interrupted my student. "Cuatro! That's fantastic. I've listened to cuatros many times on *musica andina* records. And I've heard great Andean groups in Berkeley and San Francisco and Paris and Rome. In concert halls and clubs and on the streets. I *love* this music. And the cuatro is such an important part of it. And you play it!" I realized I was gushing again, so I cut myself off. "But excuse me for interrupting you. Please explain to your new classmates what a cuatro is. Maybe they don't know."

Jackie then proceeded to describe her instrument in a

manner that was part explication, part ode. A cuatro, she explained, was smaller than a guitar and had only four, hence "*cuatro*," strings. She told everyone how popular it was back home in Venezuela as well as in other Latin American countries. This was many years before most people could just whip out a smart-ass phone and display seventy-five photos of cuatros with a few taps of a finger.

She also played several percussion instruments, she added, *and* the mandolin. But the cuatro seemed to be her main axe. She spoke of it the way one might speak of one's lover, and not a one-night stand, but the love of one's life. I had no doubt that this new student, this music lover, was a musical soul mate. Despite the moral imperative for teachers to apportion our time and attention equally among our students, there were times when we (i.e., I) got carried away. In fact, there was something else I needed to know, so I pressed on with the interview.

"Hey, Jackie, did you bring your cuatro with you to California?"

Despite her wry smile, she looked shocked, incredulous that anyone would ask her that question. In fact, she laughed and said, "Phil, did you really just ask me if I brought my cuatro from Venezuela?"

"Yes, I did." I wasn't sure what was so astonishing about my question. Most students who said they played an instrument responded that, for traveling ease and convenience, they had left it back home, not just the obviously unportable ones like pianos, but smaller ones too.

"Phil, I would *never ever* leave my cuatro behind. And, besides, I'm planning to move here. To live here. To make music here. To share the music of my people with the people here. This is my dream." This was getting more and more interesting, less and less like the typical goals of my students.

"Jackie, that's a very beautiful dream." I already knew the answer to my next question, but, again, had to ask it: "Would you be willing to bring your cuatro to class sometime? To share your music with *us*? To play for us?"

There was no hesitation. "I can bring it tomorrow." She looked as excited as I felt. Usually, if a student played an instrument or was a singer, he or she would feel too self-conscious to perform in front of all these strangers until the third or fourth week of the session, and maybe not even then. Jackie looked as if she wished she already had her cuatro with her, so she could begin right then and there to do what she loved most. I thought of Daphanie, the Taiwanese harpist who was never shy about her music and always seized any opportunity to share it with me and her classmates.

"Great, great! Fantastic! I have a feeling that tomorrow will be a special day for this class." As her huge smile lit up the room, I could see that Jackie *knew* it would be.

On the next day, Jackie kept her promise. She had

her cuatro case with her and, after my ritual of taking roll, I looked over at her, smiled, and said, "Are you ready?" She laughed as if the question were a meaningless one, since, clearly, she was just about *always* ready. I asked the other students if *they* were ready too, and they laughed too. Then they clapped *before* the performance.

Jackie carefully took her instrument out of its case, like a mother tenderly lifting her baby from its cradle, and, it *did* look like a diminutive guitar, about the size of a ukulele or mandolin.

After taking a few seconds to tune her strings, Jackie began to play. And there it was, the music, full-blooded and fully formed: instant groove. That little instrument sang out, its pulse making it difficult to stay seated. Feet were swiveling and tapping under the little seat-desks, heads were bobbing, and everyone was smiling. English lesson? *What* English lesson?

My own fingers were tapping on the top of my large oak desk—quietly, at first. The groove of Jackie's music was irresistible, fully welcoming, wide and deep enough for all who'd enter. My tapping got a little louder, but still just loud enough for me, and maybe only the few students sitting near me, to hear. As a bongo drummer for most of my life, I had no plans to abort that crescendo until it was at the right decibel level, neither too high nor too low. The goal when a musician is "sitting in" is for one's sounds to contribute to the music, not intrude, to support, not dominate—to feed and be fed by the music at the same time. You know when that's *not* happening, and you know when it is. Jackie looked up from her cuatro as she heard my drumming and, nodding, flashed her wall-to-wall smile at me: it said, "Welcome! Join me!" It's, of course, what I'd been secretly hoping for from the moment she'd accepted my invitation to play. I hadn't presumed to bring my bongos to class, but I *did* have that desk. Unleashed and happy now, I *did* join her for the first of several duets that session. What a liberation it always is to make music with a kindred spirit.

Ridiculous as it may seem, I knew the tonal qualities of that desk very well. It was like an enormous version of the Latin American wood-box percussion instrument, the cajón, which the drummer sits on while playing. Later, after Jackie had left our school, I discovered that she plays that one expertly too.

During breaks, alone in my classroom, I would often play little riffs on that desk, exploring the tonal possibilities of its various parts as they responded to fingers, palms, palm-heels, nails, and knuckles: the resonant bass of the top's center, the more treble, snappy sound at its edges, and the innumerable gradations of timbre from center to edge. Then there was the almost tympanic boom of its sidewalls, to be used sparingly. Sometimes I'd put on a little solo performance for one class or another on that instrument formerly known as a desk. But playing *with* someone, especially with someone as skillful and soulful as Jackie, made communion possible, and that was the greatest kick of all. Sometimes she'd break into song, which would take the music even higher.

Jackie brought that same intense concentration to studying English. If she didn't understand something perfectly, she was never shy about asking me to clarify the point in question. As I did that, I could feel her concentration, her focus. Then, when she got it, she would always respond with a wonderfully musical sound which slowly and smoothly rose in pitch for at least an octave, a tone that sounded more interrogative than conclusive: "Aaaaaaaaaaaaahhhhhhhhh?" It was as if she were saying, "Is this clarity really as amazing as it seems? How could I not have seen this before?" Whenever I heard that rising tone, I knew that that portion of my teaching mission, at least as far as Jackie was concerned, had been accomplished. It was yet another groove we inhabited together; only the genre was different. And when you come right down to it, groove is more important than genre every time.

I didn't remember ever hearing anyone else express comprehension in that particular way, but I knew I had heard that tone before; I couldn't, however, remember where or when.

On the following Saturday night, I took a BART train to San Francisco to attend a concert. Entering the train at the North Berkeley station, I chose a seat, plopped down, and opened whatever book I'd brought to accompany me on that short trip. I had just started reading it when the driver (engineer? conductor?) distracted me with his P.A. announcement: "The doors are closing. Please stand clear of the closing doors." Technically, that announcement was just a tad premature; the doors hadn't yet begun to close, and wouldn't until a tone sounded, an electronic tone that gradually rose in pitch for at least an octave: "Aaaaaaaaaaaaahhhhhhhhh?" It was like a question from the doors themselves: *Are you fool enough to mess with us?* But, of course, for me, it was something more too. I suddenly knew why Jackie's glissando had rung a bell (or perhaps I should say "generated a tone") when I'd first heard it. I had heard that door-closing warning tone countless times before in years of BART riding, and though I'd always found its tinge of inquiry oddly pleasing, even comforting, its meaning was always purely pragmatic, protective. It was no wonder that I couldn't make the connection immediately when I'd first heard Jackie intone it. What were the odds that a train's safety signal and the sound of a young Venezuelan woman comprehending a point of English would be the same? I laughed a bit too loudly for a sane person, and several of my fellow passengers turned their heads in my direction to check me out; I did my best to look mild-mannered, a *harmless* lunatic, not the type of wacko who threatened anyone's safety. (Today, most of my fellow passengers would probably be under headphones and would never even notice a chuckle coming from a lone man in the "real world.") I didn't really care: this was too rich, too astoundingly loco. It was as if Jackie were right there, singing into the conductor's microphone. It was exactly the same key, the same rise, the same music.

At each station, the same sound was repeated, and, every time, the Jackie-link upstaged BART's intended message. I was eager to share this discovery with her as soon as we returned to class on Monday.

Jackie laughed when I reported my BART revelation but said that, during a couple of BART trips, she hadn't noticed that she and the train sang the same song. Of course, being new to the area, she hadn't taken that many rides yet. She assured me that she would listen carefully the next time she took BART, and several other students, intrigued and probably more than a bit skeptical, said that they would be listening for Jackie on the train's speakers too.

The next time Jackie entered a BART car, she told me, she took her seat and waited attentively for the pre-door-closing announcement and the tone that would follow it. She didn't have to wait long: "The doors are closing. Please stand clear of the closing doors. Aaaaaaaaaaaaahhhhhhhhh?" There it was, that unmistakable glissando of the Venezuelan "aha experience." Now she could hear with her own ears that her teacher had not been exaggerating: it was as if someone had notated her one-word song and transcribed it electronically. It's easy to imagine her sitting there, smiling, with this new understanding dawning on her, and responding (how else?): Aaaaaaaaaaaaaahhhhhhhhh?

In subsequent years, I had several other Venezuelan students who, in fact, expressed the dawning of comprehension in that same way, so I realized it was a Venezuelan trait, not one unique to Jackie, but, truly, hers was, hands down, the sweetest, most musical version of them all.

Coda

To say that Jackie has realized her dream would be an understatement. Like Moe, Kourosh, and Naveed, but for very different reasons, she was in the small minority of my students who chose to put down roots in this country. Not surprisingly, she has become an important part of the Bay Area music world, doing exactly what she set out to do: inspiring audience after audience as a soulful ambassador of her country's music—as well as playing music that can't be easily categorized. (Check out her website: http://www.jackelinerago.com).

Joan and I have several of her CDs and have been to many of her concerts over the years. Listening to that music always brings me back to the month that I first met her, as student, musician, and person . . . and to those joyous classroom jams. The right place at the right time? Oh yes.

She's been a valuable member of various groups, and

whatever the genre, mixed genre, non-genre, or instrumentation, that oh-so-solid groove is always there, as dependable as a sunrise, and as bright. More than once, as Jackie and I have chatted after a gig, she'd bring up the funny revelation of her special kinship, nay *twin*ship, with that BART glissando, and it's never failed to make us laugh.

For years, during countless BART excursions, the train's rising tone consistently evoked Jackie and her music; it was comforting, like having an old friend along for the ride. Then, suddenly, a few years ago, some heartless soul on the BART board decided to eliminate it, making each train ride feel a bit colder, less personal: the "distant past" had suddenly become more distant. Much of the time, what one now hears is just that computerized safety warning, a poor imitation of a woman's voice, the intonation all wrong, delivering what now comes off (to *my* ears) as a darkish, somewhat heavy-handed metaphor: "The doors are closing . . ."

Indeed.

But, of course, Jackie's music, filling a club or concert hall, or soaring out of my car's speakers, is *sufficiente* to pry those doors back open. At least for a while.

Roll Over, Beethoven

On a rainy night in the seventies, I was sitting with Joan in one of my favorite restaurants, Warszawa, a Polish place in Berkeley's "Gourmet Ghetto," with perfect pierogi, tranquil eastern European decor, friendly unpretentious waiters, and classical piano music floating out of well-placed speakers. Most of the time, that music was by Chopin, apropos of his Polish origin, but, at one point that evening, the music that came on and filled the place was Beethoven's *Für Elise*. In addition to the mix of longing and fulfillment that Beethoven's melancholy bagatelle had always inspired in me, there was something new for me in the music that night, an image so clear I could almost smell it: Taiwanese garbage. Not the most appetizing association to have in a Polish (or any) restaurant.

I can explain.

In ESL conversation classes, one is always hunting for new topics to talk about, just to practice the language. Sometimes, organically, as we chatter on about whatever, we land on subjects which seem to have virtually no potential—like the day in Oakland when the topic segued into, most unpromisingly,

"What's the garbage collection system in your country?" That was really scraping the bottom of the barrel, or, in this case, the garbage can.

The subject arose after I'd mentioned to them that, in Berkeley, once a week, we always rolled our cans to the curb on the night before the morning of the garbage pickup. Yawn. "Is it similar in your countries?" I asked, not optimistic about receiving any memorable answers. As expected, most of the responses were rather boring reports of the modes and schedules of transferring refuse from households to garbage trucks. However, when Andy Chen, from Taipei, spoke, I had to ask him to repeat his account, just to be sure that I had understood him correctly.

"In Taiwan, when garbage trucks come to our street, we hear music that go like this . . . " At that point, he scatted the opening notes of *Für Elise*.

"Dada dada dada dada daaaah,
Da dada daaaah,
da dada daaaah . . ."

Andy went on, quite in key, for a few more bars before I interrupted him.

"That's Beethoven!" I exclaimed. *"Für Elise!"*

"Yes, that right. Is Beethoven. Yes."

"The garbage trucks play Beethoven? Really?"

"Yes, that right. Yes. Dada dada . . ."

"Okay," I cut in again. "And then?"

"When we hear music, we take bags outside and throw garbage in truck. Sometime, if we wait too long, we must to run because maybe truck no wait long time."

"So when you hear Beethoven's beautiful music, you go outside with your garbage."

"Well usually my mom, she do it. Truck usually come when my sister and me we in school and my father he usually working. So my mom take bags and walk, sometime run, to truck."

"Wow, I don't think Ludwig would be too happy having his music associated with garbage," I couldn't help saying, kind of thinking aloud.

"Ludwig is Beethoven?"

"Yes, that's his first name."

"But he dead for long time, right?"

"Yes, that's right."

"So it no bother him."

"True, but what I meant was that *if* he knew, it would probably bother him."

"But why?"

"Well, in the early nineteenth century—that's the eighteen hundreds—he dedicated this very romantic piece of music to a woman he was in love with. Her name was Thérèse Malfatti, who, like too many others, rejected poor Ludwig's proposal of marriage. *Für Elise* means "For Elise," but musicologists, people who study music and musicians, are pretty sure that the person who discovered this piece of music many years after Beethoven's death, made a mistake: they think it should have been titled *Für Thérèse*. Anyway, as you can see, for the composer, this music is tied up with the deepest of human feelings, with love. Not with garbage collection."

"Yes, I see that. But Beethoven dead and, what's her name . . ."

"Thérèse?"

"Yes, Thérèse. She dead too. And, love is just feeling. It die too. But we always have garbage."

"I guess you have a point, Andy."

Over the years, I have spoken to quite a few other Taiwanese students about those garbage trucks playing *Für Elise*, and most of them confirmed the truth of it, so, clearly, these curious vehicles are not in the same category as Susie's magical lampshade or Fernanda's green rabbit. Checking it out further, I learned that most Taiwanese people who have cared enough to look into the phenomenon, believe the following, possibly apocryphal, story about how this unlikely conjoining came to be: During the early eighties, Hsu Tse-chiu, a former director of the Department of Health, was asked by a mayoral committee to come up with some music to blare out of its garbage trucks to spur the populace to come running. One day, his daughter, a young piano student, was practicing Beethoven's world-famous piece. Because of both its irresistible appeal and its near universal recognizability, Hsu chose his "garbage music" right then and there. Of course, now, as I write this in 2012, it's easy to see and hear several clips of these musical trucks generating their electronic-beep renditions of the classic melody (as well as a few less famous tunes) on the internet.

As we sat in Warszawa, listening to the original *piano* version of Beethoven's piece, it's not as if I actually expected that cozy refuge to be invaded by a horde of Taiwanese families wielding garbage bags, but I know I'll never be able to hear that piece again without envisioning those melodious (and probably malodorous) garbage trucks. Such is the nature of memory: we are its mere vessels, at its mercy.

Note to foodies: if I've stirred your interest, and your taste buds, by mentioning Warszawa, I have to let you know that you can't just rush off to Berkeley for a hearty Polish meal anymore. Sadly, for me and certainly many others, that restaurant closed in 1979. At the time, I thought it was gone forever, but I recently discovered, by googling it, that it had simply moved to Santa Monica, alas hundreds of miles away in southern California, where, at least according to their website, it's the most popular place to eat excellent Polish food in that area (how many Polish restaurants can there be?). I expect they still play *Für Elise* from time to time, but, even if they don't, one can still hear it in a thousand other places, even on the streets of Taiwan.

Unthinkable

1

Ezra and I stepped out of our Orinda house into the late-summer morning: sunny, cool, clear, what's sometimes called "classic Bay Area weather," the kind of day that reminds me of one of the reasons I moved from New York to California in the first place. We were going through the paces of our weekday routine: on most mornings, we would get into my Volvo, roll down our steep driveway, and proceed to Miramonte High School, where I'd drop Ez off. I would then continue alone on woodsy back roads toward the hill in Oakland on which sat Holy Names College and the various classrooms where I'd be spending another day.

Typically, it took about fifteen or twenty minutes to get from our house to Ezra's school. That little stretch of morning with my son was perhaps my favorite part of each day; Ez and I could chat, listen to a CD or the radio, or just enjoy the simple fact of being together. At about eight o'clock on this particular morning, as we turned right onto Camino Pablo, the tree-lined road we would take to the high school, I turned the radio on and tuned in to KQED, San Francisco's NPR station;

the announcer's voice was reporting a story that was so outlandish, so implausible, that I suspected it was a dramatization, a fantasy, an imaginatively delivered con like the famous Orson Welles radio adaptation of H.G. Wells' "War of the Worlds," which had freaked out so many of its listeners, who were convinced that Earth was being attacked by Martians. That was in 1938. This was 2001. September 11, 2001.

After a few seconds of listening to the familiar voice of the NPR commentator (I don't remember which one), we realized that this was *not* radio theater. All the reportage was in the present tense, so it seemed to be about events that were happening in New York right then, unfolding as we rolled safely through slow-moving traffic three thousand miles away. Of course, because of the three-hour time difference, we were actually listening to a re-broadcast of what had already, horrifically, become a fait accompli much earlier. When I had turned the radio on, the report was in medias res, right before the South Tower, the second tower, was hit. I pulled over to the side of the road and called Joan to tell her to turn the radio on (we had no TV reception in our house). She had already done that. Neither of us could find many words to say, so we hung up in order to continue listening to that report which couldn't possibly be real, but was.

We re-entered the stream of cars and, of course, continued listening to the radio, to the horror of what had happened and was still happening. As with Joan,

Ez and I could find little to say to each other. Mostly, we'd just shake our heads incredulously and repeat phrases over and over, like, "This can't be real. This is unbelievable. What the . . ." We sounded like shock victims, which, in fact, along with millions of others around the world, was exactly what we were.

When we arrived at his school's parking lot, I gave Ezra a stronger-than-usual hug before he got out of the car. I watched him walk away into the swarming crowds of students, toward the school buildings; he turned a corner and disappeared.

Listening to the ongoing radio accounts, which had now switched to live reportage, I drove through the neighboring town of Moraga and then through the unincorporated, and seemingly unpeopled, gold and green expanses that eventually wind up in the forested hills of Oakland. Oak-land. A canyon plunged steeply to the left of that road. A few small cumulus clouds, their whiteness stark against a dense blue sky, floated high above the tops of the hills on the other side of that canyon. Even on a "normal" day, even on a day when that distant city was not under massive and deadly attack, this nameless place was the antithesis of New York's congestion, busyness, noise, pollution, madness, and concrete. On most days, as a transplanted New Yorker, I enjoyed this contrast, marveled at it; on this surreal day, the polarity was wider than my mind could contain. This was not going to be a typical working day.

Rolling into a spot in the Holy Names parking lot, I

couldn't stop thinking about my family and friends in New York, some of whom worked or lived near what would quickly be dubbed "Ground Zero." Teachers, like actors, routinely have to push thoughts and concerns of the "outside world" out of their heads in order to be fully invested in the created world of the classroom or theater. I was certain that, on this day, I would be incapable of pulling that off.

I walked extra slowly toward the building that housed the teachers' staff room and tried calling several people in New York to somehow set my mind at relative ease by learning of this one or that one's safety. Repeatedly, I got the same phone-company recorded message that all circuits were busy. Of course they were: the whole world was calling New York.

When I got to the staff room, my colleagues were, of course, buzzing with talk of what had eclipsed their lesson plans along with everything else. The school's director informed us that we'd been instructed by the company brass to assure our students that they were safe, go on with our lessons, and not dwell on events that were, after all, on the other side of the continent. Administrators are expected to, well, administrate, to say something, anything, even when feeling speechless, to direct others even when feeling lost, to somehow maintain control, or the semblance of it. I could empathize with the motives behind their directive and, at the same time, I was sure that neither I nor my students would be capable of putting this ongoing catastrophe on a back burner. We teachers looked at each other, and I knew by their faces, grunts, head-shaking, and sardonic laughs that we all (probably the director as well) were having the same thought: *Are they kidding? Not* dwell *on this with our students? Just go on with our lessons? The show must go on? Not this time. Not this show.*

As we all met with our classes, we spoke about little else than the events in my besieged hometown. I rolled a TV into the classroom and sat before it with my students, surrendering fully to what refused to be anything but the center of all our attention. At every break, I'd try calling New York again, but, each time, came up against the same recorded announcement: "All circuits are busy. Please try your call again later." There was more information pouring out of that television than any of us could process, but I could learn nothing about the fate of anyone I knew. I wouldn't find out that all my relatives were okay until later that evening when I spoke to my sister Anita, who lives on Long Island.

The press had initially reported that there were eighteen men who had hijacked those four commercial planes and used them as missiles in their coordinated suicide attacks: two against the World Trade Center towers, one against the Pentagon, and the other never reaching its target, winding up in that Pennsylvania field. Of those eighteen men, fifteen were from Saudi Arabia, two from the United Arab Emirates, and one from Egypt. I couldn't help but think about all the Arabic students I had had over the years, many of whom had been in the States with the goal of studying aviation.

On September 14, my birthday, three days after the attacks, a nineteenth name appeared on the list for the first time: Mosear Caned, not a typical Arabic name. But later that day, mysteriously, it was replaced by the name Hani Hanjour, whose photo was added to the press's eerie gallery of the faces of his fellow hijackers. He looked somewhat familiar, but, after teaching so many Arabic students over the years, why wouldn't he?

It wasn't until that evening, when I heard from my colleague Robin, that an astounding connection was made. She was, she told me, in the midst of contacting all the teachers and staff members at the school to jog our memories, so we'd know what she already knew. Well, actually, she didn't call *all* of us, just those who had been at the school for five or more years, those of us who might remember a Saudi student who had studied with us for two or three months during the spring of 1996: his name was Hani Hanjour.

That was shortly before he attended an aviation school in Oakland, where he spent one day before dropping out; he then attended a second flying school in Scottsdale, Arizona, where, after receiving low marks for three months, he again dropped out and returned to Saudi Arabia. In 2000, he sent in another registration fee to our school and obtained an F-1 (student) visa in Jeddah, Saudi Arabia. This time, however, he never showed up for classes.

As I've noted, ESL teachers rarely learn anything about the futures of their students after they leave us. This was a glaring exception, another part of the developing horror story that simply could not have happened but did: Hani Hanjour was the "pilot" of American Airlines Flight 77, the plane that flew into the Pentagon on that kamikaze mission. Our student Hani was dead, had *chosen* to die. And to kill. All sixty-four people on that flight and one-hundred-and-twenty-five others in the Pentagon had perished.

I pulled out my *San Francisco Chronicle* and turned again to the page with the photos of the hijackers. Examining Hani's face more carefully, I thought I remembered that quiet student moving through the halls of Holy Names College or sitting in the language lab practicing his English. He may have even been in one or two of my classes, though, unsettlingly, I wasn't and still am not sure about that. This fuzziness is perhaps due to more than just the faultiness of my memory and the passage of time; by all accounts, Hani Hanjour was not a man who stood out from the crowd. In an Associated Press article, "How Hijackers Led U.S. Lives," published a few days later, on September 20, David Crary wrote:

> Susan Khalil of Miramar, Fla. remembers one of the suspected hijackers, identified as Hani Hanjour, from back in 1996, when he stayed

> with her family for a month before going to flight school in California . . ."Of all my husband's colorful friends, he was probably the most nondescript," she said. "He would blend into the wall."

In that photo in the *Chronicle*, Hanjour, although only twenty-nine at most, had a dramatically receding hairline; his short curly hair formed an almost perfectly oval frame as it connected to a trim beard that just covered his jaw lines and the tip of his chin. Inside that oval were long thin eyebrows mimicked by a wide mustache with a gap at its center. His large sleepy-looking eyes made him seem almost serene. By imagining that face five years younger, maybe with a little more hair on top, my memory of that young man as student, rather than as suicide attacker, seemed to sharpen. Maybe that's just a trick of the mind, maybe not; even today my thoughts and images of Hani Hanjour refuse to stay put: everything about him keeps shifting, morphing, going in and out of focus.

Yes, it had always been a given that anything could be true of *any* of our students, but Hani Hanjour's link to 9/11 had redefined my concept of "anything." It's easy to picture Hani on the first day of a session, standing in front of the classroom, introducing himself to his new classmates and teacher, telling them about his family life back home. Reportedly, in the five-year period leading up to his 1996 arrival in the U.S., he had been managing his father's lemon-and-date farm in

Ta'if, Saudi Arabia, not far from Mecca. Lemons and dates. Such pleasant images to add to the expanding global montage of an ESL teacher: sunny landscapes of fields lined with date palms and lemon trees, our student quietly breathing in the thick hot-fruit air. But. Fast-forward five years, and see that same student in the cockpit of the plane he was "flying" toward the west side of the Pentagon, and there's no place in that montage to put this new picture. In fact, at least for a while, the montage is nowhere to be seen.

2

> History, Stephen said, is a nightmare
> from which I'm trying to awake.
> James Joyce, *Ulysses*

After the news of Hani Hanjour's involvement with 9/11 broke, our school was all over the news. Not long after, we were visited by FBI investigators eager to see if any of us had information that might link our former student to terrorists who might still be walking—and plotting—among us. Of course, they had to check every possible angle, but it seemed sadly clear to everyone at the school that all this bustling about was tragically late, and, as far as prevention of future attacks was concerned, almost certainly futile.

Incredibly, the larger political context in which these investigations took place was actually getting weirder:

only a few days after 9/11, George W. Bush and his cohorts had already begun pointing fingers at Iraq, attempting to link Saddam Hussein's regime to the devastation back east, positing since-disproved collaborations between Iraq and Al-Qaeda. Since none of the hijackers on those four planes were *from* Iraq, those allegations had the off-key ring of non sequitur, of shoddily constructed propaganda. Bush also implied that Iraq presented a potential terrorist threat to other targets on U.S. soil. I tended to trust his assertions about as far as I could throw Dick Cheney, yet a weird and troubling coincidence involving one of my students prevented me from summarily flushing those domestic-threat remarks from my mind. Thinking about that time is like remembering a bad dream; it still makes me squirm.

Although I had taught thousands of international students over a stretch of about twenty-seven years, I had never had any students from Iraq, not one . . . until that session. An Iraqi man in his forties, slightly portly, serious-looking in thick black-framed glasses, was one of the students in my 107 grammar class. This guy's showing up just as those logic-deficient Iraq-as-suspect statements were being aired by the Bush White House was an unsettling coincidence, but, without a doubt, I told myself, *just* a coincidence. It would change nothing in the simple game plan I used for relating to *all* my students: appreciate each person as a unique individual and enjoy the alchemy of nationality taking a back seat to humanity; any perceived cultural or political barriers tended to crumble as our knowledge of each other grew and our personal/pedagogical relationship developed and deepened. But there was a fundamental problem with that approach in this case: the more I learned about this guy, the more I got the creeps. It started on the first day of classes.

As was typical for the first class of each session, I asked the students to answer a few basic questions about their lives. When this soft-spoken Iraqi man came to the routine query about his occupation, he told us that he was a chemical engineer. Hmm. Well, okay, no problem. Probably.

Just keeping the conversational ball rolling, I responded with "Uh huh, that's an important profession. And what company do you work for in Iraq?"

"Actually, I don't work for company. I work for government. For my president."

"Oh, I see. And what kind of work do you do for your president?"

"You know what is R and D? Research and development?" He seemed a bit uptight; as I've said, nervousness on the first day was a normal condition for many students, but his dead-serious version of it was making *me* uptight too.

"Yes, I do. I do know R and D. That must be interesting. And what are you researching and developing?" I realized that I wasn't quite hitting the relaxed notes I was aiming for.

His face got even grimmer, all business, as he shot me a look which said, *please stop asking questions about this subject, Teacher. Please stop right now.* Then he spelled it out for me:

"I can't tell you my R and D. My government work is secret. I am not permitted telling that."

"You're saying it's classified?"

"I don't know what means 'classified,' but it is secret. Completely secret."

"That's what 'classified' means. 'Secret.' In other situations, in other contexts, it has other meanings, but in this context, yes, it means 'secret.'" My impromptu vocabulary mini-lesson had done nothing to ease the pressure, which, I assumed, everyone in that room was feeling by then.

"Okay. I understand, Teacher. 'Classified' mean 'secret.' So, yes, my work for my president is classified. I cannot tell nobody about it. I cannot tell *you.*" That "*you*" was strained and a bit too loud, and he then looked almost peeved as he glared at me, his silent imploration like a shout: *All right, Teacher, that's enough! Now that we both know what 'classified' means, and that my work* is *classified, can we just drop this subject? Now?*

Why couldn't he just be a chef, so we could pleasantly discuss some fine points of Middle Eastern cuisine? We were about a thousand miles from the relaxed amiable tone I liked to hit at the beginning of each session. Clearly, my scalpel had hit a nerve: it *was* time to stop pushing this line of inquiry. For everyone's sake. We moved on to chatting about inconsequential subjects: his family, hobbies, etc. But the combination of his profession, his boss, and his grave secrecy had unnerved me and, I guessed, everyone else too. If his work were innocent and safe, why couldn't he talk about it?

Yes, I know, some projects might be "classified" for innocent enough reasons, economic safeguards for example, but my mind, heedless of my will, jumped to thoughts of "Chemical Ali," Saddam's cousin and cohort, Ali Hassan al-Majid, the man who had given the orders that led to the genocide of thousands of Kurdish civilians in northern Iraq in 1987, whole villages at a time. Many men, women, and children had been slaughtered by summary execution. Majid was also called "the butcher of Kurdistan," but he earned his primary nickname through his extensive use of chemical weapons like mustard gas, sarin, and tabun. Chemical Ali was neither a chemist nor a chemical engineer, so to whom did he turn for expertise in designing, producing, and implementing those weapons? Who was doing the R and D?

I tried to rein in these grim associations, but, during the next few days, the engineer made it increasingly difficult for me to do so. During class discussions, he casually dropped comments about Saddam, little gushes of adoration for his employer, a man whom the whole world knew as dictator, torturer, and mass murderer. My usual modes of banter deserted me at those times, and the tongues of the other students seemed similarly tied. What snappy rejoinder would be appropriate? *Ah well, to each his own?* The fact that he never smiled didn't help. Not that smiling proves anything. I didn't trust myself to stay cool when he casually delivered those paeans, and none of his classmates seemed inclined or equipped to deal with that either, so I would just nod, mumble something, and steer us toward something more comfortable.

But I just couldn't get this guy out of my head: his stone cold demeanor and the creepy parts of his bio haunted me. I still thought it highly improbable that he might be part of a new terrorist plot against American civilians, but, after the incredible horror of 9/11 and the revelations about Hani Hanjour's connection to it, the realm of what was possible seemed frighteningly expanded. It didn't seem farfetched to imagine Saddam Hussein thinking (in Arabic, of course): *Well, Bush is already accusing us in front of the whole world of complicity in the 9/11 invasion. He already sees us as an enemy, so what do we have to lose by acting like one? On his soil. In his cities. If Al-Qaeda can do what* they *did in the U.S., we can do it too. And better! Chemicals are so much tidier than jumbo jets, and, against our chemical weapons, Americans will be as defenseless as Kurds.* If Saddam and Chemical Ali could use chemical weapons on civilians in Iraq, on their own people, why not on us?

I would go to bed at night and, instead of finding an easy sleep there, I'd imagine future post-disaster newspaper articles, accounts of chemical mass murder in American cities, photos of streets strewn with corpses. Of course, in every report, the technical mastermind behind those atrocities was my Iraqi chemical engineer. Outraged statements of journalists filled front pages and boomed from TV newscasts in my dreams and half-dreams: *How is it that nobody at that Oakland school noticed this guy? And if someone did, how the hell could he have remained silent? There were FBI agents on that campus at the same time that he was attending their classes, and nobody thought they'd be interested? From what we now know about him, it's clear that he was not shy about openly declaring his love for Saddam. And he was a chemistry expert. Chemistry for God's sake! Had no one ever heard of Chemical Ali? My God, this chemical engineer was at the same school that Hani Hanjour had gone to. You'd think those teachers would learn* something *from experience. At least* one *of them . . .*

It was true: those FBI guys *were* still sniffing around at the school. But I was not about to go to "The Man" simply because an extremely remote possibility, a near *im*possibility, was giving me no peace, simply because I needed to get a better night's sleep. Besides, I was not the sort of man who *went* to "The Man" anyway; I was no rat. But, I reasoned (rationalized?), if someone had tipped off the FBI that they ought to check out Hani

Hanjour, and if the FBI *had* checked him out, and if that *had* played a part in thwarting the 9/11 attacks, saving thousands of lives, would anyone (other than Al-Qaeda members and sympathizers) have considered that tipster a "rat"?

If, if, if . . .

I weighed and weighed the pluses and minuses of talking to those agents, whoever they were, and finally landed on this: if I didn't tell them my thoughts, and if my highly improbable nightmare scenario actually came to pass, how would I live with myself?

If, if, if . . .

Only one thing seemed to matter in the wake of Hani Hanjour, on a campus and in a world where "feasible" had been radically redefined: if there was *any*thing one could do that seemed to have even the slightest chance of saving lives, one had to do it. Everything boiled down to keeping the body count as close to zero as possible.

In general, I tended to steer clear of politics, but the prospect of talking to those FBI agents seemed neither right-wing nor left-wing. It felt thoroughly apolitical (or perhaps *meta*-political), a visceral reaction to a minute but stark possibility. It was probability theory, not conspiracy theory, which held me in its grip—unless you count the conspiracy of circumstances I sensed piling up around me: *Why now? Why here? Why me?* I still didn't buy Bush's allegations, but that was hardly relevant. If, against all perceived odds, speaking to those FBI guys actually prevented something awful, how good that would be, and if it turned out to be futile, a spinning of wheels, well, so be it. If I wound up feeling and looking like a gullible fool, well, so be that too.

If, if, if . . .

I'd approach the whole subject, I'd decided, like a doctor who ran tests on a patient to "rule out" a suspected disease. It seemed like the only way to get free of it. So, in a world in which so much was suddenly changed, I hardly recognized myself as I made the call.

I arranged to get together with them in one of the school's administrative offices during the second half of my lunch hour. I got there first, closed the door, and, while waiting for them to arrive, I still had conflicting thoughts. *What the hell was I doing here? Was this even me doing it? Why hadn't I just ignored the whole thing?* Then there was a quiet knock at the door. Ridiculously, my body jerked in the chair, and I could feel and hear my heart pounding hard in my chest, in my head.

"Come in," I said, as they were already *com*ing in. Weirdly, they were the only part of all this craziness which *didn't* feel unfamiliar. These human Twin Towers looked like stereotypes of FBI men, straight from Central Casting: wide shoulders in gray suits, slim subdued ties, marine crew cuts, one blond, one brown. It was as if they had aimed at duplicating Hollywood's stock image. They were even wearing regulation G-man shades since they had just returned from lunch on that sunny Oakland day; I had a measure of relief when they took those off and showed me that they had eyes, which made me hopeful that they also had souls, an idea which the ensuing discussion didn't do a lot to confirm.

I rose to greet them. We shook hands, and they handed me their business cards, each embossed with a shiny gold FBI emblem. Unnecessarily, I swept my arm toward the two chairs on the opposite side of the desk, an invitation. After we all took our seats, I had the unsettling feeling that they were still standing.

They began with some small talk about where they'd gone for lunch, and how the food was, and how nice the weather was in the Bay Area, a textbook approach designed to put me at ease, which, in *my* case, wasn't working so well.

Then we got down to the actual business. The blond guy pulled a little spiral pad and ball point pen from the inside pocket of his suit jacket and asked me to spell my name and the name of my Iraqi student. I did so, and he jotted them down. I then went into why I felt compelled to speak with them, emphasizing the medical-ruling-out approach I'd used to coax myself into this uncomfortable spot; I let them know I hoped they *could* eliminate him as a suspect just by researching whatever sources were available to them, without inconveniencing or worrying him—in other words, without his ever finding out that this investigation had ever occurred.

As I went through the few but troubling details, I

kept expecting the blond agent to continue entering notes in his pad, but he and his partner just nodded and mumbled mostly nonverbal indications that they'd heard and understood me. I also expected them to ask me some routine questions, and perhaps they did, but I can't recall them asking any. When I told them that I'd appreciate remaining anonymous, they assured me that that would be no problem. In fact, I already *felt* anonymous, almost non-existent.

When I was done with my account, they told me, unconvincingly, that they would perform the necessary "follow-up work." Our meeting was over shortly after it had begun. We exchanged quick pro forma thanks, shook hands, and they left, leaving the door open. I got up, walked slowly over, and closed it.

Returning to my seat, alone in that office, I thought about how those agents had seemed almost bored by the whole thing, barely going through the motions of an investigation. I had the feeling that they'd never give me or my Iraqi chemical engineer another thought after they left the school that day, and that my student would, in fact, be left in peace. Of course, what they did or didn't do is something I'll never know. Looking back, I sometimes even wonder if those guys already had more than an inkling, while they *weren't* taking notes, that the Bush-Cheney rumblings about Iraq were, from the start, oil-based smokescreens, like the fictitious WMDs that two years later, in 2003, became the major premise for the American invasion of that country. Of course, I'll never know *that* either.

On the next morning, I returned to the classroom. As I took attendance, I checked out my Iraqi student a little more closely than usual, and he seemed no different to me (why should he?). Did he see any change in *me*? Did *I*?

Somehow, we all made it to the end of that session, and, as usual, I bade farewell to my students, including the engineer. I hoped more than ever that my Hani-Hanjour-induced uneasiness about him had been groundless, that nothing evil would ever spring from his work, that it was boringly benign, and that *if* it was, he'd simply get on with it, unhindered and unharmed.

If, if, if . . .

More than a dozen years have passed since the maddeningly-timed arrival and departure of that engineer, my first and, as it turned out, my last Iraqi student. This is a story without an ending—or, at least, not one that I know. It has more than the usual number of missing links; it's as if they are hidden away in a locked vault. Stamped on the door of that vault is a word my student learned in Oakland: CLASSIFIED.

3

After 9/11, several years would have to pass before students from any Arabic country would again be routinely admitted to this country. The lives of the Arabic students who were already here during that mad September would, of course, be permanently and radically changed. One of our Saudi students, a twenty-five-year-old man who was at the school for about three months, is a good example. I don't remember his given name, which was probably a typical Arabic one like Abdullah, Ali, or Mohammad. I do, however, recall his nickname, probably because it was such an improbable choice for a Saudi: Bob. That name seemed a perfect emblem of his infatuation with the American lifestyle, as he perceived it. When he introduced himself on his first day in my class, in July 2001, he told us his real name and wrote it on the board in English letters; at my request, he wrote it in Arabic too, its meticulous calligraphy so pleasingly foreign to the non-Arabic eye. Immediately after writing it, he added, with a big grin, "But you can call me Bob." That made me and everyone else laugh, Bob more loudly than any of us. He relished being anomalous, and it didn't take long to see that Bob's love of anomaly extended well beyond his choice of a moniker.

Like Carlo Spadaccini before him, he fell in love with one of our Japanese students. Yukari was a slim, very pretty twenty-something woman with shoulder-length ink-black hair that always looked like it had just been washed. Probably no one had ever gone as totally nuts over her as Bob had. Maybe nobody had ever gone as nuts about *anybody* as Bob had. And by all indications, it was mutual. When Yukari looked at Bob looking at her, she seemed thrilled and amazed that this friendly handsome guy was so taken with her.

They looked just right together: he was a couple of inches taller than she was and had light brown skin and super-curly hair that was as black as hers. She enjoyed, as we all did, his natural spouting of American idioms, including the newborn slang of the streets. To Yukari and the rest of us, Bob sometimes seemed more American than Americans, but with more than a pinch of Middle Eastern seasoning. It didn't take long for them to become an "item" at our school.

Bob and Yukari were in my 106 grammar class that month. It seemed like everything Yukari did or said was a source of amusement and delight for Bob, even her struggles with English pronunciation, maybe especially those. It didn't bother her that her boyfriend laughed so much at her Japanese-isms, since, clearly, that laughter had not a shred of ridicule in it; it was the sound of cherishing. Bob seemed continually astonished that his journey to California had brought him together with such a lovely woman, one whom he couldn't have even dreamt of back in Jeddah.

One of Yukari's more persistent challenges in speaking English was a fairly common one for Japanese students: making an "h" sound instead of the intended "f" or "ph." Getting it right is just a matter of touching one's lower lip with one's top teeth while pushing air through that constricted opening. Yukari often didn't make that contact. If I pointed it out to her and she concentrated on that simple configuration, she could pull it off, but when something excited her or distracted her, which was most of the time, that voiceless labiodental fricative didn't stand a chance.

For example, in telling the class about a comedy that

she had enjoyed, Yukari might say, "Ooh, it was so hunny!"

"Yukari," I'd interject as gently as I could, "not hunny. Funny. See my mouth? See how my top teeth touch my bottom lip? Fffff. Fffffunny."

"Fffff. Fffffunny."

"Perfect. You see, it's easy."

"Yes, it is. That's hantastic!"

"Yukari?"

"Just kidding, Hil-san." She laughed, and the rest of us did too, especially Bob. My Japanese students had often called me Hil-san, or, sometimes, its translation, "Mister Hill," which is as close as I've ever gotten to the illusion of gentile respectability.

During a class discussion one morning, she expressed concern about her weight: "I'm eating too many dessert, especially ice cream, in cafeteria. Maybe I'm getting a little hat."

"What does buying a little hat have to do with eating too many desserts?" teased her disingenuous teacher. Yukari and I had gone over this pronunciation point so many times that session that everybody got the joke immediately and we all enjoyed yet another communal laugh, my favorite part of *any* class.

"Okay, okay, I know, Phil-san, it's 'fat.' I'm getting a little fat."

"That's still not right."

"What? I really concentrate on "f" sound this time. I was *sure* I say it right."

"Oh yes, your "f" was perfect."

"So what is problem?"

"The problem is with the *content* of your statement, not the form. You are *not* fat, not even a little bit." Which was true. One had only to look at her in her snug pink tee shirt and blue jeans to confirm that. Everybody, except Yukari, agreed that her chubbiness existed only in her mind; Bob, of course, took the lead in assuring her that, especially in his eyes, she couldn't look better, didn't need to lose an ounce. There was no doubting the sincerity of her dazzled lover. Even *she* looked almost convinced.

Sometimes, as I'd get ready to repeat my usual pronunciation directions to Yukari, Bob would jump in laughing and take over the lesson. He knew the steps by heart and got equally effective results. I was happy to take a little breather and let him do the work, a labor of love for him as he focused on Yukari's lower lip.

During one of my standard what-did-you-do-on-your-weekend Monday class conversations, Bob was eager to tell us all a story about his. A broad smile on his face, he began: "On Friday night, Yukari and I came back from having late dinner in a restaurant. Japanese restaurant. Very cool place. Sushi place. Sushi is raw fish, you know? We was walking on the campus, just chillin', and it was beautiful night. The weather was . . . how you say it . . . mild?"

"Yes, 'mild' *is* the right word. I remember Friday night was, in fact, *very* mild. Go on, Bob."

"So we was just strollin'. You know, takin' our time. Suddenly, Yukari get a very excited look on her face, like she is out-of-her-gourd happy, and she is pointing up at the sky." Yukari, red-faced and smiling, now pointed her finger at Bob and waggled it in mock warning, in playful threat. Which only egged him on.

"Yukari was pointing at night sky, and she's bananas, she's so excited, and she says so loud, like yelling, 'Bob, look! Hull moon! Hull moon!'"

We all totally lost it, laughing maniacally, and none more loudly than Bob and Yukari themselves. That's just the way it was with that pair: whoever happened to be in the same room with them on any given day got a hit of their joy. It was, in a fundamental, almost physical way, irresistible.

Bob and Yukari were again in one of my classes during the session that included September 11. Like everyone else at the school, they were profoundly shaken by those attacks. Bob confided in me that he felt like people were looking at him in a different way, as if he were somehow part of the terrorist conspiracy, or at least an endorser of it. He assured me, unnecessarily, that he loved this country, loved *being* here, that he saw the hijackers as murderers, madmen, religious fanatic "nutcases" (a word he'd heard in an American movie), that he hated what they'd done, and was ashamed that most of them had come from his country.

"Please, you must believe me, Phil."

"Of course I believe you. I *know* you."

"But you had that other student here from Saudi.

That Hani Hanjour. How do you know I'm not like him?"

"I didn't really know him. I hardly remember him. Of course, I admit that, even if I *had* known him better, there's no way I could have imagined or predicted what he would do on 9/11. But that does *not* mean that I don't trust you, just because you're a Saudi. I know and admire the kind of *person* you are. It's important that you believe me about this, Bob. It's very important that you trust me."

"Thank you, Phil. I do believe you."

"Good. Besides, there's no way I can imagine you as part of a suicide mission: with a great girlfriend like Yukari, you'd have to be even crazier than those Al Qaeda guys to kill yourself." This provoked a small smile.

"I could never. I love her."

"I know."

"And she loves *me*. She really does."

"Yes, I know that too. I think everyone who knows you knows that. And everyone who knows Yukari."

"Maybe, but not everybody *knows* us."

We nodded, looked solemnly into each other's eyes for what felt like several seconds, and shook hands, as firmly as people can grip and stay below the pain threshold. I added before he left for his next class, "Don't worry, Bob. Everything will be okay." He nodded, a gesture which, in this case, expressed comprehension, not necessarily agreement.

As it turned out, about a week later, it couldn't have

been clearer that not only had I been a second-rate comforter, but a resounding flop as a prophet too: what was in the offing for Bob was, emphatically, *not* okay.

The formerly carefree couple entered my classroom looking very troubled. In fact, Bob looked more than troubled: his face was a map of several black, blue, and violet bruises.

"What happened, Bob? What happened to your face?" I think I knew his answer, in a general way, before he gave me the specifics.

"I was in cafeteria, and these guys come over to me. Holy Names students. Tall guys. Basketball players. On school team. And they says to me something like, 'Hey, you happy now?' I could see they was very angry. Anyway, I ask them why they ask me was I happy and they say, 'You know damn well why we ask you that, you fucking A-rab.' Of course, I knew they was talking about 9/11 and making big mistake. So I wanted to set them straight right away. I told them that just because I was from Saudi did not mean I approve that killing, that crazy murdering innocent people. I told them that I was ashamed that men from my country were part of this terrible action. I told them that I was sad and angry too. I told them that I loved their country. I told them what I told you, Phil. But that made them even angrier. They shouted at me in middle of cafeteria, so loud that everyone was looking at us, and everyone could hear: 'DON'T LIE TO US!'"

I could see that every student in the class was as

glued to Bob's story as I was. Rapt and incredulous: how could anyone so miscategorize their friend? This was no religious fanatic: this was Bob, Yukari's boyfriend. Bob, who delighted in life, not in destroying it.

"I told them I wasn't lying. And of course I wasn't. But they refused to believe me. Like they was sure I was Al-Qaeda. They got angrier and angrier when I insist they was wrong. They was like nutcases. I saw that nothing was going to change their crazy idea, so I go like this (here he gave a palms-up shrug) and I start to walk away. I was walking to the exit door of cafeteria when one of those guys ran to me and grabbed the back of my shirt. And now he was screaming louder than ever: 'WHERE THE FUCK YOU THINK YOU'RE GOING? YOU THINK YOU CAN JUST LEAVE? JUST WALK AWAY? THE PEOPLE IN NEW YORK COULDN'T WALK AWAY FROM THE TOWERS. THEY WAS BURNING AND JUMPING OUT OF WINDOWS! YOU FUCKING A-RABS GONNA GET SOME PAYBACK . . .' And then they start punching me. Other students in cafeteria run over and pull them off me, and some of them know me and said kind words, I think, but I'm not sure. I can't remember clearly that part. I just wanted to get away from there. And that's what I did. I ran out the door and looked for Yukari."

His classmates were, without exception, shocked. And compassionate. Hugs, hands on shoulders, pats on his back. I was witness to this international community reaching out to one of its citizens, pouring balm on the wounds of a good man who had stepped into the quicksand of bigotry and seriously mistaken identity. Now it was my turn to feel ashamed of the actions of *my* countrymen. I was to hear later that those American guys were not simply on the basketball team; they were its stars. Somehow that made more sense to me, as if they saw it as their God-given role to lead the avenging forces against the "enemy," just as they had repeatedly led the HNC team to victory. Of course, in basketball, with its life-simplifying uniforms, it's impossible to make a mistake about the identity of your opponents.

The incident was an embarrassing one for the college, and we heard that the offenders were called to the dean's office, where they were merely chided and made to apologize to Bob. I was not there, of course, so this is just hearsay, and I can't have an opinion about whether those apologies were obligatory capitulations, sincere reversals, or a combination of the two. Things seemed to be simmering down a bit for Bob. But, in fact, that was just the lull before a greater storm.

A few days later, Bob and Yukari arrived in class looking even more despondent. Bob told us that his father had phoned him from Jeddah and told him to return to Saudi Arabia at once, that America was, obviously, an extremely dangerous place for a Saudi man at that time, that he would be remiss as a father if he permitted his son to remain in harm's way. He made it clear to Bob that this was his command, that it was absolutely non-negotiable; there was nothing to talk about. Bob knew enough not to protest or even mention that returning to his country would entail tearing himself away from the love of his life, especially since that love was neither Arabic nor Muslim. His great romance with Yukari was possible only outside the perimeter of his homeland. Unlike Carlo Spadaccini before him, he would not be taking Yukari home with him to "meet the family." A brutal verb tense lesson loomed before him: his entire Yukari-filled present and future were about to be thrown, weeping and flailing, into the past. Fighting that would be like holding up a hand to divert a tsunami.

Bob told me and his classmates that he wished there were something he could do or say that might reverse his father's decision, but, he was sure, there was nothing. His death sentence had been pronounced and the only option he saw for himself was to walk to the gallows like a man.

"I want to thank all of you for being such good friends. I have to say goodbye to you now. I hate to do that, but I have to do it. This is all so terrible, so bad. I need to go to the office now. I won't stay for today's class. I'm sorry, Phil. I really want to stay, but my father say to do all this as quickly as I can. I think maybe all this will make *me* a nutcase too."

His brown eyes glistened with pooling tears, and, once again, his faithful classmates gave him, one by one, big bear hugs, this time to bid him sad farewell.

Yukari, expressionless, already widow-like, stayed in her seat.

Before he left, he bear-hugged me, shook my hand, then hugged me again.

"Thank you, Phil. For your friendship and your kindness."

"You're welcome, Bob. I will miss you."

"I will miss you too."

Then he turned and looked forlornly at Yukari before stepping out of the classroom. Although it would be a week before his Saudi-bound plane would actually depart, I never saw Bob again. Yukari looked catatonic as she sat through the rest of that day's class.

After that day, Yukari never returned to her classes either. It was clear to all of us that she wanted to spend as much time as possible with Bob during his last week in Oakland. Her friends reported that she continued to look as if she were in shock, and how could she not be? Her fantasy love story, that improbable coupling of Middle East and Far East, had crumbled in the West, like the Twin Towers themselves. Collateral damage.

I had no idea if those lovers would ever see each other again. I doubted it. It's almost impossible to imagine Yukari, cloaked with abaya, hijab, and niqab, visiting Bob in Saudi Arabia. And, of course, because of greatly heightened international security measures, Bob's (or any Arab's) boarding a plane at that time was suddenly a much more complicated affair, and, in many cases, undoable. So it seemed equally unlikely that Bob might reunite with Yukari in Japan or any other country, certainly not this one. On the other hand, mere unlikelihood no longer carried as much weight in a world where the unimaginable had already happened.

STRANGE

Beauty is truth, truth beauty,—that is all
Ye know on earth, and all ye need to know.
John Keats, "Ode on a Grecian Urn," 1819

You know from the time frames set out in the Prologue, and from many of these stories, that my life among my students—and the pleasure I derived from it—continued for more than another decade after the cataclysms of 2001. Yes, the enormous darkness of 9/11 dominated for a while, but it does not give my memory of that thirty-eight-year span its defining characteristic; it does not submerge or extinguish what came before or, perhaps more importantly, what came after. My teaching life, in all its joy and madness, did go on. It's what life does.

In fact, in some ways, it got better. For several years, for example, in my Masters' classes in San Rafael and Berkeley, I had the freedom to design my own curriculum. A long time had passed since my 1974 search for a job teaching literature, but here, finally, was a chance to try my hand at it—in, to say the least, an unanticipated context. I wove grammar drills and speaking/listening practice into a course whose main component was the reading of an American novel or, in one case, a theatrical piece. I felt like the book-loving part of my soul was finally being fed in the classroom; I was determined to share that meal with my students. Or at least try to.

Whatever I chose for those groups to read, it had to be short enough for them to get through in three-and-a-half weeks, usually not more than 120 pages. When the time came to order the books, I always insisted that these were *not* to be "special student editions," abridged and simplified for ESL students or for native-English-speaking high school students with presumed limitations of attention span, literacy, and experience; we worked only with the unadulterated originals. It's not cool, in fact not even legal, to call sparkling wine "champagne" unless that bubbly was made in Champagne, France, so how is it okay to slap Hemingway's name on the cover of a book that maybe vaguely follows the arc of one of his novels but drains the blood from its characters, the soul from its prose? Yes, yes, I know, as many of my former colleagues insist, "It's a teaching tool. And it gives the students a feeling of accomplishment: hey, they've finished a whole book!" That's true enough, but the "whole book" they've knocked off is at best a forty-eight-page intimation of *A Farewell to Arms*. I can imagine students who have read those "special editions" going back to their countries and mentioning the

"Hemingway" or "Steinbeck" novel they'd read in class and adding, in Japanese or Italian or whatever, that they'd found the characters rather thin, the plot undeveloped.

Some of the works I used in those classes were John Steinbeck's *Of Mice and Men* and *The Red Pony*; Philip Roth's *Goodbye, Columbus*; Truman Capote's *Breakfast at Tiffany's*; Thornton Wilder's *Our Town*; and Ernest Hemingway's *The Old Man and the Sea*. It was exhilarating but often daunting to dive into these books with my students. Most of them (it seemed like at least 90%) simply didn't read literary fiction, either in English or in their own languages; if they took the time to read at all, they generally gravitated toward articles in technology, business, or entertainment magazines. Few were those who'd had the pleasure of meeting characters who had sprung, four-dimensional and breathing, from an author's head. On those rare occasions that a fellow bibliophile landed in one of these classes, I felt as if I'd been visited by a long-lost soul mate. It's hard enough to coax a student whose *first* language is English into loving, or even liking, this stuff, but attempting it in a second language stacks the odds significantly higher.

One summer in 2005, I was teaching *The Old Man and the Sea* to a group of about a dozen Masters' class students in San Rafael. We were in a bunker-like room with thick grey concrete walls and just one small window. From the teacher's desk, I could look through that window at a lovely old gnarled oak tree at the edge of one of the many super-green well-watered lawns that grace the campus of Dominican University. The students' view as they faced me was, sadly for them, limited to their teacher, the white board, and a couple of posters on the walls advertising the school they were already attending, ads for a service they'd already bought. Hemingway had the job of creating the sea and—an even more formidable task—the old man, Santiago.

Abby, née Chen Yu, was a Taiwanese woman in her early forties. She approached my desk at break time after our first class. Clearly, something was bothering her; she had the mien of a penitent: head tipped down, eyes avoiding mine, lips pursed as if in a futile attempt to hold back saying what she was about to say.

"Teacher, I'm so so sorry." I couldn't imagine what she could possibly be apologizing for.

"Excuse me, Abby? What's wrong?" She now looked close to tears.

"I must to leave your class. I think I also will leave your school. I'm finished with this studying English." She'd been clutching Hemingway's novel in her right hand, and now she raised it to eye-level like an attorney presenting Exhibit A. "This is too too difficult for me. Too strange. I understand nothing in this book. Absolutely nothing! This is like no other reading I ever do. Why this man Hemingway write like that? So strange. Why he can't just write like normal person? Why so strange?"

Now her tears spilled over and rolled down her

cheeks, those moist trails glistening under the fluorescent tubes.

So, even Hemingway, so famous for revolutionizing American fiction by creating prose of starkly beautiful simplicity, had written something that was as cryptic to Abby as a manuscript in yet a *third* language.

"Well, Abby, a writer's work can seem strange when we read it for the first time. Every good writer has a unique style, and because it's unfamiliar to us, it can be hard to relate to. At first. That can affect our comprehension. But the more we stick with it, the more familiar it gets, and the easier it is to understand." Her hopeless-looking face seemed to silently say: *maybe what you say is true for other people, but it is not true for me.* Her next words confirmed that impression:

"Not for me. I don't think I can do this. I don't think I can stick with this. I don't think this ever going be clear for me. I'm so so so sorry, Phil. I'm ashamed for myself. It's too embarrassing. It's big humiliation."

"Abby, do me a favor, try to continue, and see what happens, see if it gets easier to understand as you get to know Hemingway's style better. And as you get to know Santiago better. Think of it as an experiment?"

She looked no less hopeless and, now snuffling quite loudly, pulled a handkerchief from her purse, wiped her wet cheeks, did an about-face, and blew her nose with such force that it seemed that she was trying to propel the sea, the old man, the classroom, and me into oblivion with one strong blast. No such luck. We were all still there when she turned back around. She stashed her hanky and looked up at my face. On hers was a look of utter defeat; her escape attempt had failed. She was in for at least one more day of torture. Was this worth it? My faint hope was that it was.

"Okay, Phil. I try. I come back tomorrow."

"Good, Abby. *Tsai-chien* (Bye-bye)."

"*Tsai-chien*, Phil."

On the next day, we went over about another ten pages; Abby was silent and withdrawn throughout the class. Whenever I looked at her, she averted her eyes. I didn't have the heart to call on her. Her face had turned to steel. I didn't expect to see her on the following afternoon. Enough, after all, was enough.

But she *was* there. Cut off but present. And the next day. And the next. By Monday of the second week, she began to look less tortured, less hopeless. On Tuesday, she even started to participate a bit in the lesson; was Santiago's monumental battle with the giant marlin finally starting to become real to her? She didn't visit me again with questions or laments, and I asked no further questions about her own struggle to haul in Hemingway's "strange" mutation of the fish called English. Another week passed.

The third week began, and there she still was, in her adopted seat. We had made it beyond the halfway point, and she hadn't yet abandoned the fight. It appeared that my prediction about familiarity breeding comprehension, even in Abby's extreme case, might actually be panning out. Right after that class ended, she returned to my desk. Judging by the look on her face, relatively free of agony, I was somewhat hopeful, but I had no idea what she was about to say.

"Hi Abby. How're you doing? Better, I think, huh?"

"Yes, Phil, better. Much better. Hemingway not so difficult now. I get more used to him."

"Great! I thought so. I'm very glad. Tell me about it."

"Well, on Saturday, I had no plans, so I read the ten pages you assign for today's class. It go much faster than before. I forget that I'm reading. I get so interested in story I forget I'm sitting in chair holding book, reading book. I want to know what will happen with old man, with poor old man Santiago. So I keep reading. Another eight, maybe another nine pages. I feel like I know Santiago, like he is real person. He is like my grandfather. Not Taiwanese of course but that not important." She surprised me by actually chuckling at her little joke—a first. I chuckled too: laughing together was a miracle I hadn't dared to hope for. She went on: "I really care about that old man. I even cry a little when I reading that. He is like actual man to me."

"That's fantastic, Abby. That's exactly what's supposed to happen when you read a novel. You really got it. I'm very proud of you. That Hemingway is a pretty amazing writer, don't you think?"

"Yes. But I have a little question about that. Maybe stupid question."

"I'm sure it's not stupid, Abby. I want to hear it. Please. Ask."

"His English. Hemingway's English. His writing is so

different from anything I read ever ever before. So strange, as I say before. Strange, strange, strange." She was smiling as she repeated that adjective, almost chanting it as she swung her head left and right. "But now I can understand. It is strange in *good* way. Like way Santiago say it."

(That casual reference gave further evidence of how far Abby had come as a reader. In fact, as the old man engages in that tug of war with his enormous foe, the greatest endurance test of his life, he proclaims: "'I told the boy I was a strange old man . . . Now is when I must prove it.'" And then, a bit later, to the marlin itself: "'If you're not tired, fish,' he said aloud, 'you must be very strange.'")

"Very good, Abby. You're right. When Santiago uses the word 'strange,' it represents the greatest kind of distinction."

"Distinction?"

"'Distinction' is what makes someone, or some*thing*, special."

"Yes, I see. Thank you, Phil. It's clear. But there is something else, Phil. Something else about this book."

"Yes? What else, Abby?"

"Hemingway's writing is now pretty clear to me. Maybe *very* clear. But there is something else. I thought about this a lot. This writing is not only clear. I think . . ." Here she hesitated. She was suddenly looking unsure of herself again.

"Yes? Go on, Abby."

"Well, you didn't say anything about this, so I not sure. But I think this writing is not only clear, but, in a way, it is kind of . . . maybe . . . beautiful? You know what I mean?" Abby blushed and laughed, a nervous embarrassed titter. "Is that right?"

"Oh yes, that's exactly right, Abby. Like every language, English can be a lot more than just a way to communicate practical messages. It's easy to forget that while you're busy doing grammar exercises. It *can* be beautiful, like a poem, like a song. I'm so glad that you've seen this. It shows that you too are a very strange person."

She laughed and nodded with a satisfaction that instantly became mine too, that unscheduled non-monetary paycheck that makes teaching feel like the greatest gig in the world.

"So, yes, yes, Abby. 'Beautiful' is the *perfect* word."

"Uh huh. I thought so. Just checking."

Al Dente

It was one of those magical Marin County days, with sunlight that seemed almost liquid and air that somehow smelled like apples despite the absence of apple trees. We were reading Steinbeck's *The Red Pony* in my Masters' class during a summer session on the campus of Dominican University in San Rafael. The months without rain had turned the long grass of the nearby hills gold, like the wild grass in Steinbeck's novella.

We were up to the part where Jody, the young protagonist of that book, had just been surprised by the arrival of a mysterious old man, Gitano, at his family's ranch near the Gabilan Mountains in Monterey County. This odd stranger was more than the boy felt he could handle alone, so into the house he ran and found his mother, as usual, in the kitchen, where she was using a hairpin to clear the clogged holes of her colander.

Before continuing to discuss Jody's plight, I was sure that at least one vocabulary word in that passage needed explanation.

"Do you know the meaning of the word 'colander'?" I asked the group. I had taught this book several times before, so I knew this was a trick question, a setup with one very likely result.

Predictably, several hands shot up, and I called on a French guy, Guillaume. He answered confidently: "Yes, sure, is something you 'ang on a wall. It tell you the date and the day and the year. Is not an unusual English word. Is normal." Almost all of the other students were nodding in agreement with Guillaume's apparently perfect answer.

"Well, Guillaume, I have to confess that I kind of set you up."

"Set me up?"

"Well, tricked you. You have just given an excellent definition of 'calendar,' not 'colander.'"

"Calendar, not calendar?"

"No. Calendar, not *col*ander."

I then proceeded to write the two words on the board, pointing first to "calendar" and then to "colander," emphasizing the pronunciation difference between "cal" and "col." I told the class that I could not improve on Guillaume's definition of the former, so I'd just describe the kitchen contraption that Jody's mother was holding. I explained its shape, its basic function, and even drew a poor rendition of one on the board. I went through a few food prep scenarios: rinsing vegetables, draining spaghetti water, etc. There was a mixed chorus of ohs and ahas as the students put the word together with the object, which was familiar to most of them. After making sure that everybody also understood "clogged," we were ready to go on with the more intriguing business of solemn old Gitano's unexpected appearance at the Tiflin ranch.

Or so I thought.

Angelina, an Italian student in her thirties, was shaking her blond head as she erupted:

"Ah, the mother, she should not 'ave to cleana da holes in da colander. Dey should never *be* clog-ged."

She had certainly gotten everyone's attention.

"Da problem is Americans. Dey don' know 'ow to cooka da pasta! Dey always cooka too much. Dey murder da pasta. Eeta falls aparta. Dat'sa why in da colander da holes dey getta clog-ged. In Italy, it never 'appen because in Italy everyone know 'ow to cooka da pasta. Notta too much. Notta too longa time. So eet is still food when you eat it. Notta, 'ow you say? Mooshy?"

"You mean it's al dente, right?"

"Exactly! You know Italian expression, al dente. It mean in English 'to da teeth.' Your teeth can feel somma-ting. Somma-ting to bite. Notta moosh!"

"Of course, of course, Angelina. I like to cook. And whenever I cook pasta, I'm very careful about the timing. Because, believe it or not, it's very important to *me* that my pasta is al dente. I know many Americans overcook pasta, but not the better chefs. We serious cooks all agree with you. Al dente is the *only* acceptable condition for pasta."

"Aha. Yes, yes. You see."

Apparently back in her good graces, I elaborated:

"And yet, from time to time, I still have to unclog those little holes in my colander."

She looked shocked and freshly disappointed in me. "No, not possible! Eefa you cook it righta, no clog. You say you cook it al dente, so eef is true, no clog! Never clog! Because never moosh!"

"I agree. What you say is completely logical. But, of course, even the best chefs can sometimes get distracted. They can get an important phone call. A friend can unexpectedly show up at the door. One's child may need immediate attention. Or one's spouse. One's mind can simply wander, one can get lost in thoughts and daydreams. When something like this happens, one can temporarily forget about the pasta bubbling away on the stove and not remember until it's too late, and the poor *fusilli* has turned to mush. It could happen to anyone, even in Italy, even to the best Italian chefs."

I had felt good about my calm reasoned explanation and expected Angelina to bow graciously to its clear unassailable logic. But, judging from the shocked look on her face, all I had done was re-stoke Vesuvius. Apparently, I had said something unconscionable, not merely about Italians but about *i grandi chef d'Italia*. Angelina placed both palms on her desk and half rose from her seat as if she were about to fly across the room and sink her teeth into my al dente throat. The word that exploded out of her mouth was thunderous in its finality:

"Never!"

Epilogue

On the night of October 12, 2012, a Tuesday, Joan and I were walking in downtown Berkeley. It was about six months after my final day of teaching. We had just enjoyed an invigorating concert by Carlos Nuñez ("the Jimi Hendrix of the bagpipes"), a Spanish wizard on recorders, pennywhistles, and, yes, bagpipes, at Freight and Salvage. We were feeling less tired than we might have at almost eleven o'clock, partly due to the bracing bay-infused night air, but probably more to the adrenaline that was still racing through us after that wild foot-stomping music.

We had just said good night to our friend, my former Oakland colleague Misha, who had enjoyed the concert with us, and were heading north on Shattuck Avenue, downtown's main drag, toward Hearst, where our car was parked. After crossing University Avenue and going about twenty or thirty feet past that busy intersection's northeast corner, I heard, mixed in with the groaning, squealing, and honking of traffic, someone call out, "Phil!"

I stopped walking and looked around, but with all that traffic noise, I wasn't sure where that voice had come from. It rang out again, this time more loudly:

"Mr. Phil! Over here! Mr. Phil!"

It had come from behind us, near a lamppost at the corner. A bright pair of headlights shone into my eyes from just behind a couple of male figures, one short and one tall, silhouetting them, keeping them anonymous. As that car completed its turn and went on its way, I could make out their faces: the short guy's rang no bells for me, but I knew the broadly smiling face of the taller one very well. I hurried over and gave him a hands-on-top-and-bottom shake.

"Hey, it's amazing to see you!" It *was*.

"Do you remember me?"

"Of course, of course. How could I forget you?" But the truth was that, as I was about to introduce him to Joan, I was embarrassed to realize that, although I remembered *him* very well indeed, I couldn't remember his name. Not that it was unusual for that to happen: I've calculated that, over the years, I've had more than 28,000 students, a statistic I sometimes employ to try to cut myself some slack when I'm unable to retrieve one of their names.

"This is my wife Joan, and . . ." *Shit! What* was *his name?* I really did remember this man very clearly, his soft impish voice, his slight stammer, his deadpan riffing during class, his unwavering friendliness—but his name? Try as I did to break into my own memory bank, the name just wouldn't come. I had little hope that I would be as lucky as Robin when she'd correctly guessed that her old Iranian student's name was Abdullah. It was time to concede defeat. I put my hand on my student's shoulder and confessed: "Oh, this is ridiculous and embarrassing. I remember you so well, but this old brain of mine can't remember your name. I'm sorry."

"Oh, it's not problem, Phil. I am Kareem. Now you remember?"

That missing piece snapped right into place: it felt so obvious that only an idiot could fail to remember it. I reminded myself again about the 28,000.

"Of course, of course. Kareem. Short for Abdulkareem."

"Yes, yes, that's right. But maybe you remember me more as Question Man. Remember? Question Man?"

"Yes, of course. Question Man. You were certainly the only student I ever had with *that* name."

Kareem laughed and then introduced us to his friend, who was from Syria, and we commiserated with him about the great woes that his country was going through. We also chatted a bit about Kareem's current situation. He was going to another language school in Berkeley to prepare for one of the standardized tests that torture countless students, foreign and domestic. We also got around to reminiscing a bit about the "good old days" when we were both at the same school.

"Phil, do you remember what my special saying was?"

"Yes, *that* I *do* remember. How could anyone in our class forget it?"

"Okay," Kareem said, grinning, delighted to put his

old teacher to the test. "What was it? What was my special sentence?"

"Your motto, your special sentence, was, 'I have a question.' It was so funny because you said it every day, at least once, maybe more than once. It was also *how* you said it that made everybody laugh; you were serious and not serious at the same time. You were a very funny guy. All the students enjoyed Question Man."

Raising my right index finger in the cool night air, I tried my best to imitate his riff: with the pitch of my voice elevated a smidgeon and adding just the dash of Arabic accent that *he* had, I intoned with mock-seriousness, taking my time, trying not to smile, "I have a question."

He laughed his hearty laugh at hearing a passable approximation of his routine coming from the mouth of his teacher. "Very good, Phil."

"Thank you, Question Man."

He had heard that I wasn't teaching at our school anymore and asked if I was teaching somewhere else. I explained that I wasn't, that I was working on a book.

"Is it a novel?"

"No, not a novel. It's a book of true stories about some of my students."

"Wow. Fantastic. I want to read that."

"I hope you will."

"I hope so too." Then Kareem got a funny look on his face, an impish smile I remembered well. He paused for a couple of beats before raising *his* right index finger in the air. There could be no doubt about what was coming.

"Phil?"

"Yes, Kareem?"

"I have a question."

All four of us laughed at what felt like Kareem imitating me imitating him.

"Yes, Kareem?"

"Will you put *me* in your book?"

"Maybe. You *are* in my notes, but I haven't decided yet if you'll be in the book. There are lots of decisions to make."

His grin broadened. "Oh, but you must. If you write a book about your students, you *must* put Question Man in it. How can you not?"

"I might just do that. I'd like to, but I really don't know yet." I really didn't.

"Oh, you will. I *know* you will put me in it."

"Inshallah."

I knew that was a word against which he could have no argument. He laughed, nodded, and replied, "Yes. Inshallah." His entreaty had been gently put to rest.

Kareem and I had a farewell hug, and we all said our goodnights and farewells. Joan and I took our time as we resumed our cool-night stroll toward the car, up that stretch of Shattuck, past its little shops and restaurants, most of them dark, closed for the night. With Question Man's voice echoing in my head, past and future merged and melted—as they tend to do—into the verb tense of the always-now, the simple present, which is not as simple as most grammar books would lead us to believe.

Or perhaps it *is*.

We arrived at the car, and for maybe the thousandth time, I marveled at the life my accidental career had given me, one in which nationalities are never abstractions—one in which there is always the possibility of someone on a Berkeley street corner shouting hello at me from anywhere in the world.

Acknowledgments

Special thanks to those who gave generously of their time and care to read the initial versions of my manuscript: Mark Breckler, Joan Chomak, Mitch Covic, Jay Humphrey, and Tom Webster . . . and to Ezra Chomak and Ross Mitchell too, who read it further down the line. To each of you I'd tip my hat if I ever wore one. Your encouragements kept me going—and your suggestions made this a better book.

It would be foolhardy to attempt to list all those who have cheered me on, so I won't even try—you know who you are. Nevertheless, I would be remiss if I didn't single out the person who's done it the longest, in writing and in life, my sister, Anita Moyal, who, literally, has always been there for me. Sure, when we were kids, we had occasional skirmishes, like all siblings—like the time, during a spat about who-knows-what, that I dared her to dump a full sugar bowl over my head and she *did* it, covering me and the floor with what seemed like billions of those tiny white grains, more than we could clean up before our parents returned, and that sweet residue turned out to be an invitation to several families of cockroaches to make their first visitations to our Brooklyn home, but that's another story . . .

CPSIA information can be obtained
at www.ICGtesting.com
Printed in the USA
FSOW02n1804201216
28759FS